D1250898

Play of a Fiddle

Play *of a* Fiddle

Traditional Music, Dance, and Folklore in West Virginia

Gerald Milnes

THE UNIVERSITY PRESS OF KENTUCKY

Publication of this volume was made possible in part
by grants from the E.O. Robinson Mountain Fund
and the National Endowment for the Humanities.

Scholarly publisher for the Commonwealth,
serving Bellarmine College, Berea College, Centre
College of Kentucky, Eastern Kentucky University,
The Filson Club Historical Society, Georgetown College,
Kentucky Historical Society, Kentucky State University,
Morehead State University, Murray State University,
Northern Kentucky University, Transylvania University,
University of Kentucky, University of Louisville,
and Western Kentucky University.

Editorial and Sales Offices: The University Press of Kentucky
663 South Limestone Street, Lexington, Kentucky 40508-4008

03 02 01 00 99   5 4 3 2 1

Library of Congress Cataloging-in-Publication Data

Milnes, Gerald.
    Play of a fiddle : traditional music, dance, and folklore in West
Virginia / Gerald Milnes
        p.   cm.
    Includes bibliographical references (p.   ), discography (p.   ), and
index.
    ISBN 0-8131-2080-2 (alk. paper)
    1. Folk music—West Virginia—History and criticism.   I. Title.
    ML3551.M55   1999
    781.62'1307546—dc21   98-40733

This book is printed on acid-free recycled paper meeting
the requirements of the American National Standard
for Permanence of Paper for Printed Library Materials.

Manufactured in the United States of America

Contents

Acknowledgments

Many have helped me with this project. Foremost I want to thank all of the generous people who were the subjects of my interviews and research efforts, especially those who became musical buddies. Because I met and befriended many of these people in their twilight years, I've had to suffer the loss of some good friends. This becomes an impetus to add their thoughts to the permanent record.

A Mellon fellowship from Berea College and a research fellowship from the West Virginia Humanities Council were important in documenting source material. Loyal Jones, former director of the Appalachian Center at Berea College, along with the Augusta Heritage Center's Margo Blevin, supported and encouraged my interests. Writing projects for former *Goldenseal* editor Ken Sullivan and projects with folklorist Michael Kline aided and sustained my work. John Cuthbert at the West Virginia and Regional History Collection carried out useful projects. Steve Green, who has researched Appalachian fiddling traditions, was a willing correspondent. Peter Silitch of Braxton County made helpful suggestions. Bill Rice assisted with courthouse research. Jim Costa's knowledge about and collection of material culture was beneficial. I have carried on a continual conversation with Dwight Diller about the Hammons family and their music. Ron Hardway's diligent genealogical work was useful. Joe Bussard helped with his staggering grasp of facts regarding early recordings of country music. Armin Hadamer and Suzanne Kohler provided insight into German influence on Appalachian folk music. Ethnomusicologist Drew Beisswenger was a helpful reader. I continually looked to the exceptional work of Samuel Bayard and Alan Jabbour to understand the vagaries of American fiddle music.

Last but not least I thank my wife, Mary Alice, who encouraged my work, helped revise my drafts, often heard "We're just going to play one more tune," and endured that lie many times.

Introduction

"Across the Blue Mountains to the Alleghenies"
Appalachian folk song

No person has had more influence on the folk culture of West Virginia than William Penn. In 1681 Penn began his famous "Holy Experiment," and throngs of Europeans responded to his promise of religious freedom in a "good and fruitful land." They flooded across the Atlantic to Pennsylvania (Penn's woods), arriving at Penn's City of Brotherly Love (Philadelphia) in the late seventeenth and eighteenth centuries. English Quakers were first, followed by their Welsh counterparts, to join a small number of Swedes and Finns already in Pennsylvania. German Anabaptists arrived in significant numbers and settled beyond the Quakers. Waves of Scots-Irish Presbyterians soon followed, pushing farther west on the Old Philadelphia Road (now Route 30) that pierced the wild Pennsylvania countryside.

Many of these pioneers and their progeny traveled west in Pennsylvania-made Conestoga wagons on what became known as the Great Wagon Road. The route, now Interstate 81, turned southwestward when it reached the Appalachian chain and ran parallel to the ridges. The emigrants crossed a narrow band of western Maryland and the Potomac River and headed into the Great Valley of Virginia. Westward-traveling English settlers and African slaves from the tidewater areas of Maryland and Virginia joined the movement. These pioneers sought passage into and across the Allegheny range to become the principal ancestors of the people introduced in this book. Most of the folk culture discussed in this book arrived through this course of migration.

An early group of German Pietists, seeking the biblical "Woman of the Wilderness,"[1] settled along Pennsylvania's Wissahickon Creek in

1694. Three immigrant brothers, the Eckerlins, joined the community in 1725 and later moved with a faction westward to Lancaster County. Much has been written about the extraordinary a cappella harmonic music sung by this group.[2] The Eckerlins left Lancaster, followed the Great Wagon Road west and south, and eventually arrived at Dunkard's Bottom on the Cheat River (now West Virginia) in 1753.

My own immigrant ancestors, who were from England, Germany, Northern Ireland, and Scotland, sought a better life in America through this great migration. They desired a friendlier climate in which to practice their Methodist, Mennonite, and Presbyterian beliefs. I began life on the banks of Wissahickon Creek, where the Eckerlin mystics had first located. I later lived in Lancaster County and in 1975 came to the banks of the upper Cheat River, unconsciously completing a replication of their life's journey. Like the Eckerlins, my impetus was an idealistic movement (in my case, a small tide of people seeking a more meaningful existence through the back-to-the-land movement of the 1960s and 1970s).

By 1976 my base of operations was a mountain farm in southern Webster County near Birch River. I've played string music since the age of nine, and this new setting fired that lifelong interest. In proximity to fiddlers I greatly admired, I fed my musical appetite while befriending numerous older players.

Henry Glassie said it is impossible to keep one's life and research from flowing naturally together.[3] Indeed, mine have been one and the same. My interest in traditional folk music stirred a curiosity about the context surrounding that music and the traditions of my West Virginia neighbors. These new friends, mostly people born between 1890 and 1920, enthralled me. I wondered if others had been exposed to the unique information I was hearing and recording. I determined through a literature search that publication of these musical performances and expressions of opinion, fact, and fantasy was sparse.

In 1976 I was hired to help teach a class in old-time music at the Augusta Heritage Arts Workshop. I've been affiliated with the program since as co-producer of audio recordings and coordinator of the Appalachian music program and since 1989 as a full-time coordinator of Folklife Programs. The Augusta Heritage Center (as it is called today) became a program of Davis and Elkins College in 1981 and is a focal point for people interested in folk and traditional art and craft. They learn from experienced practitioners and witness folk art and craft as practiced by tradition bearers. Often Augusta is the first place these older folk artists have been given recognition for their talents and skills.

In 1988 Loyal Jones, former director of the Appalachian Center at Berea College, encouraged me to expand my musical research and rectify the gap in the literature I had found by writing about the music I was hearing and musicians I was meeting. So I began to work more seriously toward that end.

I set out with a few objectives for this work. The foremost goal is to provide an overview of the folk music, folk dance, and associated folk culture of West Virginia. The spotlight has never illuminated West Virginia as a pivotal area for traditional folk music (early recording and performance centers in Bristol, Atlanta, Nashville, and elsewhere have brought recognition to other states). Nor was the state in the forefront of a more recent old-time music revival. Lack of recognition notwithstanding, West Virginia has made extensive contributions to early and recent noncommercial traditional folk music. Nationwide, people who play old-time music play many tunes of West Virginia origin. The state maintains a traditional music environment that rivals that of any region.

My inquisitiveness about the music led to a contextual interest in social history, regional traditional life, folklore, and material culture. These facets of West Virginia folklife cannot be separated from West Virginia folk music. I set out to investigate West Virginia's musical heritage by identifying traditions and folk artists while seeking to understand comparative works others have contributed. When a look at other regional traditions seemed appropriate, I consulted published references from my own pieced-together library and at the Booth Library at Davis and Elkins College. The Augusta Collection housed there contains important collections of field recordings from around the region as well as my personal field recordings, which are referenced throughout this work. Occasional trips to the state archive in Charleston and the West Virginia and Regional History Collection at West Virginia University were useful.

The "field," however, would be my main direction of inquiry. It was my rural neighbors and their music, folkways, and traditions that caught my attention and sustained my interest. The thoughts and actions of these people, as documented here, will contribute to a wider understanding and knowledge of regional traditional music and life. I used Braxton County as a microcosm on certain topics when survey-type research (throughout the state or across counties) would have been too large a proposition. Most of my field research is in central West Virginia, an area to which I had easy access but that also is particularly rich in terms of traditional folk culture.

A description of terms used in this work is necessary. I use the term "folk" (with music, dance, art, lore, or life) to mean music, dance, statement, and activities that represent the shared expressions of traditional, regional, and cultural values of older people in West Virginia.[4] Operative terms for the music include "traditional," "Appalachian," "old-time," "mountain," and "early hillbilly." I differentiate traditional folk music from popular folk music (the genre of music brought about through the national folk revival of the mid twentieth century). While I focus on traditional folk music, I do not dispute that the national movement has affected traditional folk music.[5] Many now realize that the "folk revival" of the mid to late twentieth century renewed interest in traditional folk culture, encouraging documentation and revival of many traditional music genres.[6] Many people became enamored with traditional music through regional music festivals and other events of the period. The movement also encouraged many traditional players to rejuvenate their art form. But they were not "reviving" something that was dead; rather, they were rejuvenating something they had never lost. Some argue that the recent revival of old-time music continues, but some people have continuously played traditional old-time music since early in this century. This work focuses on these people—the older people who needed no national revival to spur their interest. Many of the folks I write about still actively make music.

I may be accused of presenting only the quaint, old, and/or nostalgic elements of West Virginia rural folklife in this work. I don't deny that what interests me falls largely into the area of generally positive aspects of traditional folk culture and folk art. A fair share of social problems exists in West Virginia because of a long history of labor struggle and economic difficulty. A strengthened identity brought about through recognition and celebration of rich and positive aspects of traditional folklife can only help in that regard.

1

Chills of Hilarity

"Time and space is everything."
Randolph County proverb[1]

"When I moved to Wirt County, I got acquainted with an old man who loved music," recalled Brooks Hardway, an old-time banjo and guitar player from Braxton County, West Virginia. "He told me one day, he said, 'I was at a fiddler's contest one time back in the twenties at Clay Courthouse.' He said there was six fiddlers in that contest, six of the best. Ed [Edden] Hammons was one of 'em, and he said Ed Hammons was a champion fiddler at that day and time. He said there was some old man in that contest that played left-handed, and he said he took first place over Ed Hammons and the other five a-playin' a tune called 'Piney Mountain.' I said, 'That's my Grandpap Santy's brother.' That was Frank Santy who winned that contest over Ed Hammons. That's pretty much something to be proud of, I'll tell you. Frank Santy could fiddle 'Piney Mountain' till it would bring chills of hilarity throughout your body."[2]

Hardway's story hints at some of the concepts that are integral to any discussion of traditional folk music in West Virginia. These concepts include the emotional relevance of the music, legendary musicians and musical lore, origins and influences related to the music, and playing customs. This chapter will explore each of those areas and their intricate interplay.

While some people think old-time fiddle music "all sounds alike" and are not affected by it, others like Brooks Hardway admit the fiddle moves them in significant ways on occasion. I am one of those people. At times I have experienced a strong emotional reaction to the music that is at once euphoric and melancholic. Old-time folk musicians I know relate similar sentiments. Melvin Wine of Braxton County told of being deeply moved as a child by certain tunes his father played. When his father played "Lady's Waist Ribbon" late at night, Melvin cried in bed.

Something in the music "touched me all over," Wine recalled. "Dad would play that, and I'd wake up a-cryin'. I just couldn't stand the sound. I don't know what about it, but I'd just cry every time he'd play it."[3]

For many people, traditional folk music, both tune (instrumental) and song, expresses emotion unequaled in the realms of performance and visual arts. An element of truth in the music touches some essential place deep inside. Traditional folk music involves an ageless musical expression of feeling and emotion over which, at times, the artist seems to have little control. Because of its profound emotional effect and despite a continual barrage for more than a century and a half of popular musical forms, the music of Frank Santy and other traditional folk musicians lives on.

The emotional aspect is much of what attracts people to traditional folk music. Old-time fiddle music isn't fiction. It represents real emotions long held by the people and culture from which it originated. The tune "Piney Mountain" undoubtedly was not composed to intentionally create an emotionally charged atmosphere that would bring "chills of hilarity" to listeners. Instead it developed through a process whereby human experiences materialize as sound created on musical instruments in many capable hands. The oldest fiddle music in West Virginia and other regions captures a disposition of people, a representation of time, and a portrayal of place.

Folk music is folk art. It is faithful to cultural values and identity. It reflects tradition and expresses emotion found in the folk community from which it comes. Songs, by their nature, express values more overtly than tunes, but even in tunes, certain values can be obvious. Barnyard tunes, such as those that mock chickens, traditionally have been part of the repertoires of rural fiddlers. Since imitation is an ultimate form of flattery, we can deduce that playing tunes that mock barnyard creatures is a way in which rural people express the significance of these animals in their lives. This is also true of fox chase, bear chase, train, highway, and other such tunes that pervade old-time music.

Music that brings "chills of hilarity" goes even further to convey the listener to another mental state, just as folk music in all cultures has done for thousands of years. Folk music from less modernized cultures is almost always associated with dancing (as most traditional fiddle music is) and often has some deeper purpose and meaning.[4]

Other aspects of old-time music are calming. People identify with nostalgic feelings captured or portrayed in the music. Instead of eliciting feelings of the unknown, as may be suggested by "chills of hilarity," the music brings about nostalgic feelings of the known, affording comfort and security.

Harking back to another time and place is another effect of traditional folk music that creates positive emotional experiences for many of its listeners. This aspect of traditional folk music can unite people of diverse cultural backgrounds perhaps by transporting them to an earlier time when they were united culturally. After all it is often said that music is the universal language. One does not have to be African American to feel the emotion in blues, or Cajun to feel the undercurrent of emotion in that music. Perhaps fiddle music that helps listeners transcend a state of mind is the result of an unconscious attraction to aspects of the music that in our racial memory[5] had deeper meaning and purpose. When Brooks Hardway experiences "chills of hilarity," is he affected by music in ways that likewise inspired and motivated his ancestors in much the same way that music is used today in some religious settings?[6]

Furthermore cultural, ethnic, regional, and racial groups continually borrow from one another, causing most musical forms to be related and in constant states of change. Mountain music uses African and European rhythmic, melodic, and vocal traditions, while using melodic forms that display Celtic, Anglo, Germanic, and African emotion and influence. Today meaning and significance in West Virginia folk music is associated more with place and circumstance than with ethnicity.

Expressive music can also be a way of releasing emotions for the musician. Currence Hammonds recalled that his uncle, the famed Edden Hammons (family members spell the surname in different ways), at times became deeply depressed and would go off by himself in the woods, sing or play old lonesome songs, and weep. One such song, "Drowsy Sleepers," had the refrain, "There's many a bright and sun-shiny morning/that will turn to a dark and a dreary day." Edden Hammons was able to express incredible sorrow through his music, which it seems was his way of dealing with his personal depression. Braxton County fiddler Bob Wine used old-time music for similar purposes.[7]

Louis Watson Chappell was an English professor at West Virginia University and a pioneer of field recording in the state who recorded numerous West Virginia fiddlers and singers between 1937 and 1947. Chappell noted that during one recording session Edden Hammons played an old piece and started to tell about an uncle who had played the tune. As Hammons thought about the association of his uncle and the tune, his emotions overcame him and he could not continue to play.

Fiddlers often have sentimental or nostalgic connections to the people from whom they have learned in addition to emotional reactions to the music itself.

When coupled with intricately bowed rhythms and engaging melody lines, traditional Appalachian fiddle tunes can create compelling, sometimes even eerie or spooky music. A debate has gone on for years as to whether the emotions elicited by old-time, traditional music are positive and virtuous or negative and evil.

"Here a feeling for the supernatural sets in," wrote Emma Bell Miles in a 1905 description of Appalachian vocal music. "The oddly changing keys, the endings that leave the ear in expectation of something to follow, the quavers and falsettos, become in recurrence a haunting hint of the spirit world—neither beneficent nor maleficent, neither devil or angel, but something—something not to be understood, yet to be certainly apprehended."[8]

As Miles indicated, something unexplainable about the music associates it with the "spirit world," a world of the unknown when found in a secular setting. The association of fiddle music with forces of evil is widespread and has old-world precedence.[9]

Clyde Case of Braxton County acknowledged the eerie quality of some old-time fiddle music and told of a neighbor who played peculiar music. "French Ballangee up here, he had a key he played in, he called it the discord key," Case said. "He wouldn't hardly ever tune up in that, just once in a while, he'd tune up and play a few."[10]

The "discord key" was probably what central West Virginia fiddlers call "Old Sledge tuning." The DAEA fiddle tuning (high to low) allows for a droning first string accompanied by a melody on the second and resonant bass strings. This and other scordatura (unusual or "open" tunings used to create special effects) were popular in early sixteenth- and seventeenth-century lute music and seventeenth- and eighteenth-century European violin music. Forgotten among most classical musicians today, these tunings have been preserved in folk tradition in West Virginia.[11]

Mythical motifs are suggested in folk tunes through both the sound and mood brought about by the modes in which they are played. Tunes attain further mythical status through accompanying narrative and lore. The supernatural elements of West Virginia folk music are even clearer in the verses of songs.

Phyllis Marks of Gilmer County sings at least four songs with overt supernatural elements. "The Cherry Tree Carol" and "The Friendly Beasts" have a Christian context, with the supernatural element attributed to the power of God. In "Bow and Balance to Me" (Marks's version of the old Child ballad #10 "The Twa Sisters"), a fiddle made from body parts of a drowned girl supernaturally plays "by my sister I was drowned" when "on the fiddle the bow did sound." Marks's "Molly Bender" ends with the ghost of a slain woman appearing at her intended's trial.[12] A similar motif is documented in West Virginia law. The ghost of a deceased girl appeared to her mother and revealed the murder of the girl. After the body was exhumed on this evidence, an autopsy proved the ghost to be correct. A suspect's conviction in 1897 based on this evidence is a rare case in which a supernatural event convicted a murderer.[13]

Certain instruments also were identified as supposedly having supernatural powers and satanic affiliations. Stories about fiddles with mythical properties are widely known.[14] A Hammons family tale centers around a fiddle that played itself after "Old Pete" Hammons had played it later than midnight at a Saturday night dance. When Pete returned home from the dance after breaking the Sabbath, he hung the fiddle on a peg and went to bed. By itself the fiddle started playing "The Devil in the Woodpile." Pete had to burn the fiddle in the fireplace to get the music to stop. According to Currence Hammonds, Pete never played the fiddle again.[15] In a Barbour County tale an unwanted visitor was rebuked by an "evil" fiddle. Just before admitting a visitor, a fiddler placed his fiddle-playing wife behind a thin board wall upon which a violin hung. He told the visitor he could make the fiddle play itself and, on giving the proper cues to his unseen wife, spooked the fellow into never coming back.[16]

Some organized religions have recognized the powerful emotions evoked by secular folk music and use this to advantage. Others do not, but people will continue to feel these emotions. Ancient music may affect people in ways that are joyful, mournful, seductive, chilling, or mysterious, but it also may be inspirational in a positive religious sense. It remains for the listener's judgment as to whether it is a heavenly blessing or sin's enticement, whether it is a positive celebration of life or a negative reflection of evil. These dilemmas have plagued zealous Christians for centuries.[17]

Of course the emotional aspect rendered by any music depends on the forte of the musician. Certain fiddlers were expert at evoking "chills of hilarity" and other strong emotions. Jack McElwain and Edden Hammons were top fiddlers in the region, with McElwain usually receiving the nod as the best there was. Ernie Carpenter, who remembered beating Hammons in a contest one time, said no one ever doubted that McElwain would win any contest in which he played.[18] "Blind Ed" Haley, from Logan County, another old-time fiddler who gained much admiration in West Virginia, traveled around the southern half of the state playing requests for handouts and tips. Brooks Hardway remembers Haley's visits to the area:

Brooks Hardway, 1988. (Photograph by the author.)

I'm a pretty good judge of what good fiddlin' is, and Ed Haley was the slickest, hottest—he's another fellow that was fifty years ahead of his time. Ed Haley could lay the leather on that fiddle bow. And so smooth—it was out of this world.

I walked up in the courthouse at Spencer one time, that was in the twenties—there was a crowd in the courthouse yard—and I walked in and there set Ed Haley, a-fiddlin'. He had a tin cup settin' there on a little stand, and Ed Haley wouldn't play unless that tin cup kept rattlin' with nickles and dimes. . . .

Laurie [Lawrence] Hicks—was rough as a cob, but, my my, he could put stuff on a fiddle that was out of this world. He would go down to Charleston and bring Ed Haley up and keep him a week, maybe two. . . . Laurie picked up a lot of his stuff too. Ed enjoyed that. That's free board for Ed, you see, and at that day and time it was nippety-tuck to make a livin' if a man didn't live on a patch of land somewhere. . . . When Laurie Hicks was on his dyin' bed, he re-quested, he said, "I would like to have Ed Haley to play a few tunes over my grave, when I'm dead and gone." And Ed Haley made a special trip up to Stinson and fiddled over Laurie Hick's grave. They said he played some of the sweetest tunes you ever listened to. He took a little group with him, and he played the fiddle over Laurie Hick's grave. That's a true story.

One night—they had played all evening, and it was midnight—and Laurie thought of old John McCune. Old John McCune was an old-time fiddler. He couldn't play much, but he had one tune that they said he was out of this world on. I don't know what the tune was ["Wild Horse"], but Laurie thought of that and he said, "Ed, if you ain't too tired," he said, "I'd like to go down to John McCune's and have him to fiddle a tune for you." . . . They went down to old John McCune's. John got up out of the bed and fiddled that tune, and Ed Haley set there and listened to it. When John got through, Ed Haley said, "Mr. McCune," he said, "You never need to hesitate to play that tune for anybody." He said, "There's nobody a-livin' that can beat you a-playin' that tune." So that was an honor to John McCune on his number.[19]

Another story involving John McCune introduces the widespread folk belief about music traveling uncanny distances. Phoeba Parsons, an old-time banjo player in Calhoun County, described John McCune as the best fiddle player she ever heard and told of a time in her childhood when McCune and her father "beat that fiddle (with fiddlesticks) and played all night."

"There was [another] man—and he's dead and gone now—it was Riley Morris," Parsons recalled. "We knowed him well. He had done something and they's after him. He went across . . . this hill here, then it's down in and up, then another hill. It's about a mile I'd say. He took him a ladder and he crawled up in that cave. He got in there and he had him a bed in there. He's hidin' from the law. Okay, he told us every tune that they played. He knowed 'em and heared 'em, and he told us about 'em. Now, how could he of a-heared that far across the hill?"[20]

Parsons' recollection of the outlaw in a cave more than a mile away who heard every tune her father and John McCune played is modest compared to some. For example, Ernie Carpenter's grandfather played music for a young girl on Elk River one evening, and the next day a man who had been thirty-five miles away was able to tell him every tune he played. Carpenter ended that story with a qualifier: "They say music will travel a long way on water, you know."

Origins of old-time tunes are significant components of West Virginia folklore. Old-time folk musicians often try to trace traditional folk tunes to their original sources. One of Brooks Hardway's attempts went like this: "John McCune is the man who left 'The Wild Horse.' Old Noah Cottrell learned it from John McCune. Ward Jarvis learned it from John

Phoeba Parsons, 1994. (Photograph by the author.)

McCune."[21] Brooks and other old-time folk musicians base their research on personal experience and oral tradition. The histories aren't always accurate, but the lore invariably is intriguing.

Fiddler Melvin Wine, for instance, uses family lore to trace the origin of the tune "Soldier's Joy" to his great grandfather, Smithy Wine. According to Melvin, Confederates took his great grandfather to Richmond during the Civil War and imprisoned him for aiding Yankee soldiers. The Confederates discovered Smithy was a fiddler and made him play for a dance. Associating it with the dance that night, Smithy started calling the tune "Soldier's Joy."

While the "known origins" of most tunes in the American repertoire have developed through the folk process, some are discovered through theoretical knowledge of tune types, melodies, and bibliographic reference—a method which often proves the tunes to be of a much older

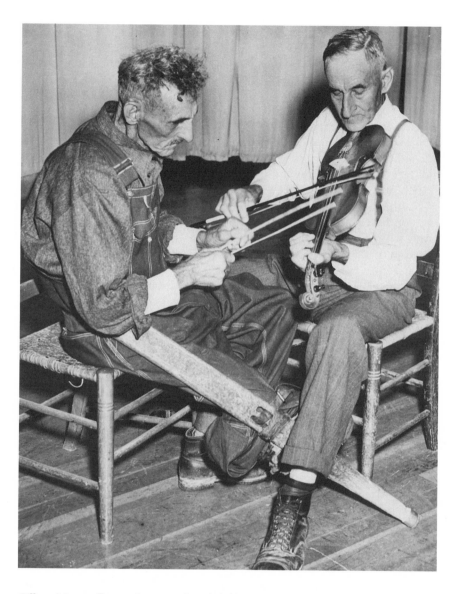

Gilbert Massey "beats the strings" with fiddlesticks while the fiddle is played by
Andrew Burnside at an early West Virginia State Folk Festival, circa 1956.
(Comstock Collection, Booth Library, Davis & Elkins College.)

vintage than suggested by the old-time folk musicians. The existence of "Soldier's Joy," for example, has been documented to well before the Civil War.[22]

Alan Jabbour has studied tunes and tune types by looking at their structure rather than their specific melodies. Much West Virginia fiddle music exhibits a tune type and structure that became prominent in published sources in the mid to late eighteenth century. Addition of the fiddle as a folk instrument in north Britain, Scotland, and Northern Ireland in the eighteenth century generated the huge body of tunes based on this model.[23] We generally recognize that Scots, Irish, and North Country British influences dominate melodies in Appalachian fiddle music.[24]

In the late eighteenth and early nineteenth centuries German influence on folk culture was considerable. Samuel Bayard, who collected tunes from Pennsylvania fiddlers and has noted melodies of German origin among his collections, said German music "pervades American instrumental folk music." He suspects some common tunes like "Buffalo Gals" to be of a German source,[25] and he notes that some common tune types, such as waltzes and schottisches, sprang from popular German sources. It is easy to find these tune types in folk tradition today in West Virginia. Germans or German Americans composed many other common old-time tunes, such as "Fisher's Hornpipe" and "Durang's Hornpipe."[26]

Most regional country fiddlers have in their repertoires two-part tunes in which each part is played in a different key. "Flop (or Lop) Eared Mule" and "Fire on the Mountain" are standard tunes of this type. In the early 1970s I knew Pennsylvania German fiddlers who played many tunes of this type. Some of the tunes still had German names. Melvin Wine's tunes of this type, on the other hand, have down-home names like "Black Cat in the Briar Patch" and "Hey Aunt Katy, There's a Bug on Me." German names, forgotten with the language, would be replaced by these down-home designations, if my theory is correct.

Tunes used for the polka, a popular dance form that swept Europe circa 1840, commonly use this two-key structure. Wine's "Hey Aunt Katy, There's a Bug on Me" is a variation of a tune also known in Virginia as "Richmond Cotillion." "Flying Clouds" is another two-key tune of this type and is sometimes called a cotillion.[27] The cotillion was not only a tune type but a nineteenth-century dance that, along with the quadrille, was the basis for our American square dance.[28]

Another obscure type of tune in Melvin Wine's repertoire also has two parts in different keys, but one part uses a major scale and the other uses a modal scale. Tunes of this type are "Lovely Jane," "Hannah at the Springhouse," and "Boatin' Up Sandy." These and a distinct group of older tunes that survived into the late twentieth century in Melvin

Melvin Wine. (Photograph by Mark Crabtree; courtesy of Augusta Heritage Center, Davis & Elkins College.)

Wine's mind surely comprise some of the oldest instrumental folk music in circulation in America today. And given the importance of such tunes among some of today's younger revivalist fiddlers, they will remain in circulation. They have that mysterious feel to them, alluded to earlier, and have origins that are anything but completely understood.

The use of modal scales is a confusing subject for many. Melvin, who has heard and played modal music in his home all of his life, remarked that it is still "strange sounding" to him.[29] Old-time musicians' approaches to music, of course, do not involve theory. One old-timer told me he knew as much about music "as a hog knows about Sunday school." Melvin and other old-time musicians documented herein have an intuitive comprehension of what mode, or perhaps I should say "mood," the music is portraying. It is evident to Wine and other old-time fiddlers that tunes in modal scales are more serious and emotional than the lighthearted, or happy, type. When Melvin plays a lighthearted tune in a major scale (Ionian), he usually gives it a light or even humorous ending. He will play "Shave and a Haircut," for example, then stop and look at the backup musicians, who musically respond with "two bits." More often, Melvin ends with a humorous, screeching halt. When playing tunes in the older diatonic modes, however, he gives the endings much more respect. He plays four notes from within the modal scale, such as low to high A, C, E, and A, when playing in the key of A.

Old-time fiddlers treat intervals of notes uniquely as well. Fiddlers I have known play certain intervals that are not on pianos, at least not those tuned in a standard fashion. Lee Triplett of Clay County, for example, regularly played notes that would sound sour to the musically trained ear. His music grew on me until I expected and loved the sound he got when he played specific notes.[30]

Tracing the history of traditional folk tunes can be impeded by title confusion. One of Wine's tunes lodged in a modal scale, "The Rainy Day," is a variant of tunes found in other areas of the state and country. Musicians in the Hammons family played a related melody they titled "Hell [or Hail] against the Barn Door." Braxton County fiddler Ernie Carpenter played a variant he called "Dan Friend's Piece," after the fiddler from whom he learned it. Rob Probst of Pendleton County played an unnamed variant.[31]

Oral tradition also confuses time signature and dance description within tune titles. The word quadrille is sometimes in tune names even though the tunes may have little to do with the quadrille dance figures. Oral tradition becomes published source when these tunes get put into print. In most of central and southern West Virginia, pieces with any dance reference, besides waltzes, usually get played as hoedowns or breakdowns. These are simply fast-paced dance tunes, formerly called reels or hornpipes. In West Virginia, tune titles with a hornpipe extension do not get played in hornpipe style or with the dotted note measure preferred by an Irish step dancer. Confusion arises because many old-time fiddlers do not associate the word that designates the time signature of a piece with the meter of the tune. At one point, Melvin Wine did not recognize tunes as waltzes unless the word "waltz" turned up in the title. He did not know he played any jigs, although he had several 6/8 tunes in his repertoire. "Floating" tune titles, instances in which one title represents several tunes, add to the bewilderment.

Tunes with titles related to historic affairs, military events, people, places, local events, human situations, animal behavior, and human emotions—all ideas commemorated through fiddle tunes in West Virginia—are easily distinguished. Tunes like "Bonaparte's Retreat," which celebrate a familiar event, traditionally became widely known tunes (even before becoming popularized with words). Tunes connected to relevant stories tend to perpetuate the stories, which in turn perpetuate the tunes. Two things today have broadened the range of such tunes. One is the popularization of tunes through modern media (radio and recordings); the other is an intellectual interest in folk music that transcends regional values and cultural and geographic boundaries.

Burl Hammons had a fiddle tune in his repertoire entitled "Shanghai."[32] There is a winter solstice tradition in eastern West Virginia called Shanghai, which could be associated with the tune. At Lewisburg, in Greenbrier County, a community Shanghai Parade takes place every New Year's Day on the main street of town. Marchers parade in masquerade. They bang on pots and pans and generally let their hair down in the spirit of inversion associated with the ancient, mid-winter European rituals. Community historians at Lewisburg have documented the existence of the practice back to the post–Civil War era. At some point, this folk practice became a more structured community event in Lewisburg.

In Pendleton County the Shanghai tradition continued as an unstructured community event. In this setting, people in masquerade formed into small groups and went from farm to farm on horseback or on foot. They sometimes solicited food, but group mischief as well as the freedom gained through masked identity was the main endeavor of the participants. Sanctioned begging, as at Halloween and old style Mardi Gras events, was secondary, or food simply was accepted when offered. People observed Shanghai, in Pendleton County, during the week preceding Christmas. It started on the date of old Saturnalia, curiously enough, and ran through the date of the winter solstice until Christmas.[33] Many aspects of this ritual are similar to mumming traditions as found in the Old World as well as in the Maritimes of Canada.[34] I believe the word Shanghai could come from the Gaelic term "sean aghaidh," meaning "old face," and relating to the masquerade that is essential to the practice.[35]

Musical traditions associated with folk rituals are rare in the Appalachians. Along with "Shanghai," there are numerous versions of "Old Christmas Morning."[36] Ritual activities associated with this date, as in the mummer's plays, have also disappeared, but many fiddle tunes commemorate the date and event.[37]

Regardless of their names or histories, tunes always will be musical sound—the only constant characteristic they carry through time and space. And that sound is always changing: it leaves a fiddler's mind, is physically interpreted though the fingers, transfers to vibration and resonance through the magic of a fiddle, and finally is processed through another human mind. When all is said and done, old-time fiddlers learned and played the tunes they heard and liked, not caring from where they came. Ernie Carpenter, who inherited a rich fiddling legacy and repertoire from his family, once played a catchy tune for me. When I asked him what it was, he said it was the theme music from a Western television show he had just seen. Fiddler Glen Smith, who has a great sense of humor, likes to play a particular tune in situations where many people are listening intently. When he finishes, someone invariably asks what it was. Smith, who can barely contain his laughter, says, "Yakety Sax," a Boots Randolph saxophone tune of modern vintage.

Glen is a formidable adversary at modern contests. Ernie Carpenter had clear opinions about today's fiddle contests. He grew up in an age where the old unaccompanied style of playing was the rule. He complained bitterly that modern contests allowed back-up musicians to play with fiddlers. He felt that only fiddles should be played in a fiddle contest, and I agree that if contest sponsors took his advice, old-style fiddlers would be the winners. There are few contests in West Virginia where a traditional old-time fiddler has a chance to win, despite the promotion of many as "Old-Time" fiddlers' contests. Most winners play in the smooth and notey "Texas" style. Judging is so subjective, it is difficult to make it consistent, and the winner in most contests can be anybody's guess, depending on a myriad of factors.

Woody Simmons, a Randolph Countian[38] and one of West Virginia's very competitive fiddlers, once played at a Ritchie County Fair contest. There were cash prizes given out for first, second, and third places. The judges announced that there was a tie for second. Woody wound up in the tie and they had a play-off, which Woody lost. When the judges announced the three top finishers, Woody was not among them. They had not given him third, even though he had tied for second, ahead of the third place finisher.

The West Virginia State Folk Festival at Glenville promotes a traditionally based contest. In 1974, Kanawha County fiddler Mike Humphreys scored low in the contest because he "did not play the old-time style." Humphreys' style was anything but modern, but was not as archaic as some of the central West Virginia fiddlers there that found favor with the judges. Humphreys stomped off with much ado, never to return. I distinctly remember the rendition of "Katy Hill" that he played. It was some of the hottest, most powerful fiddling I had ever heard. Was it old-time music? You bet it was, but everything is relative.

Emery Bailey of Calhoun County was a great old-time fiddler, who, if playing in legitimate "old-time" fiddling contests today, would often walk away with top honors. Around 1930, officials accused Bailey of playing something other than old-time music, as Brooks Hardway relates:

Emery Bailey was fifty years ahead of his time in what he could do with a bow on a fiddle. They had a contest at Sutton one time, old-time fiddler's contest, and Emery went. . . . When Emery come back, I asked him, "What did you do in the contest?"

Emery said, "Upon my honor, Brooks, they didn't let me play." He said, "They wouldn't let me enter the contest."

I said, "Did you play a tune or two for 'em Emery?"

Emery said, "Yea."

I said, "What did you play?"

He said, "Upon my honor, I fiddled 'Sally Gooden,' Brooks."

I said, "Why didn't they let you play?"

He said, "They couldn't call my way old-time fiddlin'."

I said, "What was wrong?"

He said, "I think I's a-puttin' too much diddle on the bow." Now, Emery's a-layin' the leather to "Sally Goodin." I'd give anything on earth if I had a tape of that tune that he played that day.[39]

I do not know exactly what kind of "diddle" Bailey was putting on his bow. Melvin Wine told me about an old fiddler named Pat Cogar, who has won the Glenville contest and is one of a line of fiddlers from that family in Braxton County. Melvin says that Pat's father, John, was a better fiddler, that Pat had a "sheeptail-wag" on his bow.

An important concept in old-time fiddle music is the way tunes are combined to form a music session. In a good session, from a fiddler's viewpoint, tunes follow each other in a way that is logical, orderly, and sensible to the ear. For Ernie Carpenter, the sound, key, and phrase links one tune to the next tune in a good session. Session etiquette is important too. A banjo player following along is expected to suggest only tunes that fit the pattern. A listener's request is often rejected because of nonconformity in sound, key, feeling, or other provenance to the previous tune. This tradition of etiquette results in tune sessions in which fiddlers call most of the shots. The fiddlers approve the tunes, often in deference to the key in which the banjo is tuned if a banjo player is present.

Singers are in charge and take "turn about" in a folk-singing session—a rare occurrence today in a traditional setting, other than at a festival or formal gathering. Just as there is a separation of instrumental music and singing in older Irish music, the separation was in place in older Appalachian music in West Virginia. Singing with the fiddle or between fiddled melodies was uncommon in West Virginia until recently. Through the years in Melvin Wine's family, for example, people were singers or fiddlers, but not both. Frank George noted this situation in southern West Virginia.[40] Ballad singer Maggie Hammons also played a banjo, but she never sang and played at the same time. In fact,

Patrick Gainer (left) with fiddler Pat Cogar. Gainer introduced many traditional musicians to a public stage through his organization of the West Virginia State Folk Festival in 1950. (Courtesy of the Comstock Collection, Booth Library, Davis & Elkins College.)

according to Dwight Diller, Maggie used different melodies when singing and playing some tunes. Brooks Hardway noted how unusual it
was when French Carpenter once sang a song while fiddling. Although
everyone present was familiar with old-time music, none had ever witnessed that. Singing while playing an instrument is an African American contribution to American folk music, spread primarily through the
minstrel stage. It did not significantly affect white tradition until the
twentieth century. Cecil Sharp, who sought out 281 traditional singers
in 1916 and 1917, met only one person who played an instrument (a
guitar) while singing. That was in Charlottesville, Virginia, where there
has long been a substantial African American population.[41]

In modern country music, which evolved from traditional folk music, instrumental tunes have nearly disappeared. They are still prevalent,
however, in the less-evolved bluegrass music. Modern country singers
normally sing in the first person rather than expressing a group senti-
ment, as is often done in traditional folk music. Venues for modern music
forms differ from those of traditional folk music too. Performance-ori-
ented settings, such as jamborees, roundups, and media broadcasts,
are the usual venues for modern music,[42] while old-time music is played
at less formal affairs. Festivals and fiddlers' conventions provide important performance venues for old-time and bluegrass music. With
old-time music, in particular, the focus is not a stage; rather the main
attractions are the informal aspects of these affairs, the jams, the social
interaction, and sometimes dances. Attention turns to the stage only
when the event is a contest.

The content of modern country songs also departs from traditional
folk music. Most modern country songs are about romance or its con-
sequences, only one of many themes in traditional folk songs and ballads. Fiddler Charlie Daniels' relatively recent recording "The Devil Went
Down to Georgia" is an exception. It uses motifs and tunes commonly
found in traditional folklore. The piece touches on what Emma Bell
Miles described as "a haunting hint of the spirit world." For years, it
was the most requested number encountered by fiddlers performing
for children at school programs in West Virginia. Kids latched on to
that tune/story, confirming an ageless attraction to the traditional elements of genuine folklore and folk music. While old-time music has a
much rougher edge to it than Daniels' rendition, his song still reflects
those aspects of folk music that elicit intense emotions (like Brooks
Hardway's "chills of hilarity") and command the attention of listeners.

2

Choking the Goose

"If anybody couldn't play of a fiddle, dance of a jig, or shoot of a gun, he wasn't worth a damn."[1]
Braxton County fiddler John McNemar

Areas of West Virginia with strong fiddling traditions, such as Webster, Pocahontas, Clay, Calhoun, and Braxton Counties, celebrate highly esteemed players. Often these legendary fiddlers account for the musical legacies of those areas and are the sources of many tunes in local repertoires. Even some published sources of nineteenth-century West Virginia history mention prominent fiddlers. Late in the century, William Byrne wrote accounts about many of Webster County's illustrious characters in his book about fishing, *Tale of the Elk*. He mentions, for example, "Jack McElwain, then and now far famed fiddler" among the county's most prominent citizens.[2]

Indeed, numerous old fiddle tunes played in an old style in central West Virginia are attributed to Lewis Johnson "Uncle Jack" McElwain (1856-1938). Writing about Webster County fiddlers, Sampson Newton Miller observed, "there was Jack Wayne[3] of Erbacon, hard to crowd."[4] McElwain's death in 1938 was untimely—by 1939 Louis Watson Chappell was trekking into the area with a recording machine collecting traditional music. Although primarily recording ballad singers, he also recorded prominent fiddlers.[5]

Jack McElwain made his home on White Oak, a tributary of Laurel Creek, near the village of Erbacon in Webster County. Erbacon sprang up in the late nineteenth century around the railroad. Once a thriving village, it is all but a ghost town today. Local lore has it that Erbacon received its name from the cook at the local hotel who would ask, "Do you want ham 'r bacon?" In reality, the town was established by and named for E.R. Bacon, an official with the B&O Railroad.[6] For such a

"Uncle Jack" McElwain with siblings. (Date and photographer unknown; author's collection.)

small place, Erbacon produced its share of fine fiddlers, and the best known was Uncle Jack.

"Boy he could fiddle," recalled banjo player Bud Sandy. "He played 'Old Sledge' and 'Hannah at the Springhouse.' Now, that old man could play anything, boy. I don't know how he'd do it, but he'd cross his legs and both feet set right on the floor."[7]

Fiddler Ernie Carpenter seldom spoke of old-time fiddle playing without mentioning McElwain. Speaking about a tune commonly called "Dog Shit a Ryestraw," Carpenter used a popular analogy and said, "When Jack 'Wain played it, you had to open the door and let the stink out. He could really play that tune. Was beautiful the way he played it."[8]

An old neighbor of Jack McElwain's said McElwain left home for weeks at a time on "fiddlin' trips." His trips were often with fiddling friend Tom Jack Woods.[9] He was probably most noted locally for the time he took an extended "fiddlin' trip" to the 1893 World's Fair in Chicago. McElwain entered and won the fiddle contest there.

While McElwain was in Chicago, his fiddle was stolen, but he recovered it at a pawn shop before returning to West Virginia.[10] Many remember that McElwain, on being told what a fine fiddler he was, would reply in his whiney voice, "It ain't me, it's my feedle." McElwain thought his violin had been made by an original Italian master, but an appraisal after his death proved it to be a German copy.[11]

Melvin Wine, Bob Wine, Ernie Carpenter, Shelt Carpenter, Edden Hammons, French Carpenter, Doc White, and Dewey Hamrick are all notable fiddlers and members of musically prominent West Virginia families who attribute tunes and fiddling prowess to McElwain. Noted Logan County fiddler "Blind Ed" Haley traveled to McElwain's area from his home in Ashland, Kentucky. Haley's repertoire includes tunes learned from McElwain. "Old Sledge" is one such piece, although Haley's rendition of the piece is not notable.

Sherman Hammons recalled his uncle Edden Hammons meeting McElwain at the "pig's ear" at Cowen in Webster County to swap tunes. "Pig's ear" is a euphemism for a tavern where illegal whiskey could be had, a fact which suggests this interaction took place during Prohibition days.[12] As young men, and with encouragement from their fiddle-playing fathers, Melvin Wine and Ernie Carpenter made pilgrimages to McElwain's home to learn tunes. Dewey Hamrick said his father walked 40 miles to and from Uncle Jack's place on Laurel Creek playing the part of the modern tape recorder for his fiddling son. Dewey's father learned and remembered tunes like "Yew Piney Mountain" and "Big Fish" to whistle for Dewey to learn.

Reese Morris, another Erbacon fiddler of some renown, played in the old "West Fork style," which is attributed to Jack McElwain. This style refers to the West Fork of the Little Kanawha River in Calhoun County, where the McElwain family lived at one time. Erbacon fiddler Harry Scott also played in the McElwain tradition. When I met Scott, shortly before his death in 1986, he was too old and infirm to play, but he talked reverently about "Uncle Jack." Scott said that when McElwain played "Old Sledge" you seemed to rise three feet up off the ground. In fact, all the fiddlers I encountered who had heard McElwain play described him in phenomenal terms, usually as "the best I ever heard." They also attribute the oldest tunes to him.

By chance, the Library of Congress documented another Erbacon fiddler, Tom Dillon. During a collapse of the coal market in the 1950s, West Virginians left in droves to find work in other states. Dillon was an itinerant fiddler and house painter who had almost hit bottom in northern Virginia in 1956. He was fiddling for change and handouts in a park adjacent to the Library of Congress when he was noticed and invited across the street to record his tunes. Library personnel asked Dillon if he knew of other good fiddlers in West Virginia. He gave them the name of his friend Ernie Carpenter. Carpenter received an invitation to come to the Library and record, but, unsure of the motives for the gesture, he declined to go.

By all accounts Tom Dillon was an unusual character. Ernie Carpenter recalled Dillon once coming to visit in an old station wagon with a flock of chickens in the back. Dillon was a "trader," which in rural West Virginia can be an occupation unto itself. Some people whose only cash income is from trading have "raised families" in that fashion. Many trade as a sideline, dealing in everything from livestock to chain saws. Dillon supplemented his trading with whatever cash and in-kind services he could procure through his music.

Dillon often took his fiddle to local sandlot baseball games and fiddled for money or drinks after the games. He backstepped as he played and sometimes played with two bows strapped together. He used cross tunings[13] to good advantage and always kept drones going through his melodies. Dillon's droning sound sometimes consisted of three strings being played at once. He employed some astounding bowing and rhythms in a variety of vernacular tunes.[14] He called himself the "Cornstalk and Bagpipe Fiddler" and had handbills printed with that title and a picture of himself with his fiddle.

Shortly before he died, Dillon appeared at a couple of the state's folk festivals at Glenville, and some of his tunes were recorded there.[15] In fact Dillon probably garnered his title "Cornstalk and Bagpipe Fiddler" by way of Patrick Gainer, who organized the state folk festival in Glenville in 1950. The bagpipe is unknown to traditional musicians in West Virginia, but Gainer liked to hypothesize about the fiddle and bagpipe connection through the use of drones by fiddlers.

Most of the known Hammons family fiddlers were born in or came to Webster County, and Sampson Newton Miller related a story of Edden Hammons' introduction to the music-appreciating public:

> About 1899 on the fourth of July at Webster Springs, there was scheduled a platform dance and picnic near the old Salt Sulphur Spring. As a boy, I distinctly remember this event. Whoever had charge of the dance had employed Bernard Hamrick to play for it. "Burn" as he was familiarly known, brought his violin to the platform about two hours before the dance was to start. He tuned his fiddle and began to play. People flocked in from everywhere. "Burn" played only a few pieces and quit. People cheered and cheered, but "Burn" wouldn't play anymore.
>
> Jesse Hammons, father of Edden, said, "Mr. Hamrick, let my son play a tune or two." After a great deal of persuasion, "Burn" let the lad of nine have the violin. Edden tuned it and started playing with the

fiddle on his left shoulder. He played so well and the people began to cheer till you could scarcely hear anything else. "Burn" got peeved at what had happened and he gave Edden his violin and went home. So there was no dance that afternoon."[16]

Other Webster County fiddlers mentioned by Miller are George Tracy, Sampson Hamrick, Dave Baughman, Moore Hamrick, Arthur Elbon, Hans Hamrick, and Aretus Hamrick.

During his travels collecting folk music in the 1940s, Louis Watson Chappell recorded several Pocahontas County fiddlers. The collection includes Edden Hammons, who lived in Pocahontas County at the time; Bob Puffenburger, from Marlinton; and Marion Shinaberry, who was from Green Bank and recorded hymns.[17] More recent fiddlers of some renown from Pocahontas County are Hamp Carpenter and Lee Hammons. Lee Hammons is distantly related to Edden Hammons and may be heard on the recording *Shakin' Down the Acorns,* (Rounder 0018) and playing banjo on *The Diller Collection, Volume 2* (Augusta AHR-019). Burl Hammons (1908-1993) and "Mose" Coffman (1905-1994) were two other exemplary fiddlers of the region. Originally from Greenbrier County, Coffman lived, worked, fiddled, and recorded while living in Pocahontas County. Coffman credited Glen Gillespie and Dave Baldwin as major fiddling influences on him in Greenbrier County.[18]

Describing fiddle playing at a dance on the frontier in Pocahontas County, William T. Price wrote, "About 10 or 11 o'clock the 'husking' and the 'quilting' were suspended, supper served and then came the 'hoedown,' wherein heavy stumbling toes would be tripped to the notes of a screeching unruly violin, such fiddling was called 'choking the goose,' or when there was no fiddle in evidence someone only 'patted juba' about as distinctly as the trotting of a horse over a bridge."[19]

"Choking the goose" is a great description of an unruly, squawking fiddle. Modestly describing one of his own fiddle performances, Ernie Carpenter would say he was just "cuttin' and coverin' "—recognizable by anyone who has ever plowed with a horse as a fair description of how to botch up the job.[20] Price reports several slaves among the first settlers, which probably accounts for the "patted juba." This rhythmic form (similar to "hambone") from African tradition consists of hands slapped together and to various parts of the body, creating a rhythm. It was usually done to a rhyme, and Courlander suggests it included a dance used for ritual purpose.[21]

Clay County's fiddling legacy included members of the Carpenter family and was continued by others, including notables Ira Mullins and Lee Triplett. Mullins and Triplett earned status not so much for their fiddling, which in their younger days was formidable, but for their per-

Lee Triplett with Dana Perkins at the Morris Family Old-Time Music Festival at Ivydale, 1972. (Photograph by the author.)

sonalities. Older West Virginia musicians have enough stories about Ira Mullins and his contest adversary Lee Triplett to fill a volume. Clay County fiddler Doc White attributed much of his musical influence to French Carpenter and the legendary Jack McElwain. Braxton County fiddler John Johnson said that when his grandfather, Clay Countian

Doc White at Glenville, 1973. (Photograph by the author.)

Alec Hamrick, fiddled, "he could make the hair raise on the back of
your neck." Clay County fiddler Sol Nelson "was famous throughout
the Elk Valley from Clay Courthouse to Sutton."[22]

Clay County, home of these notable musicians, lays claim to some
rough places and times. In the Booger Hole area, for instance, family
feuds, murder, and mayhem sowed the seeds for a large body of folklore, including ghosts, unexplainable incidents, and general strange-
ness. Fiddler Wilson Douglas explained:

> We moved back up in there on the old Douglas place . . . on the right-
> hand fork of Booger Hole. You look right across the valley and see the
> head of Booger Hole where they killed all them people. . . .
>   You'd hear people coming up this little road, riding a horse . . .

wide open. But they'd never get there. Never get there. People'd talk all night. You couldn't understand what they's—talk all night! And you'd see people dressed in white going in every direction once in a while. You'd never catch up to 'em. They'd disappear. By God, it just beat anything I ever saw. I can tell a million tales about that place. My mother, my sister, could verify me. . . .

There's a little path where all them there travelers traveled in the old days. I looked out that path, and here come a woman dressed in white, and her hair was so black it looked like a crow. And it drug the ground. And I never could see her face. She had something over her face, and I never heard such cryin' in my life. The first thought hit me, I knew some people's makin' moonshine in that holler. I thought now there's a bunch of women down there, and they've got in a fight, and she's leavin'. She come up, I wasn't a bit more scared than I am now. She come up as far as from here to the middle of that yard. And she just went up in the air like that. Just like that. I set there and rubbed my eyes, and I said, "Now I know dang well that I seen that."[23]

Andrew Sampson, who was "run out" of Booger Hole after being charged with—but not convicted of—murder, left Clay County and moved to the Calhoun County/Braxton County area.[24] The Sampson family contributed to the traditional music of that area into the late twentieth century. One of Andrew's sons, Homer, became a shape-note singing school teacher and taught hundreds to sing in the old four-part harmony style. Homer and his brother Harvey followed in their father's footsteps as old-time fiddlers. They contributed ballads, folksongs, and fiddle tunes to recording projects I have produced. Their fiddle repertoires are distinctly regional, and their fiddling style is wonderfully archaic. Family history aside, Homer and Harvey Sampson proved to be fine country gentlemen who harbored a rich store of musical tradition.

Harvey Sampson lived near Nicut,[25] near the Calhoun/Braxton line, where the earliest settlers greatly contributed to that area's wild and woolly reputation. Four of these settlers, Jackson Cottrell, Daniel McCune, Joseph Parsons, and Alexander Turner, were convicted of the murder of Jonathan Nicholas about 1843. The four were members of the Hell-Fired Band, a vigilante group formed to discourage any civilization, settlements, roads, churches, or improvements of any kind in the area.[26] To these people, who had acquired hunting, trapping, and ginsenging as a way of life, encroaching civilization was a threat.[27] The band used intimidation, mayhem, and murder to scare off those bent on settling the new country. Only a few pioneer families were represented by the Hell-Fired Band, but the feelings that caused the conflict were widely shared on the frontier.

Cottrell and McCune were descendants of Adam O'Brien, who settled around 1800 in what is now Calhoun County.[28] O'Brien was the first white man to have resided in this area of central West Virginia, and a fair number of central West Virginia's old-time musicians are descended from him. He was a hunter, trapper, and "Indian fighter." He was of Irish birth, lived to be more than one hundred years old, fought in the Revolutionary War at the Battle of Point Pleasant, and left his initials on rocks and trees and in caves throughout the area. It is said that he sired a child at age ninety-two! O'Brien acquired folk-hero status, especially regarding his procreation capabilities.

The Hell-Fired Band drew its life's blood and inspiration from Adam O'Brien. Before his death in 1836, O'Brien's recollections were noted and later reported in the *Southern Literary Messenger* of May 1838. O'Brien said, "We lived quite happy before the Revolution, for there was no courts and no law and no sheriffs in this here country, and we all agreed very well. But by-and-by the country came to be settled: the people begun to come in, and then there was need for law; and then came the lawyers, and next came the preachers, and from that time we never had peace any more."[29]

Early historian John D. Sutton wrote about one of the area's noted settlers: "Old Pioneer Jack Cottrell who lived on the headwaters of the West Fork, was one of the noted characters of that region. The Cottrells, it is said, had Indian blood in their veins. Jack lived a typical wild, rural life. He was a hunter, seng digger, lived in the woods, followed bee hunting, roamed the mountains, crossed every low gap, followed every hog trail, fiddled and danced in every cabin, but never laid up any store ahead. . . . Old Jack told [a local] merchant one day that as soon as "the blessed root began to blossom" he would have plenty of ginseng, and his summer's living would be assured."[30]

Despite the crudeness of life in Calhoun County, Ernie Carpenter defends the area as having the distinguished reputation of producing numerous musicians.

"I expect that the county in this state that has more musicians than any other county is Calhoun," Carpenter said. "Whenever you see a guy or a girl, *anybody* from Calhoun County, you just hand them a banjo. You don't need to ask them if they can play. You just hand them a banjo or a fiddle, and I guarantee you nine out of ten of them will play!"[31]

Senate Cottrell, Noah Cottrell, Phoeba Cottrell Parsons, Jenes Cottrell, Sylvia Cottrell O'Brien, Ezra Cottrell, Emery Bailey, Brooks Hardway, Carrol Hardway, Lester McCumbers, Linda McCumbers, the Bernard McCumbers family, and Ward Jarvis are all recent musicians in the area who have been recorded, at least on field recordings.[32] Sylvia Cottrell O'Brien mentioned the fiddling of old "Uncle Marsh" Cottrell.

The Baileys were another family of remarkable musicians around

Scott Bailey (bottom right) with his family and friends. (Date and photographer unknown; courtesy of Harry Newell.)

the Calhoun/Braxton area. Scott Bailey is remembered as a fine fiddler, as was his son, Emery, whose recorded tunes were reported by Malvin Artley.[33] Emery's brother, Homer, is remembered as a top-notch clawhammer banjo player and fiddler, and Flummer, another sibling, also played banjo.

"Scott Bailey, he was so mean his father and mother couldn't do nothing with him," recalled Ward Jarvis about the unruly young fiddler. "They tried to scare him—he's just a boy. Now this is the truth. He's just a boy, and they set a day to hang him! They called the neighbors in, and they's going to hang him. Scott, he found it out some way, and that morning they got to coming in, and Scott took the hill just as hard as he could run. He run back on the top of the hill, and he hollered back at 'em, said, 'Tell 'em Scott ain't a-going to be at the hanging.'"[34]

Musical families in this neighborhood include Hardway, Santy, Sears, Case, Mollohan, McCumbers, Sampson, Hall, Tanner, Cunning-ham, Ballangee, and Jarvis. Ward Jarvis and Frank Santy were prob-ably the most respected and well-known fiddlers in the area.[35]

Sam Hacker, a fiddler from nearby Little Otter in Braxton County, was recorded by Louis Watson Chappell in 1947. Hacker was a keen fiddler who garnered respect among his peers for his musical abilities.

Emery Bailey. (Date
and photographer
unknown; courtesy of
Harry Newell.)

His father and brother were good clawhammer banjo players.[36] Hacker
often played at the Braxton County stock sale at Gassaway and danced
as he played.

"He was about six or seven years old," said Hacker's daughter, relating her father's start in music. "I've heard him tell it a-many a-times.
There was a lady that lived close to him that could play the violin pretty
good. He had—back then they called it dropsy. And the doctor said, let
him, you know, have his way. Well this woman's name—we called her
'Aunt Dolly,' and she'd come there and entertain him, and she made
him a fiddle—out of a cornstalk. Did you ever hear tell of the like? She
went out, and she got him a cornstalk, now, and she cut that cornstalk
in strips, you know, and put a bridge in under it, you know, and fixed
him a bow. Now that's how he got started a-playin' the violin. Now that
sounds kind of fishy, but they done it! They made him a bow. Went out

Dilly Wyatt. (Sketch by Porte Crayon; from *Harper's New Monthly Magazine*, September 1872.)

to the barn and got the hair out of an old horse's tail and made him a bow! What they was trying to do was keep him entertained while he had the sickness, see."[37]

Hacker had the reputation of being willing to fiddle at the drop of a hat. For starting out as a "cornstalk fiddler," Hacker went far with his fiddling. His rural neighbors valued his folksy, happy-go-lucky disposition in a way that had to do with his sporting attitude toward life. Hacker's daughter said the hardest thing she ever had to do was lower the strings down on her father's fiddle after he died at age 76 in 1976.

The Allen family from around Napier in Braxton County also were exceptional musicians. At least six members of the family fiddled, and all of them have passed on. Melvin Wine credits Tom Allen with teaching him the fine versions of "Betty Baker" and numerous other tunes he plays.

Many twentieth-century musicians in the area stem from these Braxton, Calhoun, and Clay County families. Of all the musical families and the musicians they spawned, only a few received notoriety commercially during the "golden age" of old-time country music. Budge and Fudge Mayse of Braxton County were perhaps the best known because of their radio work at WMMN in Fairmont.[38]

Although fiddling was considered a manly endeavor, several women fiddlers from central West Virginia deserve mention. Sampson Newton Miller lists Sarah Miller Gregory as the outstanding fiddler in Webster County around the year 1855, just before Jack McElwain was born. It was unusual for a woman fiddler to be held in such high esteem at that early date. In 1872, according to travel writer Porte Crayon,[39] Dilly Wyatt of Harman in neighboring Randolph County was another dominant female fiddler.[40] John Armstrong (1875-1933) of Harman was considered the "brag fiddler" of that area. Ernie Carpenter remembered several woman fiddlers in Braxton County including Gela Richards and Jessie Rhea, an African American woman. Sarah Singleton was a mainstay at Braxton County dances. Fiddler Wilson Douglas from Clay County credits French Carpenter as his major influence but commends his grandmother Rosie Morris' ability as well.[41]

While some popular musicians, like Uncle Dave Macon, played to packed houses in county seats, such as Sutton in Braxton County, noncommercial string music was still going strong in every backcountry village in the early to mid twentieth century. Talent scouts never visited central West Virginia as they did areas like Bristol, Virginia, and Atlanta, Georgia, so few area musicians were documented via commercial recordings. Some central West Virginia musicians of note were recorded by folklorists early on, but many exceptional musicians like "Uncle Jack" McElwain were never recorded. At the close of the twentieth century, a remarkable body of old folk song is still in oral tradition.[42]

3

The Carpenter Legacy

*"Music is a great gift, one of the greatest anybody can have, be-
cause it's something nobody can take away from you. . . . Money
can't buy it. . . . It's a very precious thing, I think, very precious!"*
Ernie Carpenter[1]

On a rainy night in the spring of 1979 I found myself at a square dance
at the old Frametown Fire Hall in Braxton County. I was playing fiddle
with a guitar player, Cliff Wilkie, and a banjo player, Ben Carr, who
lived nearby. We were making the most of a less-than-adequate sound
system by playing as hard and as loud as possible. A mixed crowd of
folks was out on the floor. Fire department members sold hot dogs with
slaw and chili in an adjacent room. Kids ran, shrieking in the midst of
play, in and out of the old school building. The large room was ringed
with onlookers. During brief interludes, dancers and local old-timers
would amble up and say, "Play Sally Gooden" or "Can you get that 'Jimmy
Johnson?'"

We were well into the night. The many dances called from the floor
were interspersed with a few cakewalks as fund raisers for the fire department. We were playing "Did You Ever See the Devil, Uncle Joe?"
when through the entrance walked two older gents, one of whom caught
my eye as I played. He wore a Stetson "Open Road" hat and watched
me intently as he made his way around the edge of the dance floor to an
out-of-the way spot in a far corner.

The dance eventually ended with a "promenade right off the floor,
that's all there is, there ain't no more." Right after sounding the final
note, I made a beeline for the old gent with the hat. Somehow I knew I
wanted to meet him. He complimented my fiddling and then told me
his name was Ernie Carpenter. Melvin Wine had mentioned Carpenter
to me, describing him as an "able" fiddle player. Carpenter had been

Ernie Carpenter,
1988. (Photograph
by the author.)

out that night playing music for a "fox chaser's reunion." He invited me
to his place to play and become acquainted.

I took up Ernie's offer and soon became interested in his music,
tales, and family history.[2] The Carpenter family of central West Virginia
is perhaps the best known old-time fiddling family in the state, perhaps
in all of Appalachia. Never recorded commercially in the days of early
country music, the family is known for playing noncommercial traditional old-time music. This is reflected in both style and repertoire.

Ernie Carpenter (1909-1997) was rather protective and not interested in teaching me his older tunes until he got to know me. Then,
during one visit, he presented me with a tape of tunes he had made
specially for me to learn. I was honored! The tunes on the tape contain
introductions by Carpenter that carefully place the tunes in a family
context and personalize their existence.

Carpenter was one of two people with whom I was well acquainted in West Virginia who had a direct connection to frontier life. Ernie had known his grandfather, William Carpenter, and could play his fiddle tunes and retell his tales. William, or "Squirrely Bill," Carpenter was born before 1830. Listening to Ernie, the one intermediary between Squirrely Bill and me, I felt near at hand to an American frontier experience. Ernie Carpenter somehow stood apart from the twentieth century and offered an alternative viewpoint to modern conventional wisdom. He took great interest in younger musicians like me and spoke his feelings frankly about any subject.

The family descends from William Carpenter, who traveled from England to Rhode Island in 1636. A Joseph Carpenter came from New York to Augusta County, Virginia, in 1746. Sometime after 1780, Ernie's great great grandfather Jeremiah Carpenter along with his brother, Benjamin, found the wilds of Elk River in central West Virginia to their liking. Only a few white hunter/trappers, including Adam O'Brien, had traversed the area since two brothers accidentally found the river in the seventeenth century.[3] According to Ernie Carpenter, Jeremiah gave Elk River its name after killing a large elk along the river soon after the family settled.[4] The Carpenters had traveled from the Jackson River country of old Virginia. Historians and genealogists differ over who was who, what the dates were, and exactly when these early Carpenters settled on the river.

Reputed to have all been fiddlers, the Carpenter family has left a legacy of recorded oral history that goes back to before the period when they settled Elk River. Ernie Carpenter is a fifth-generation Carpenter on the Elk and the receiver of much oral history from his grandfather, Squirrely Bill, and father, Shelt.

The family had considerable conflict with Native Americans in old Virginia. According to Ernie, Jeremiah was captured and held for several years in Ohio before escaping and returning to the family.[5] Ernie believed Jeremiah's father to be William Carpenter, who was killed by Native Americans on the Jackson River in 1764. In *Chronicles of Border Warfare*, by Withers, and in McWhorter's *Border Settlers*, the death of William Carpenter is reported. But Withers also reports that William's son, who was captured by and then escaped from Native Americans, was a Dr. Carpenter who lived in Nicholas County. Other genealogists identify Jeremiah's father as Solomon Carpenter, possibly a brother of William.

Another younger Solomon Carpenter, known as "Devil Sol," was in the Civil War, imprisoned at Camp Chase, and inspired a tune-tale, known in the Carpenter family as "Camp Chase."[6] In this incident, Devil Sol, a man named Bowie, and others were engaged in a fiddle contest

Ernie Carpenter under Solly's Rock, 1980. (Photograph by Doug Yarrow; courtesy of Augusta Heritage Center.)

at Camp Chase, a Union prison camp near Columbus, Ohio. Devil Sol won his freedom by playing this tune. It is often noted by West Virginia fiddlers who still relate the story that Devil Sol added a few extra notes, giving him an edge on his competitors and leading to his liberty.[7] Sol had to sign an oath of allegiance to the Union upon his release, but he headed straight south and joined another Confederate outfit.[8] Alan Jabbour traced the "Camp Chase" tune to the early nineteenth century under the title "George Booker" in America and earlier to an eighteenth-century Scottish strathspey, "The Marquis of Huntly's Farewell."[9]

At the Carpenter's new home on Elk River, conflict with Native Americans continued. During a raid, placed by Withers in 1793 and others earlier, Indians killed Benjamin Carpenter and scalped his wife, who survived. Then, or possibly during an earlier conflict (as early as 1782), Jeremiah took his wife and other family members to a large, overhanging "shelf" rock on Camp Run. This is a tributary of Laurel

Creek, itself a tributary of Elk River, and is near what became the Braxton County village of Centralia.

Ernie related that sometime in the late eighteenth century, a child, also named Solomon or "Old Solly," was born to Jeremiah Carpenter and his wife, Elizabeth Mann Carpenter, under that rock. Some Carpenter family members still living near the rock-home call it "Solly's Rock." Jeremiah gets credit as author of the fiddle tune, "Shelvin' Rock," made to commemorate the birth of his son under the rock. Folklore has it that this baby never cried after its birth until long after the immediate conflict with the Native Americans dissipated and he was brought out into the sunlight.[10] Not verified is Ernie Carpenter's claim that Solomon's mother, his great great grandmother, was an Indian.

"Shelvin' Rock" is a tune entrenched in Carpenter family lore, but "Shelvin' Rock" is also a floating tune title. It is even used for the title of a different melody in Braxton County.[11] In this case, it seems possible that an older tune title perfectly illustrated an incident the Carpenter family fiddlers wanted to commemorate. Through the folk process, the "Shelvin' Rock" tune and the incident became one and the same. Ernie Carpenter took me to this remote location, took out his fiddle, and played the old tune while standing under the rock where his ancestor was born.

Several Carpenter family stories stem from the period when the family lived under the rock. One legend is about a Christmas tree, reputed to have been made for Solly. Ernie Carpenter recounted this tale for me, and a published account from 1885 is attributed to James L. Carpenter, a son of Solomon Carpenter, the baby born under the rock. A ten-foot pitch pine cross was made to decorate the top of a holly tree that stood down the slope from the Carpenter's rock-shelter home. The cross was coated with rosin and bear grease and secured to the tree with hickory widths. At dark the cross was lit so it burned and glowed in the top of the tree, much to the delight of young Solly. When the strips of hickory bark burnt through, the burning cross cascaded down the tree and down the hill.[12] This is reported as the first Carpenter family Christmas tree, but Christmas trees were unheard of in America at this time (the late eighteenth century).[13] The Carpenters, if they had any religious affiliation, would have been of the Protestant persuasion. At that time Protestants were denouncing Christmas celebrations as nonsense. Christmas trees were not common in America until the mid nineteenth century.[14] If there is validity to this story about a burning cross on a holly tree in the eighteenth century, the event probably descended from Celtic tradition. Many references to this practice exist among the ancient Celts.[15] While the Carpenters were not practicing an ancient Pagan religious rite, the tradition, just as in the German Christmas tree tradition that is still popular, stems from such a source.

The Carpenters were intricately tied to Elk River as raftsmen, boatsmen, and fishermen. Ernie's forced removal from his Elk River homeplace to make way for the Army Corps of Engineers' Sutton Dam Project in the 1950s was a bitter pill to swallow. He anguished over the tragedy into old age and confided to me one time that no one knew how close he came to murdering the authorities who came to evict him.

One old family story, narrated by Ernie, has his great grandfather, Solomon, standing along the Elk when a man came floating down atop a set of barge gunwales. These gunwales were hand hewn from old growth timber on the upper reaches of the Elk and floated down to Charleston for barge construction. These barges were loaded with salt by slaves on the Kanawha River at Malden. They were taken down the Ohio and often on down the Mississippi where, after the salt was sold, they were sold and sawn for lumber.[16] As this raftsman approached, Solomon called out to him, "You ain't got enough manpower on them gunwales to handle them. I'd like to tell you a little something about this next shoal down here that you're going through."

"I don't thank God almighty for advice on this river," the man yelled back. "I know all about it. I'll eat my supper in Sutton or [I'll eat it] in hell."[17]

Ernie said the gunwales struck a large rock just below there at the "Breechclout Shoal." The man, a Gibson, drowned, and it took three days to recover the body.[18] Such tales within the chronicles of Carpenter family history and lore allude to great respect for the river, its power, and the sustenance it afforded the Carpenters for five generations.

The Elk has its birth in Pocahontas County and makes a long curve through Webster County before entering Braxton County, where it becomes a navigable (by johnboat) stream. Until the "Coal and Coke" railroad, built by turn-of-the-century industrialists Henry Davis and Stephen Elkins, came to Braxton County in the late nineteenth century, the Elk and the Little Kanawha Rivers were the avenues of transportation in and out of the area. Having established themselves at the highest navigable point along the Elk, the Carpenters and other settlers became engaged in the freight business. All supplies and provisions were brought up Elk River in dug-out canoes up to sixty feet long. The Carpenters and the Taylors were Braxton County families who made these canoes. Ernie Carpenter described them:

> My grandfather made canoes and sold them. They got a dollar a foot.
> If it was a thirty-foot canoe, they got thirty dollars for it; fifty-foot,
> fifty dollars; sixty-foot, sixty dollars. One time he had completed two
> canoes and he had one old canoe, and they took all three canoes with
> them on this one trip to Charleston. They sold one new canoe and the

one old one to two brothers just up the river a little ways from Charleston. The brothers had a freight line of their own, and that is what they wanted them for. They paid fifty dollars for the new canoe and I think my grandfather said twenty dollars for the old one. The brothers got into an argument about which one was going to get the new canoe, and finally got into a fight over them. A few days later, my grandfather came back up the river and saw the canoe setting there cut in two down the middle. He got to inquiring what happened and found out those two boys had got into a fight and the one sawed it in two. There it was, not worth a cent to nobody. . . .

They would be several days making the trip to Charleston and back to Sutton. In the summertime they would camp along the river. In the wintertime, when it was real bad weather, they had certain houses where they had engaged rooms to stay and eat. They would finally make their way back to Sutton with their load of goods and unload them. There would be a few weeks in between times, and they would go back and do the same thing over. They did that for years and years.[19]

Squirrely Bill Carpenter told Ernie about an incident involving fiddle music and a young girl that happened on one of these river trips. "She showed up at the camp with a fiddle just as they were finishing up their dinner," related Ernie. "She told my grandfather she was trying to learn how to play the fiddle and wanted him to play a few tunes to her. He tuned it up and played some. She was very much excited about it so just as he was about to leave he played, 'The Pretty Little Girl I Left behind Me.' They got along the river a quarter mile or so and they looked back, and she was standing back there on the river, a-waving and crying with that fiddle in her hand."[20]

Shelt Carpenter, Ernie's father, was well known as a guide to fishermen on the Elk. He also entertained at the fishing camps with his fiddle and his tales. Ernie Carpenter quoted his father continuously and retained an affinity for him long after Shelt's death. While being presented with the Vandalia Award, West Virginia's highest folklife honor, the eighty-year-old Ernie turned to me and said, "I just wish my dad could be here." During later visits with Ernie at a nursing home, his mind seemed to come and go, but he still reflected on his father's opinions about various matters.

There is a reverence among the older generation throughout Braxton County for Shelt Carpenter, but more as a person than as a musician. He was well known by the professional class of doctors and lawyers from Charleston who brought him to their fishing camps on Elk River. Shelt showed them where to fish, when to fish, and what bait to use. He told tales, played music, and drank their whiskey. There are many stories about Shelt and numerous quotes attributed to him. Following are some examples:

> "I've been all over Europe, Stirrup, Asia, Africa, and parts of Hell, but Braxton County is the best God damned state in the university" (said after Shelt returned from the longest trip of his life, to the 1893 Chicago World's Fair).
> "Bread is potato's mother."
> "I could eat soup [even] if it was made over a lizard."
> "It's just my luck that if it was raining soup, I'd have a fork instead of a spoon."
> "In the old days we did everything by hand-power and awkwardness."
> "They say that money talks, but all it ever said to me was goodbye."
> "I've been as lucky as a one-legged man at an ass-kicking!"
> "You have to believe in yourself, even if you know you're wrong."

Fiddling traditions run deep through various branches of the Carpenter family. Family lore has it that Ernie's great great grandfather Jeremiah and his son Solomon were fiddlers. Ernie's grandfather Squirrely Bill (Solomon's son) was his earliest fiddling influence. Ernie's father, Shelton, learned tunes from Squirrely Bill and passed on tunes to Ernie.

"[My father] was a good old-time fiddler," recalled Ernie. "He used to keep that fiddle in a large safe[21] that we had. The safe was never locked. He kept that fiddle on the top shelf. Just kept it laying in there on a cloth, never had a case for it. Not a kid on the place ever touched that fiddle or ever even went close to it. I was the first one to take an interest in it when I got big enough. As soon as I hit my first note on the fiddle, he said, "The fiddle is yours. I'm through. I won't be a-playin' no more. You're going to do the playing from now on."[22]

The way Shelt helped and encouraged his son's musical interest is not the normal story heard about how fiddlers get started. Ernie's good friend, Melvin Wine, is a fiddler who has gained wide attention for his musical prowess. He had a more typically Appalachian introduction to the music, jokingly called the "Appalachian Suzuki method" by some. He was forbidden to touch his father's fiddle, but curiosity and the urge to make music got the best of him and he "snuck" the fiddle out. Like Peter Rabbit being forbidden to go into Mr. McGregor's garden or Adam and Eve being forbidden to partake of the fruit, "the one forbidden thing" is exactly what people want, human nature being what it is.[23]

Among the elite of West Virginia's old-time fiddlers, there is a reverence for old-timers who played the older, lonesome, crooked, often modal, archaic-sounding tunes. This is the music of the old Carpenter fiddlers. Fiddler Wilson Douglas recalled that Clark Kessinger, West Virginia's most famous old-time fiddler, had this opinion of the particularly old-style music the Carpenters played:

> [Kessinger] said, "There ain't nobody get music out of a damn fiddle like them Carpenters." Said, "I can fiddle, but I can't get that music out like they could. I can't get that sound. . . ." Oh, he liked Carpenters' fiddlin', Clark did. He said, "Now I've tried to play a few of them tunes, but I can't. . . ."
>
> When [French Carpenter] played that fiddle, it was just a part of him. You know what I mean. He was like myself. He put everything in it he had. Nothing else was on his mind. And when them frogs would sing in the spring of the year—French didn't want nothin'. He was smart. He could of had anything he wanted. He wanted an old shack with a split-bottom chair and that danged old trunk that he made that stuff out of leather, and four or five old trap fiddles to work on, after he quit filing saws for these lumber companies. He'd pull that fiddle out about dusky dark up there in the head of Otter Creek. Them frogs a-hollerin'. You know how they do. He'd cut down on that "Christmas Morning" or "Little Rose," and I believe it was the saddest doggone fiddlin' I ever heard in my life. Them people would say, "My God, French Carpenter can fiddle. You listen to that, would you."[24]

Banjo player Brooks Hardway also remembered French Carpenter:

> I used to be at my Grandpa's house, I nearly stayed there, they just lived six, eight hundred yards above us,[25] . . . . I was there one day, never will forget it, I was ten or eleven, twelve years old and looked down the road and seen a man comin' up with a flour poke in his hand. We watched him till he got up in front of Grandpa's house, and it was French Carpenter with the fiddle in a flour poke and about four inches of the neck of it a-stickin' out of the top of that poke. He had his hand around that fiddle neck with that fiddle in a flour poke. Well, Grandpa never let a man with a fiddle or a banjo pass the house without stoppin' him and bringin' him in. So he halted French Carpenter, and French Carpenter stayed all night with Grandpa Santy. They had music, and the house was full of people that night. . . .
>
> [It was] the first time I'd ever seen French Carpenter, and he played the fiddle, and he sung with it. He's the first man that we in that part of the country ever heard sing with the fiddle. And he played some of the sweetest tunes that I ever listened to, and sung 'em. [He] fiddled to twelve or one o'clock in the night and held the attention of them people. You could a-heard a pin drop, a-listenin' at French Carpenter sing them pretty songs.[26]

Wilson Douglas recalled the exploits of French's father, a fiddling preacher named Tom Carpenter:

> Tom Carpenter could get some of the awfulest sounds out of a fiddle that you ever heard. He was a preacher. . . . He was a big man you know. He'd go from Clay to Cowen, Cowen to Webster Springs. He'd preach awhile. I have to tell you this tale. He'd get a revival meeting a-going somewhere and he was a smart man. Oh, he was a smart man on the Bible. Preach like the devil. There would be a bunch of young people, bunch of women, and they'd mention a square dance. There was a big cornfield down there then where that there church was. Old Tom said, "Now anybody got a fiddle?" One boy told him yea, he had a fiddle. He said, "You bring it up there and hide it in a corn shock. After the service we'll have a little dance down there." Old Tom would fiddle for that dance. Oh, he was something. He didn't practice what he preached really. Oh Lord, he could fiddle.[27]

Long after the golden age of old-time country music, when the industry moved from its folk roots to the slickly packaged studio sound of Nashville, a few people looked back over their shoulders and realized there were musicians cut from a different cloth. There were a few fiddlers who did not change their style or repertoire: they did not care what the public thought. They played to please themselves and perhaps their ancestors, but they did not play to please the general public.

Two members of the fiddling Carpenter Family, French and Ernie, lingered long enough to be noticed and recorded. But many in the family, although the technology was around, escaped musical immortality.

Wilson Douglas mentions Tom and Harmon Carpenter of Clay County. Many people in Braxton County speak of an Angie Carpenter Cowger, who was a fiddler. Arlie Carpenter, of Webster Springs, still plays some of the old family tunes. Another Webster Countian, Columbia Carpenter, was well thought of by fiddling neighbor Alf Hall. Charles Carpenter of Webster County fiddled and once played on the radio at Oak Hill. Prudie Carpenter and her father, Alden Carpenter, played fiddle music around Richwood in Nicholas County. Lloyd Carpenter, a son, played in Webster County before relocating to Pennsylvania. Hamp Carpenter and Wes Carpenter played fiddle, carrying on the family's music traditions in Pocahontas County. All of these fiddlers descended from old fiddler Jeremiah Carpenter of Shelvin' Rock fame. The music of this family seems likely to last into the twenty-first century—weathering the storm of ever-increasing waves of "pop" competition and media-promoted styles—if only among a few traditionalists.

4

"Upon My Honor"

"No fools, no fun."
West Virginia proverb

West Virginia has a folk hero in fiddler Edden Hammons. The mystique surrounding Hammons isn't found in many published sources; rather it exists in the minds and oral tradition of older people of the region. As a member of the common people, Hammons is talked about, lied about, joked about, admired, fictionalized in print, and generally remembered by his peers as much as were public figures of the region. I've heard anecdotes about the man along with praise of his musical ability from Wirt County to the west, Mercer to the southeast, and Randolph to the north. This encompasses a geographic area greater than twice the size of Connecticut.

Dwight Diller made an enormous contribution to the study of American and Appalachian folk culture when, as a college student, he was the first to notice the music of the contemporary members of the Hammons family. The life of this family on the frontier is well documented because of Diller's achievement.[1] The Library of Congress' Hammons Family study reports the migratory state of the family throughout the last 200 years and suggests the possibility that they were from the older "fully established American stock" known to populate the Virginia tidewater. This implication runs contrary to immigration trends in the Appalachian region, which show an eighteenth-century tide of immigrants of Scots-Irish and north British origins,[2] along with a sizable portion of Germans, all coming by way of Pennsylvania.

Marion O'Brien, a family descendant whose information came from his grandfather, Sampson Hammons, related family oral history that concurs with the more normal immigration pattern. He says an ancestor, Edwin Hammons, immigrated from Belfast, Northern Ireland.

O'Brien did not recall a date or port of entry in this country, but related that Edwin Hammons settled in what was referred to O'Brien as "the canebreaks." Charleston, South Carolina, was a distant second to Philadelphia in terms of numbers of immigrants from Northern Ireland,[3] and the "canebreaks" may be a reference to a South Carolina port of entry. This would concur with established patterns of immigration to America. The date of immigration would be before the American Revolution, because the war brought a quick end to passage from Belfast. The immigrant ancestor Edwin Hammons, mentioned by O'Brien, would be a father or grandfather of the Edwin born ca. 1777 and identified in the Library of Congress study.

According to O'Brien, Edwin Hammons was a school teacher who received a milk cow for teaching his first term of school in America.[4] At some point after this, information from the Library of Congress study has the family hovering on the frontier, including stays in Pittsylvania County, Virginia; Hawkins County, Tennessee; Whitley and Knox Counties, Kentucky; and eventually (1847) the Big Sandy/Tug Valley area of Kentucky and Virginia. However, at least one family of Hammonds (surname is spelled in different ways) was in the Big Sandy Valley in 1791.[5]

Burl, a modern-day Hammons, played a fiddle tune titled "Old Christmas Morning," which is similar to a tune collected in Kentucky as "The Brushy Fork of John's Creek." The family of Hammonds who lived in the Big Sandy Valley in 1791 settled at the mouth of John's Creek. Another family, the Marcums, settled in this neighborhood at the same time, and a Hammons family tale involves this surname.[6]

Daniel Hammons, another family member, was born in North Carolina about 1830 and immigrated to West Virginia from there, showing that the family group stayed on the move, with different members catching up in leap-frog fashion throughout their frontier experience. The family included uncles, grandparents and cousins, whose general migratory course was as a unit but with different factions of the family playing catch-up.[7]

In her book *Feud*, Altina Waller's claim that the inhabitants of the Big Sandy/Tug Valley were models of social cohesion in the antebellum period, is challenged by Hammons family history.[8] The valley has had a reputation for lawlessness from its early settlement. One 1855 account described it as "a wild mountainous half civilized region [where] deep glens, and mountain gorges, and dense, unbroken forests, made it the home of a daring, reckless race of individuals . . . the horse thief, and gambler, and counterfeiter."[9]

Maggie Hammons Parker and Marion O'Brien, both descendants of Big Sandy Hammonses, gave some indication of their family's expe-

"Crooked Neck John" Hammons, circa 1858. (Courtesy of Marion O'Brien.)

rience on the Sandy. A family fight/feud occurred there that, according to their accounts, determined a major move in the family's history.

In Maggie's (and her brother Burl's) account of the fight/feud that preceded the family's departure from the Sandy River country, the family was engaged in floating logs down river.[10] They followed the logs on a raft, guiding them, presumably, to market. At a certain point on the river, for whatever reason, another party "got to shooting their lights out." The ensuing fight, reported Maggie and her nephew James, "was a tough time." They added that Uncle John Hammons "cut one man pretty near plumb right in two."[11]

In Marion O'Brien's account, the fight ensued near the mouth of the Big Sandy and the other family involved went by the name of Fluty. A "Buck" Fluty and an Edwin Hammons, O'Brien's great grandfather's brother, died in the fight. Edwin Hammons actually was drowned during the skirmish, according to O'Brien, due to being drunk and attempting to swim from a raft to the shore to participate in the fight. O'Brien also remembered that his grandfather, John Hammons, was hit in the side of the head with a "stick of dye wood."[12] O'Brien pointed out that John's head "listed" to one side for the rest of his life. An old family photograph bears this out. John acquired the nickname "Crooked Neck John," according to Currence Hammonds. John's father, Jesse, survived the fight, despite having sand "ground into his eyes" and a knife broken off in his skull. Fearing trouble with authorities for the killing of Fluty, the family decided to flee upstream and continued up the Tug Fork. This led to the family's stay in Wyoming County and eventually took them to Nicholas and Webster Counties in central West Virginia.[13]

For whatever reason, there was quite an immigration to central (West) Virginia from Kentucky and Wyoming County just prior to the Civil War. The Sizemore, Robinet, Patrick, Short, Cline, Perdue, Hammons, Roberts, Clifton, Mullens, and Riddle families were part of that movement. Many of them came from areas in North Carolina, southwestern Virginia, and Tennessee and ended up neighbors in the Sandy River Valley. Leaving there, they stopped in Wyoming County and then came to what is now Webster County in central West Virginia.[14]

Moves by members of the Hammons family in West Virginia, including Edden, continued in a graphic visual maze that swirled around and crisscrossed itself. This route, as with a maze, had no outlet other than to retrace and retreat. But bridges were burned behind through modernization, and the future was a world unknown. The onslaught of the Industrial Revolution was as disdained as the black plague to these people, who were desperately trying to avoid an end to their lifestyle. A few Hammons family members, along with members of other central West Virginia families, escaped from West Virginia to Montana around the turn of the century in one last attempt to flee the uncertainty they felt in the face of encroaching industrialization and modernization. "Old Uncle Pete" Hammons made that trip near the end of his life and realized his last life's goal, to kill a grizzly bear, before he died.

Ronald Hardway called the mountains of central West Virginia, where much of the Hammons family lived out their lives, "the last frontier." The feuding and fighting, exploding population, and legacy of conflict (as well as possible legal trouble) provided incentive for the Hammonses to leave their former homes.[15] In the new world of central West Virginia, the mountains were higher, the population was thinner, and the prospects for the future seemed much brighter.

Fiddler Edden Hammons' old-world ancestors probably went to Northern Ireland in search of a better life, and his immigrant ancestor came to America for the same reason. Once the family was in this country, however, things did not change much. The American dream to the musically inclined Hammonses of Pocahontas County was just that, a dream. While many immigrants went on to find the world of opportu-

Edden Hammons (with fiddle) and his son James. (Courtesy of the West Virginia Regional History Collection, West Virginia University Libraries.)

nity and prosperity they hoped for, these Hammonses did not. They continually sought and fantasized about a future that did not exist. In the late twentieth century, much of the family who remained in the region still experienced life at the low end of the socioeconomic scale.

Such was the world into which Edden Hammons was born around 1874. Edden was the youngest son of Jesse, one of the fight/feud survivors. His real name was Edwin, but he always went by Edden. When pressed, he claimed his name was "Edn, and nothing elst."[15] Hammons was born on the Williams River, died in 1955, and is buried on Stomping Creek in Pocahontas County.

Edden Hammons' exploits were portrayed in a work of fiction, without much notice. In his essay "That Hammons Boy" from *The Last Forest*,[17] Douglas McNeil, a high school principal from Marlinton, West Virginia, portrays Hammons as "Elam," a backwoods kid who drew his fiddling expertise from the land upon which he was raised. (His script is suspiciously close to "The Mountain Whippoorwill, Or, How Hillbilly Jim Won the Great Fiddler's Prize," published fifteen years earlier, in 1925, by Stephen Vincent Benet.[18]) McNeil's "Elam" was "aloof" and "alien" to his brothers and sisters. He worried his concerned parents because of his "effeminate ways." McNeil, with an attempt at a back–country dialect spoken by the main character's father, portrays Hammons as an unusual mountain child: "Thet e-e-lim boy uv mine will never be worth a damn," vowed old Josh [actually Jesse] Hammons. "He-e will not fish; he-e will not hunt; he-e will not sang; he-e will not do a single cursed thing the God's blessed day long, only set, humped up, a-playin' on the fe-e-dle."[19]

Through a fantastic set of circumstances in McNeil's short story, "Elam" winds up on a concert hall stage in a big city where he is to make his debut after receiving proper training as a violinist. On the big night, under the stress of the stage and the pressure of the huge attentive audience, his senses go blank. His mind reverts back to the natural wonders of Pocahontas County and, as if possessed, he fiddles the music of his race. He does this not to the crowd, but to the birds and green slopes in the mental image of his homeland. Upon completion, feeling a moment of uncertainty and uneasiness at the ludicrous thing he just did, his fears are assuaged by the thunderous applause of the crowd.

Benet's work came at a time of national journalistic propaganda that ballyhooed the early 1920s fiddle contests in Atlanta, Georgia. Benet wrote "The Mountain Whippoorwill" about a contest in 1922 when fiddler Lowe Stokes beat "Fiddlin' John" Carson at the big Atlanta contest.[20] His work ends in much the same way as McNeil's. McNeil, a native of Pocahontas County, was much closer to his subject than Benet, and no doubt much of his characterization of Hammons was based on local narrative and personal experience. Both works, however, are wildly fictitious.

McNeil and Benet, making literary efforts to create folk heroes, incorporated poetic license to produce successful works of literature (at least in Benet's case). However, both works went unnoticed by the basically nonliterate folk, who are the only ones capable of recognizing their own heroes. Even so, such published attempts to esteem Hammons and his talents could only add fuel to the fire, and the works have been noticed by Hammons' admirers of recent years, who have an intellectual interest in aspects of his life.

In addition to all of the oral discussion about Hammons within the folk communities of central West Virginia, some folk poetry about the man, from an unknown pen, has come to light:

Hammons and the Ass

Near Campbelltown,[21] one summer's day
A strong lunged ass was heard to bray.
The mountains echoed back his voice;
To hear it made his heart rejoice.

"What a pity," said the ass,
"That I should have to live on grass.
My lungs are strong; my voice is loud;
At dances I could draw a crowd."

"Hear my music. How it fills
The valleys lying among the hills.
It is sweet, I know, for see what
Great ears for music I have got!"

A man named Hammonds heard the din
While passing with his violin.
He stopped a while upon his way
And bid the old ass cease to bray.

"My long eared friend," Mr. Hammonds said,
"This neighborhood must wish you dead,
For worse than any sounding brass,
Is your braying, Mr. Ass."

"If you want music cease your din
And listen to my violin."
He rubbed the rosin on the bow.
He tried the notes both high and low.

Using a large stone for a chair
He played a grand soul-stirring air.
Before the fiddler ceased to play
The ass again began to bray.

No violin or song of bird
Could for a moment then be heard.

> At last the old ass dropped his head
> And unto Mr. Hammonds said:
>
> "Music is sound, my friend, you see.
> Therefore all sound must music be.
> Of mine the world will be the proudest,
> Because mine, my friend, it is the loudest."
>
> What more could Mr. Hammonds say?
> What further do than let him bray?
> He wandered off through twilight dim:
> Ass wisdom was too much for him.[22]

Currence Hammonds spent much time with his uncle, Edden Hammons, and spoke of him in endearing terms as his role model, often defending his peculiar ways. Edden was known to be a crack shot with a rifle, a much-touted attribute among the family and in the region in general. Edden taught Currence to shoot when Currence was a young boy on Williams River in Webster County. Until Currence's death in 1984 in the Tygart Valley, he was known as a shooter to be reckoned with at area matches. Currence won his first match on Williams River as a boy under the tutelage of Edden. At that contest, held near Cowen about the year 1905, Currence, shooting Edden's gun, beat his father Neal (Cornelius), which caused some family discord. Neal was a well-respected marksman with a mountain rifle and didn't enjoy being beaten by his young son. First prize was a bred ewe sheep, which Currence promptly donated to the family stock to ease tensions.

Most old-timers in the Tygart Valley of Randolph County remember that Currence Hammonds and fiddler Woody Simmons were two of the best shots in the valley. The manly traits of shooting and fiddling went hand-in-hand and were held in high esteem in many pioneer families. This is especially true in central West Virginia where the Hammons, McElwain, Hamrick, Cottrell, Carpenter, and other families were respected hunters and marksmen, as well as renowned fiddlers.

Among the most often told tales on Edden Hammons are the accounts of his passion for fiddling (one winter, a fellow said, Hammons sat in a corner and fiddled so much that the shadow of his elbow wore a hole in the wall) and the related traits of unemployment and neglect of his family, particularly his wives.

The story of Hammons valuing the fiddle more than his wife is so widespread in central West Virginia that it has achieved folktale status, complete with numerous variations. The variations include assorted situations, different wives (Hammons had more than one), and miscellaneous sexual innuendoes. The general theme is that Hammons gives his new wife the strong impression that all he ever plans to do with his life is play the fiddle, whereupon Hammons receives the ultimatum to choose between her and his fiddle. Most all accounts have Hammons declaring at the end, "Upon my honor, I'll not lay my fiddle down for no damn woman!" At which cue the wife leaves for good.

"He wanted [music] too much," said Millie Johnson Hammonds, a distant relative who told several Edden-leaving-his-wife stories. "And he'd go play for dances. Now, his woman didn't want him to do it. . . . And, [Edden said] 'Now God damn it Betty, I'm not going to a rowdy-house, I'm a-going to a civil dance!' . . . Now Betty said, 'If you want me, you'll have to lay that fiddle down.' He said, 'I'll lay my fiddle down for no damn woman!'"[23]

Hammons' reactive, often quoted response to his wife's ultimatum no doubt actually happened and is substantiated by the fact that he only lived with his first wife, Caroline Riddle, for three weeks after they married.[24] The motif here is much older than Hammons and his disgruntled wife. Consider this rhyme from an early "Mother Goose" collection:

> John, come sell thy fiddle,
> And buy thy wife a gown.
> No, I'll not sell my fiddle,
> For ne'er a wife in town.[25]

Nor is the plight of these fiddlers a motif only out of antiquity. In recent years, Clay County fiddler Wilson Douglas found himself in a similar situation. Like Hammons, he opted for the fiddle with little hesitation.

Hammons also had marital problems with his second wife, Betty. Things must have worked out, but there is plenty of humorous tension in the stories told by Millie Johnson Hammonds. "She left him one time, and she was pregnant," Millie recalled. "And he said, 'Now damn it Betty, would you leave me after me a-scrapin' around in that wet grasses and finding you them little plumses?"[26] The humor here, found by those who knew this to be typical of Edden, was his recall and expression of what to him was a very tender moment.

Although she made fun of Hammons and strongly disliked his treatment of his women, Millie admitted that she liked to see him come around because of his entertaining antics, and she shows obvious, though understated, endearment. As with everyone who knew the fiddler, she has numerous comical stories about him:

> He come to our house one time and he wanted to borrow one thing off us. He said, "Mrs. Johnson, I got me a nice bunch of beans and cooked them, and I need cornbread." So Mom, course, she give it to him. And when she give it to him, he said, "Now let's see what else I

want. I want a little lamp oil so to have a light." To eat the stuff after
he got it cooked, you know. And Mom got it for him. And he said,
"Now I want a little bit of snuff. It'll taste pretty good after I get done
eating." And when he started [to go], he said, "Perry, could you give
me a grist to grind tomorrow? I'm just about out of bread." Dad give it
to him. I would've too. . . . Oh you'd laugh your sides sore at him. And
he'd dance! Old Edden could dance, boy. And he'd come to the house
and he'd play music. Do all kinds of things, but work. He wouldn't
work.[27]

At times, Hammons' indifference to his family's needs was not toler-
ated by the community. A Webster County musician remembered a time
when Hammons was given a good thrashing by neighbors for not looking after his family. After this, the perpetrators gave him a large sack of
groceries to take home to feed his family. Upon reaching home and
plopping it on the table, Hammons is reported to have said, "Now you
kids touch light on that; your Pap took a good thrashing for it!"

Minnie Hammonds, wife to Edden's nephew, Currence, railed about
Edden's non-providing ways. She spoke in despicable terms about vis-
iting him one time on Cheat Mountain when there wasn't a single thing
to eat in the house except bear meat. She also went on about how he
dressed in dirty, ragged clothes. One time when he came to visit—dressed
as usual—Minnie was "boiling clothes" (washing) in a kettle in the back-
yard. She told Edden to go inside and hand out his clothes so she could
wash them. Upon receiving them, Minnie threw the ragged clothes in
the fire and burned them! She then gave the furious Edden some of
Currence's clothes to wear.

The most distasteful accounts of Edden seem to come from women,
probably because they felt sympathy for those of their sex who were
legally attached to him. An older woman on Birch River once told me
in rancorous tones that Edden "would steal kindling from his mother!"
Not that she thought he had, but in general she thought he was that
kind of person. It says something about values, and in particular, the
value of a steady supply of kindling.

Almost everyone who remembers Hammons mentions his appearance, which tended to be ragged. Some take pity, but fiddler Gus McGee
indicated that Hammons' pitiable condition was second to a personal
vice. "I played at the fiddler's contest one night over here," McGee said.
"He's kind of down. Didn't have nice clothes on or nothing. They give
me the first place; then the fellow came around and asked me if I cared
if he'd give it to Edden, and said he looked like he needed some money.
I told him, 'No, I didn't care.' So they give it to him, and he went right
straight down there to the liquor joint and stayed there till it was
gone. . . . Give [other] fellers drinks and stuff."[28]

Hammons' lack of work was renown, and it wasn't just his wives who tried to get him to earn a living. Currence Hammonds remembered a time when the Ku Klux Klan visited Edden. "They come and wanted him, said he has to go to work," Currence related. "'Now Mr. Hammons, if you don't, we're going to take you out and give you a whipping. You've got to work. Lay that fiddle down, and go on to work.' Edden looked at them a little bit, he said, 'Now you just klu kluc all you please,' he said, 'I'm a-going to play my fiddle.'"[29]

Hammons' daughter remembered that the Klan also left switches on his doorstep one time to warn him to get to work. She felt it wasn't a serious threat, however, because Hammons himself was a member of the Klan.[30] Other Hammons family members were involved with Klan activity too. Some actively participated in violently discouraging a black family from settling in Webster Springs.[31]

Not only are Hammons' expressions such as his byword "upon my honor" parroted in the telling of such stories, but his long, slow, and drawn-out dialect also is mocked. Through tale after tale from so many people, I felt as though I had heard Hammons speak even though I never had. When the collection of Louis Watson Chappell became available to the listening public at West Virginia University, I heard a recorded Hammons say, "Ain't that nice?" at the finish of one tune. It sounded as natural to me as if I'd heard him talk all my life.

Although there are countless anecdotes about Hammons' laziness, humorous ways, and strange (possibly just old) pronunciations, most people have a fondness for Edden the man and all have respect for him as a musician. Hammons didn't accumulate much in the way of material possessions. In one of Millie Johnson Hammonds' tales, she described Hammons' shoes as having "the sides tore off 'em and strung up with groundhog-hide strings." Hammons clearly was not a materialistic person. This is not just a diplomatic way of saying he was lazy. Today he would be characterized as a "starving artist." As an artist he could express himself eloquently and in sensuous ways. Depictions of his musical experience begin with accounts of him starting to fiddle at an early age on a homemade "gourd fiddle."[32] His art was very meaningful to him, and he pursued it from early childhood to old age. Hammons' attitude may have been a vestige of bardic tradition.[33] Is it possible that Hammons represents the generation of musicians (or minstrel/bards) who went from being highly valued members of society to being regarded as lazy ne'er-do-wells?

Although Edden Hammons is most often the subject of the stories and tales, the Hammons family in general has been immortalized in the same way. Such tales are told by county natives, who noticed the Hammons had peculiar, perhaps old-fashioned, ways.

According to one humorous (and fictitious) tale, a turn-of-the-century census taker was on the Williams River and called at the door of a family member. Incredulous at the Hammons woman's lack of knowledge about current affairs, he asked if she could name the president of the United States. She answered that she didn't have the least idea who the president was. He then asked if she had ever heard of God. She replied that yes, her "husband spoke of someone named God Damn all the time!"

In another story, a family member serving time in boot camp, wrote home that he was planning to come for a short visit. Since the family couldn't read, it was customary for the postmaster to send for a family member to come to town so he could read the letter to him. This was done, and the Hammons fellow went home to inform his wife that according to the letter, the Army would be sending their son home on a furlough. The woman expressed dismay before saying in disgust that the least they could do is send him home on a train.

William Byrne wrote of another family trait related to Daniel Boone's "elbow room" theme:

> About the year 1895 it was "norated around" that a railroad was to be built from Camden-on-Gauley up the Gauley and thence up Williams River to an eastern connection. The next time Mr. Mollohan visited Webster Springs, Old Pete [Hammons] came all the way over from his home in Williams to see him, in great perturbation. He said, "Mr. Molly-hawn, they tell me they are goin' to run a railroad up Williams right by my place, an' I come over to see if you wouldn't let me have a place furder back—over on the head of Cherry, maybe, er Cranberry— somewhere that no railroad can't go to. I'll tell you, Mr. Molly-hawn, if things keeps on like this, this kentry won't be no fitten place fer men like me an' you to live in."[34]

A patriarch of the family in West Virginia and one of the oldest family members from whom most of the musical family members are descended was Edden's father, Jesse Hammons. He was born about 1833. His grandson Currence Hammonds remembered Jesse's death at the family home:

> The night he died, I'm a-telling you, he played the "Bonaparte's Retreat" and the "Drunken Hiccups," I believe it was. I's sitting there playing, you know, trying to play on Daddy's fiddle. He was setting over on a chair. He was clear out of his mind. He didn't know me, nor he didn't know nobody. And, I was playing that . . . trying to play that "Bonaparte's Retreat." He just looked over at me, said, "You ain't a-playing that right. Your fiddle ain't in tune. Give me the fiddle."

Well, Dad was sitting there. About twelve o'clock at night. "Dad, will I give him the fiddle?" I's afraid he'd throw it down, you know. You give him anything, and if he didn't want it, you'd better get a hold of it or it'd hit the floor right now.

I said, "Dad, will I give him over the fiddle?"

Well Daddy said, "Yes. Give it to him." I just reached it over to him. He just set there, and his fingers seemed limberer than mine. Just as limber as they could be, he just tuned that fiddle, and now he *tuned* it too. It was in tune, and he went to playing the "Bonaparte's Retreat." I mean he played it. He played that piece, and he just rolled over on that "Drunken Hiccups," and you never heared nothing like that in your life. Now, honest to God, that was the prettiest thing you ever heard, or I thought it was.

And he played that, and he just shoved the fiddle over at me and he said, "Here." And I just grabbed it. "Now," he said, "You can play it."

I said, "No, I can't." I just went back and put the fiddle in the case and went on in and set down.

He died that night . . . next morning about four o'clock. Now, that was something. People wouldn't believe that. But that's the truth. . . . Yes sir, he played them two pieces. My mother got up out of her bed. She's laying in the next room. She got up and come to the door and stood and listened at him play. And there was another fellow there, he's dead now, that was my first cousin. His dad and him played the fiddle some. He got up and listened at that playing. After he died, next morning—next day, he said to me, Bernard did, that was his name, he's named after my uncle, he said, "Did you ever hear a fiddle sound like that last night?"

I said, "No I didn't."

He said, "That was the prettiest thing ever I heard."[35]

The story about his grandfather's death likely had a settling effect for Currence in that the fiddle was "given over" to him as he requested. A long-held belief among old-timers is that a dying man should have his last wish.

The facts in stories told by Currence Hammonds (1895-1984) were questionable at times. For example, it doesn't seem probable that Jesse Hammons played "Bonaparte's Retreat" and then rolled over onto "Drunken Hiccups" because these tunes are played in different tunings on a fiddle. Nevertheless, apart from some minor details, Currence's family stories seem grounded in fact. His stories were fixed in his mind as he told them and were not changed, other than minor embellishment, from one telling to the next.

Currence Hammonds grew up among frontiersmen. For a man who died in the late twentieth century, he was unique in many ways. As a youngster, he wore the handspun and woven "wamas," an eighteenth-century-style hunting shirt, and was shod with homemade moccasins during the seasons when the feet needed to be covered. He was a fine ballad singer and banjo player, also a moonshiner, marksman, hunter, fisherman, and excellent storyteller.

People told stories about Currence concerning his departure from or bending of the truth. Fiddler Woody Simmons recalled the time Hammonds lost control and ran his pickup truck into a ditch. Hammonds was standing at the ditch when Simmons came upon him. Simmons asked him how the old truck's tie rod ends were. Currence replied that they were "brand new." Simmons said that upon inspection he noticed the whole steering mechanism was held together with baling wire!

On one occasion, Hammonds employed this reputation to try to wriggle out of a sticky situation. The Hammonds family at times has been at odds with the game laws, always fishing and hunting for food when they needed it as they had done for centuries. In one story, Currence was out squirrel hunting before the season started and bagged several squirrels. Later, as he told men at the community post office about his hunting that morning, a stranger asked how he made out. Currence replied that he shot "a whole mess of squirrels." The man asked, "Do you know who I am?" Hammonds replied that he didn't, and the man told him he was the game warden. Currence coolly responded, "Do you know who I am?" The surprised man replied that he didn't, and Hammonds retorted, "I'm the biggest liar in Randolph County!"

Many and varied branches of the Hammons family included fiddlers. George Hammons, who was well loved by the Carpenter family of Braxton County, traveled between the mountains of Webster County, where he stayed all summer, and Clay County, where he tended cattle for their owner all winter. Ernie Carpenter remembered how the family watched for George Hammons every fall and spring as he trudged along Elk River making his way between his summer and winter quarters. Hammons would stay about a week with the family and play music. This went on for years until one time when Hammons was at an advanced age. Shelt Carpenter, Ernie's father, took old George out to the "poor farm"[36] to stay and be cared for. Hammons didn't stay at the poor farm for long, but continued his usual route.

"That was in the fall, and when spring come, we expected every day to see Uncle George come along you know," said Carpenter. "Goin' back to the mountains. So I guess he went back down to Clay and died down there somewhere. He was a good old fiddler. He knowed an awful lot of tunes."[37]

Such small but cherished events brought together those who played traditional music through a folklife that was directly tied to natural rhythms. These traditions are deeply missed by those who remember the experiences. Countless old-timers tied to agrarian pursuits that brought people together at harvest or other seasonal times express these nostalgic sentiments.

Many twentieth-century musicians in the Tygart Valley were named Hammon(d)s, or were related to the Hammonses, or were influenced musically by the family. Among them are Currence Hammonds, Minnie Hammonds, Dona Hammonds Gum, Arthur Johnson, Cletis Johnson, Millie Johnson Hammons, Jesse Arbogast, Pearl Arbogast, Wren McGee, Gus McGee, Woody Simmons, "Partner" White, Russell Higgins, Ernest Higgins, Anthony Swiger, and Silvie Pritt.

Edden Hammons, his family, and its music have been relatively well documented by folklorists. *The Edden Hammons Collection*, an LP record drawn from field recordings made by Louis Watson Chappell,[38] includes an accompanying booklet edited by John Cuthbert and Alan Jabbour and was produced by West Virginia University. This record, and other field recordings at the West Virginia and Regional History Collection at West Virginia University, prove Edden Hammons to be an awesome musician.[39]

Chappell also recorded Nancy Hammons from Nicholas County, singing thirty ballads and songs.[40] *The Hammons Family of Pocahontas County* is a recording of family music with an accompanying booklet that was produced by the Library of Congress.[41] Another recording, *Shakin' Down the Acorns*, produced by Rounder Records, included these family members.[42] I recorded Currence Hammonds and Dona Hammonds Gum on an old-time banjo anthology that included Russell Higgins, another family descendant through his mother.[43] Several field recordings of the Pocahontas Hammonses, made by Dwight Diller, have been produced and released on the Augusta label.[44]

Currence Hammonds believed that "Little John Hammond," who recorded on the Gennett, Challenge, Champion, Supertone, and Silvertone labels, was his second cousin. He told a long story about this cousin getting in trouble with the law about 1912 and leaving in a hurry with the law after him. Currence never heard from him again, he said, until his wife's brother played a recording of "Purty Polly" and "Little Birdie" for him by "Little John Hammond." Although I was able to verify through family members that it was not the same man, Currence believed the musician was his cousin until his death.[45]

Old people puzzle over where so-and-so could have gotten his or her musical ability, always attributing it to the fact that it "runs in families," such as the Hammons. Not considered in their pondering is the fact that not just talent, but tradition runs within families. There has to be inclination and motivation on the part of the musician, and this is

Sherman Hammons (shown here in 1981) carried the
Hammons family's music traditions into the late twentieth
century. (Photograph by Marte Clark; courtesy of Augusta
Heritage Center.)

supplied by tradition. A prominent musician will leave a legacy of good
musicians in his or her community who are not blood related. An all-
inclusive answer as to why the Hammonses (or other families) are
musically gifted is held by many older West Virginians and provides
hard-to-refute reasoning: "It's a gift from God."

5

Go Ye Forth and Preach the Gospel

"Dance on sir; and after a while you will dance down the red hot pavements of perdition to the tune of damnation played upon the violin of destruction with the devil for a fiddler!"
Dr. Roszell, Lewisburg, West Virginia, 1845[1]

To understand music traditions and lore in West Virginia, it is important to survey the religious beliefs and related ethnic backgrounds of the region's people, especially the early settlers who formed the basis of the culture. Histories of the state's counties document a strong representation of Pennsylvania Germans and Scots-Irish among the pioneers of the region. These Scots-Irish settlers, or their foreparents, mostly immigrated to America between the years 1717 and 1775 and included many who descended from "covenanters," or people who bound themselves by oath to Presbyterian doctrine.[2]

The "Test Act" of 1704 precipitated the massive immigration to America from Northern Ireland. This act excluded non-Anglicans from public office. The absence of freedom of religion also played a part in this mass exodus. Combined with a land system of absentee landlords, high rents, and general economic insecurity, these factors caused the great flood of immigrants to the colonies, spurred by William Penn's experiment.[3]

Typically, Scots-Irish immigrants landed in Philadelphia and settled with their families in the back country of Pennsylvania. Often the sons or grandsons of these early settlers came to the frontier of western Virginia, but many from the Old World, especially in the mid to late eighteenth century, made it to the frontier. An example is John Jackson, the pioneer of the large Jackson family in central West Virginia. He was born in Londonderry, Northern Ireland, in 1719 and died in Braxton County.[4] Many of the earliest settlers of Pocahontas County were Scots-Irish and shared similar religious beliefs. Isaiah Curry's remote ancestors were among the people who suffered for their religious views in the north of Ireland and came to the Valley of Virginia seeking a place of worship, unmolested by civil and religious tyranny. George Poage loved to "wail with judicious care" the hymns and tunes sung by the Covenanting ancestry in Scotland.[5]

Just what were these hymns and tunes that Poage wailed on the eighteenth-century American frontier in what is now Pocahontas County, West Virginia? John Powell makes the case that the religious music of Presbyterians, even prior to coming to the New World in the eighteenth century, was music gathered from the common folk, albeit with poetry that suited their purposes. In Wedderburn's hymnal, published in Edinburgh in 1560, it is stated, "Ane Compendius Booke of Godly and Spirituall Songs, Collected out of Sundrie Parts of the Scriptures, with Sundrie of other Ballates Changed out of Prophane Songs, for Avoiding Sin and Harlotry."[6] This music was not the formal church music heard in the Presbyterian church of today. It was pure and simple folk music, with the tunes and melodies revised with religiously acceptable poetry. Powell reports another scholar's synopsis of the situation as, "Why should the devil have all the pretty tunes?"[7] George Pullen Jackson noted the use of several fiddle tunes in early religious music, even including the obviously secular melody "Turkey in the Straw."[8]

It was not long before settlers were changing from their ethnic identities to a new American identity. They changed from their old-world Presbyterian, Episcopal, Lutheran, and Anabaptist affiliations to the Baptist and Methodist persuasions of the frontier's circuit-riding, evangelizing preachers. Presbyterian ministers attained their positions through extensive formal training; therefore, ministers were not generated fast enough to keep pace with the demand of the population and religious explosions on the American frontier in the early nineteenth century.[9]

Not only was the frontier changing the mores and religious value systems that came from England, Ireland, Scotland, and Germany, but these new Americans also were redefining their musical tastes in relation to their evolving new forms of worship. A new and distinctly American form of religious folk music was coming into existence.

Three great revivals of religious influence occurred in America before the Civil War. The first, known as the Great Awakening, introduced an evangelical type of hymn from the British Isles to Colonial America. The second movement, known as the Second Awakening, brought about a wave of religious fervor at "camp meetings" in the back country and on the frontier. The third movement, recognized as the City Revival, is of less importance here.[10]

Whereas the Great Awakening may have brought about the first American break from established religious musical form, the Second Awakening and the rise of evangelical religious fervor, mostly in the Pennsylvania backcountry and southern mountains, left us with the spiritual folk songs, or folk hymns, that have a lingering legacy in West Virginia. This musical form developed during the period from the 1780s to the 1830s. The camp meeting was an old-world form brought by the Scots-Irish to America.[11] The new spirituals that developed along with this form of worship on the frontier directly contributed to the religious fervor generated through the camp meeting.[12]

"One might well remember, for example, that the camp meetings began and remained in nature surroundings, in the wilderness," wrote Jackson.[13] Camp meetings in America (also called bush meetings, field meetings, and, today, brush-arbor revival or tent meetings) spawned a new emotion which materialized in song as the spiritual. At this point the chorus was introduced to the songs and became an identifying mark.[14]

Choruses were repetitive, and verses were simplified for easy memorization by illiterate participants and where songbooks were nonexistent. Often only the introduction of a new person, as in mother, father, sister, and brother, differentiated one verse from another. Additional verses could suggest more people such as sinner, preacher, playmates, etc. But it is the music—the old folk tunes clinging to all the sensitive and moving traits that attract many to folk music—that has caught the attention and held the fancy of West Virginians for as long as two centuries. These folk hymns are the predecessors to the "gospel hymns" that began about 1870 in the Protestant churches and continue to be sung today.[15]

My introduction to folk hymns of this type was through Maggie Hammons Parker's "When This World Comes to an End."[16] The Hammons family witnessed camp meetings in the early twentieth century. I heard Maggie's first cousin Currence Hammonds sing "I Heard the Thunder Roaring" late one night at his home in Huttonsville. I immediately felt the powerful influence such songs had on Currence. Born in 1894, he said he remembered the song from camp meetings that were held on Williams River in his youth. An excerpt of the song follows:

> I heard the thunder roaring, roaring, roaring,
> I heard the thunder roaring, in that great day;
> Take your wings in the morning, fly away to Jesus,
> Take your wings in the morning, and sound the jubilee.

Maggie Hammons
Parker, 1986. (Photo-
graph by the author.)

Other verses introduce "lightning flashing" and various other natural phenomena.[17]

From another person, Millie Johnson Hammonds, who married into the Hammonds family in Randolph County, I collected "When the Stars Begin to Fall":

> My Lord, what a warning,
> My Lord, what a warning,
> My Lord, what a warning,
> When the stars begin to fall.
>
> Oh sinners, what will you do,
> Oh sinners, what will you do,
> Oh sinners, what will you do,
> When the stars begin to fall.
>
> The moon will be bleeding,
> The moon will be bleeding,
> The moon will be bleeding,
> When the stars begin to fall.[18]

The natural world of the pioneers is a resounding factor in these spirituals and others of this type, including some that are still in circulation. Many of these hymns have verses that predict what will happen when the world comes to an end, and some specifically allude to references in Revelations regarding falling stars, thunder, etc. In Revelations 8:7, hail and fire are mingled with blood. In 12:1-5, a woman, standing on the moon, appears in the heavens and gives birth. In 6:12, "the full moon became like blood." This may account for the many verses in these hymns that refer to a bleeding moon.

In old folklore still present in West Virginia and as with much of mythology through the ages, the moon plays a central part. The bleeding moon motif in the above spirituals appears often. However, this motif is much older than the Book of Revelation. Ishtar, the moon goddess of Babylon, was thought to menstruate at the full moon. The word "menstruate" means "moon change."[19] European peasants believed the moon actually rained blood during its period of waning,[20] and much folk song, as still found in West Virginia, supports the speculation that blood will fall from the moon. This verse from the widely known spiritual "When the Saints Go Marching In," as sung by West Virginia's Lilly Brothers, is another example:

> Oh when the moon, rains down in blood,
> Oh when the moon rains down in blood,
> How I want to be in that number,
> When the moon rains down in blood.[21]

Mythology also specifies that the moon's gender is female, as with ancient moon goddesses and as in another verse of Maggie Hammons Parker's "When This World Comes to an End," where she sings, "Oh, the moon, she will be a-bleeding."[22]

Another moving spiritual from the camp-meeting period that is revered by old-timers is "We'll Camp Awhile in the Wilderness."[23] This was the favorite of old Elmer Mollohan and has attributes easily understood as meaningful to pioneer-era life. Mollohan was an old gristmiller on Holly River who passed away in his tenth decade of life in 1993. He was an interesting storyteller who, like many his age, reacted to contemporary worldly happenings by relating them to Biblical prophesy. My interviews with Mollohan led the mind into wondrous journeys through time and space. If I may suggest a new field—folk geology—it would be the only category that might encompass Mollohan's reasoning.

I met Mollohan one day when, with a friend, I stumbled on his old gristmill by accident. We had been fairly lost on unmarked dirt roads, and this was the only house we'd seen in several miles. I reckoned I was at Mollohan's Mill upon pulling into the yard and parking near the old building. An old man with a full beard and longish hair tumbling out from under a cap walked toward us from the miller's residence. Mollohan's hands were clasped behind his back, and he approached with an air of having been expecting us forever and of being slightly perturbed at the wait. His steely gray eyes darted around while he passed us on a beeline for the mill.

> "Howdy there?" he asked.
> "Okay. How are you?"
> "Want to see the mill?"
> "Yea. How old is it?"
> "Just a few years older than me."

We had a prerequisite look at the wooden turbines, grain bins, sifters, bolters, and old cogs and shafts that four generations of Mollohans had built and maintained. But Mollohan quickly headed up a flight of wooden steps to some rickety old rocking chairs in his "office," which was actually a storage area on the mill's second floor.

We were flies in the spider's web. Mollohan, with captive audience, shut his eyes and recounted local history, Civil War episodes, fond musical memories, and prophetic happenings. His was a long, eventful life experienced through the senses of a wondrous mind.

That encounter led to other visits from me until Mollohan's death. The following excerpt, edited from some ramblings Mollohan got onto one day when I had a tape recorder going, gives you an idea of his unique point of view:

> Now, the old man who knew the history of Webster County said that the Bible said that the angels stood on the four corners of the earth and held the winds of the land around them. They said the angels stood on the four corners of the earth and held the four winds that blow upon the earth in their hands. The four corners of the earth that he spoke about was the four points of the compass: north, south, east and west.
>
> You can go out here and set a line today that was run a hundred years ago, and if you go on that line, you just as well read off five degrees on your compass. Pull the front end to your right one degree for every twenty years.[24] That's what it takes. I say that the earth is something like a generator. It's generating a current, but it's gradually turning. . . .
>
> The Bible said the world will stand a thousand years, but not thousands. The first thousand's up. The Bible says, if you put it together the way I'm a-puttin' it together, that the world will be destroyed within the next one. You can see all these other places where the earth

did explode. You can go over at the mouth of Seneca where that big hole is [Smoke Hole], you can go back on top of that and there's a big rock standing on top of that and they have been heated red hot. You notice next time you pass by that. Look at it. That was red hot. . . .

If you walk up and down these hills like I have . . . I can see periods of time. Same as you read them in a book. I don't find many people who talk on that subject because they're afraid to pass their opinion.[25]

The Mollohans were Irish and were early settlers in the region. A good idea of ethnic and thereby religious influences in central West Virginia may be formed through observing family names and their provenance as detailed in local county histories. William Griffee Brown's *History of Nicholas County* lists forty-one German family names, thirty-eight Scots-Irish, fourteen English, seven Irish, five Scots, four French, three Dutch, two Norman-French, and one Welsh.[26] Irish Catholics were rare on the early American frontier. It wasn't until the potato famine of the 1840s that they migrated in significant numbers. For the most part they congregated in the larger cities where work was plentiful. But meaningful numbers did establish rural communities, and they were poised to contribute the labor force needed at the onset of the Industrial Revolution, which heated up during the last half of the nineteenth century in West Virginia. In Randolph County in the 1840s, Irish laborers who built the Staunton-Parkersburg Turnpike stayed and established their own community at Kingsville. They contributed to the local music and dance repertoire. This typifies similar Irish enclaves of central West Virginia in the mid nineteenth century.

Once the pioneer ethnic groups settled in West Virginia, they promptly moved toward becoming homogeneous neighbors.

"How quickly these Scotch-Irish Covenanters, German Mennonites, and English Episcopalians became Baptists and Methodists," observed Brown in his *History of Nicholas County*, "how soon they adopted the same dress and modes of living; and how quickly they forgot race and language, because of common danger, common hardships, and common ambition to create a new way of life in this new world!"[27]

As these pioneers quickly moved from their ethnic identity, they took on a regional oneness of their own. An old distinction made by West Virginians separates them, by region, from Virginians, or Tuckahoes. Anyone from east of the Blue Ridge in Virginia seems to have earned the Tuckahoe tag; older people in West Virginia commonly use this term as a label for Virginians. Virginians had labeled people west of the Blue Ridge in what is now West Virginia as Cohees.[28] Being of English stock, Tuckahoes were/are culturally different from the predominant (northern) Irish and German culture west of the Blue Ridge.

The term "Tuckahoe" turns up in American minstrelsy, often connected to the "Jim Crow" songs, where it refers to the region of the famous Tuckahoe Plantation on the James River in tidewater Virginia. Tuckahoe as a place name is also found in Greenbrier County, West Virginia, where, undoubtedly, Tuckahoes settled.[29] Tuckahoe is a Native American word for a wild root, sometimes called Indian bread, which the Native Americans taught early James River settlers to eat. The word "Cohee" was used by the English of eastern Virginia (Tuckahoes) to identify people in western Pennsylvania and western Virginia, where large numbers of Scots-Irish settled. The word comes from a contraction of the Scottish term "quoth he," which was used instead of "said he" or the more modern "he said." Quoth he became Quo'he and finally Cohee.[30] The Tuckahoes are scorned in this song from central West Virginia:

> I'll sing you the best one I ever sung yet,
> All about the ragged and the dirty and the half-starved set;
> They're ragged and they're dirty and they live down below,
> Called by the Irish the poor Tuckahoes.

The often mocked Tuckahoe dialect immediately identifies a Tuckahoe to West Virginians (a Tuckahoe would pronounce the state's name Vagin-ia). The Irish mentioned in the song are the Scots-Irish, as early Scots-Irish settlers typically referred to themselves as simply Irish and they were. The song goes on to poke fun at the Tuckahoes' lowland ways:

> When they go hunting they call up their dogs,
> Chase an old rabbit in the hollow of a log;
> Bow wow, bow wow, they'll declare,
> They never seen a fatter or a finer old hare.
>
> Then they'll take him home and jerk off his skin,
> With a pot of water ready for to flop him in;
> But before he has time to stew or to thaw,
> Just let 'em at him they will eat him dead or raw.[31]

Perhaps in response, these tidewater and piedmont dwellers made songs of their own that belittled the ways of the mountaineers, including this widely known one:

> Come all you old Virginia gals and listen to my noise,
> Don't you marry those west Virginia boys;
> If you do your portion will be,
> Cornbread, molasses, and sassafras tea.

This song, too, goes on to ridicule the ways and roughness of life of the Cohees:

They build their houses of log walls,
But for windows, they have few at all;
A clapboard roof and an old slab door,
A sandstone chimbley and a puncheon floor.

They'll take you away to the blackjack hills,
There to live and make your will;
There to live and stare in space;
That is the way of the west Virginia race.

Speech patterns (Cohees) and foodways (Tuckahoe, cornbread, etc.) were used to identify, categorize, and stereotype these groups, but religion also separated them. The Anglican-leaning Tuckahoes of the eastern tidewater evidently shared the same love-hate relationship with music and dance as the Presbyterian-turned-Methodist and Baptist "Irish" west of the Blue Ridge.[32] Contingents within both groups believed fiddle music to be the work of the devil himself; many others held it in high esteem. Accounts going back to the late seventeenth century document this ambivalence involving east Virginia's clergy and their slave musicians.[33]

In some old-world reports the divisions were made clear, and "Old Scratch" seemed to be winning. A sixteenth-century English reformer complained that, "a man may find the churches empty, saving the minister and two or four lame, and old folke: for the rest are gone to follow the Devil's Daunce."[34] A Lancashire minister of the period complained that, "for one person which we have in the church to hear divine service, sermons and catechism, every piper . . . should at the same instant have many hundreds on the greens."[35] It seems fiddlers assumed their stereotypical role from the pipers.

Sutton's *History of Braxton County* gives some insight into early dancing practices and how dancing sat with the religious set. He noted that in pioneer days the people were fond of dancing. They usually danced "the single reel or hoedown" in the cabins having the smoothest floors. He related that a man present at one of these affairs was fond of dancing but had gotten religion. The man couldn't stop his foot from tapping, and, as the merriment went on, he jumped out on the floor and began to dance. The author then moralizes that the man should have stayed away from the dance, but that if he had to be there, he should have kept his foot still. The author added, "This, through grace he might have done."

Sutton further states that a lady asked a Methodist bishop if there was any harm in a Christian dancing. The bishop did not know that there was but said a Christian did not want to dance.

"A Christian under the influence and in the enjoyment of the knowledge of his acceptance with God must possess a joy that can not be harmonized by placing himself under the influence of and his body subject to emotional music without doing violence to his profession,"[36] noted Sutton, heightening our understanding of nineteenth-century religious conviction.

It seems some Methodists thought that their feet patting without their consent was of the devil. This spawned jokes by the irreverent through the years. Someone asks, for example, why Methodists don't make love standing up. The answer is, "because God might think they're dancing!"

Ernie Carpenter told me about a Braxton County fiddler who lived in the "Holly River Country" and became involved with religious practice. He "got it in his head" that his fiddling was interfering with his spiritual life and decided to take drastic action. Picking up a hatchet, he walked outside to a stump, laid down his left hand, and chopped off the ends of his fingers. He thought this would end his fiddling, but the urge to express himself musically and a breakdown of his religious fervor soon had him overcoming his handicap. In the 1960s people gathered to play music on Saturday evenings at McQuain's store at the mouth of Laurel Fork. This backsliding fellow was a regular at these sessions. People who looked closely noticed he played the fiddle with finger stumps.[37]

Self-denial has caused numerous fiddles, at the hands of those who think the instrument has evil powers, to bite the dust through the years. Many fiddlers go through periods in their lives when they "lay it down" and quit playing for religious or family reasons.[38]

Ernie Carpenter claims to have quit once but then happened upon his fiddle in a closet. When he opened the case, he found mold on the fiddle. Considering the old fiddle nothing less than a genuine family treasure, Carpenter said the incident scared him badly. He cleaned up the old fiddle and resumed playing.

Another local account has the noted Jack McElwain, one of West Virginia's most respected fiddlers ever, bashing his fiddle over a stump in a fit of religious fervor. Carpenter recalled the incident:

> Jack used to play for all the dances over his part of the country. . . . He went to church one night and got religion and came home and went in and got his fiddle and took it out where he cut a big tree in the far end of the yard and just beat it down over that stump. Made tooth picks out of it, beatin' it over that stump. When the neighbors heard about it, they thought it was ridiculous, which it was, and told him that there's no harm in that fiddle. He said, "Well," he said, "The fiddle itself might not be any harm in it, but it's the way you use things." He said if he kept the fiddle around he'd be playing for dances, and that, he thought, was harm. He was wrong there too. . . .

[His son] traded some boy [for] the fiddle Jack had [until] he died. He said he was a-foolin' around with [the new fiddle], and [Jack] just twisted and squirmed. He wanted a-hold of the fiddle so bad he didn't know what to do. Finally the boy couldn't get it tuned, and he brought it over to him, and he said, "Dad will you tune this fiddle for me?" He said he tuned it up and took the bow, and he said he just touched the "Cumberland Gap" in the high places. That's the way he described it: he said, "I just touched the 'Cumberland Gap' in the high places." He said, "I saw it was a real fiddle." From that time on till he died he played the fiddle."[39]

Some handle the religious dilemma easily, believing their talent to be a gift from God, and they even play the fiddle in church, as is the case with Melvin Wine and Sarah Singleton (1914-1995) of Braxton County. Wine did quit for one stint in his life, after he had a religious conversion. The influence of a young granddaughter whom he was baby-sitting caused him to play again. Unable to stop the young babe from crying, Wine dug out and played the old family fiddle, which amused and pacified her. He said he realized at that time that his talent was a gift from God, and he returned to fiddling in earnest.

On the whole, among the general church-going populace, the instrument and those who play it are thought to be headed in the wrong direction. Even Melvin Wine has some reservations; he refuses to play for dances, believing Satan is at work at these activities. As a basis for his fears, Wine once witnessed a man at a dance give out a "big oath" and immediately fall over dead; he also saw the accidental death of a woman at a dance who was hit with a blackjack blow meant for someone else.

Carl Davis of Raccoon Creek remembered that his grandmother, who lived with the family, would not tolerate a fiddle in the house. She believed it to be "the devil's music instrument." However, she allowed a dulcimer to be kept, and several family members played and made dulcimers. One time she was away and Davis' father brought down the fiddle from an old outbuilding. The family had a big time while the old man played for them until somebody spied Grandma approaching the house. Just as she entered, Davis' mother slipped the fiddle out the back door.[40]

The general notion that fiddlers are "thick in hell" is pervasive. I was recruited as a pallbearer at the funeral of a well-liked neighbor on Birch River. It was generally known that the deceased was a moonshiner. At the burial, after we had carried the coffin up a steep hill to a small plot, the preacher generously heaped praises on the man as he prayed for his soul. After the service, I was introduced to the preacher as one who "plays the fiddle." Quickly withdrawing his hand and moving on, he mumbled something about there being "too many of them around here."

Besides all of the great folk music instigated through worship, humor is another thriving tradition inspired by religion. There are probably as many humorous stories and jokes with a religious context as any other sort, ribald stories included. One pokes fun at the religious sects who do not believe in baptism by total immersion: Two little Baptist boys who had been to a baptism decided to baptize the cat when they got home. They filled a tub with water and wrestled around with it for a time, getting all scratched up in the process. Finally one said to the other, "Oh, to hell with it, let's just sprinkle it."

In another, a preacher ends a prayer by asking God to cause all the beer, wine, and whiskey to be poured into the river and done away with. After saying "Amen," he calls for a number in song. A voice in the back of the church offers, "Shall We Gather at the River."

Clay County fiddler John Morris related that the Elk River is still used for baptism services in that county. There was a baptism where the aspirant was a particularly large woman. It's normal for a person, upon being duly immersed, to experience a spasm of rapture and emerge from the water praising God with shouts of "hallelujah," while the congregation breaks into hymnody on the riverbank. This woman, in her state of ecstasy, sprang upright in an inspired bound and, after gasping for air and raising her arms toward heaven, shouted at the top of her lungs, "Hot dog!"

The damming of Elk and Little Kanawha Rivers caused a tremendous social upheaval in Braxton County. Ernie Carpenter, for one, carried the scars to his grave. Despite the upheaval, there are strong signs that traditional religious life in the area was too strong to suppress. Now that Elk River is dammed and public access areas have been built, boat access ramps have become the place of choice to hold baptisms. They afford smooth entry for preachers and easy access for baptismal candidates to wash away their sins.

Narratives that find humor in a religious context are endless and historical. Sarah Singleton told this tale on a local character:

> That was Hayes Cogar. He was up a-grubbin' [clearing new ground].
> My Uncle George Dean hid behind a tree, and he'd say, [in a deep,
> thunderous voice] "Hayes Cogar, go ye forth and preach the Gospel."
> Hayes would look all around. Didn't see nobody. So he started to grub
> some more. Directly Uncle George would say the same thing you
> know.
>
> Directly old Hayes just throwed that mattock down, and he run off
> the hill, and he went down to the house, and he said the Lord told him
> to go preach. He went up on Bragg Run at that schoolhouse and everybody turned out to hear Hayes preach. He got behind that desk and

he started to preach. He said, "Jesus Christ risen on the third day of Easter," he said. Directly he was preaching some more, and a big rat run across the floor. "Jesus Christ, what a rat," he said. Oh, they got the biggest kick out of that you ever saw, and Uncle George liked to died. I'm tellin' you, he's the biggest tease I ever seen in my life. He's all the time puttin' a joke on somebody. Hayes wasn't very smart. They oughta been ashamed of themselves.[41]

This scenario, whereby a person of religious persuasion takes the Lord's name in vain or swears by the very deity or damning elements he or she is supposed to venerate or fear, is common in the kind of amusing tales "told on" community characters. This has been the case since the pioneer experience, as this story from Calhoun County indicates:

On the occasion of the stars falling or constallation of the eliments in about 1833, on which occasion the Boggs household being awakened and beholding the condition of disturbed heavenly bodies, Mariah forthwith fell on her knees and fervently and eloquently importuned her God to deal as gently with her as possible and fully believing that the end of time was near at hand, noticing her husband moving cautiously from the window to the door watching the descending stars, he being of a quiet turn of mind, his erratic wife Mariah knowing no superior but her God and only under extenuating circumstances acknowledging his superiority lost all patience with her husband's apparently indifference and so carelessly neglecting to make the most of what little time appeared to remain for Mariah to meet her God in peace, railed out at William and wanted to know "why in the h—l he wasn't praying."[42]

Many rural communities have characters, such as Hayes Cogar, who aren't "too smart" and become the butt for many local jokes. For the most part, it seems, this is good-natured kidding. Strong of back though weak of mind, the person usually serves a helpful role in the community by helping farmers put up hay, butcher a hog, etc. In turn the community looks after this person. A man on Birch River for years never had a home of his own but was always around when there was a job to do and always had a place to sleep and something to eat. These people are often somewhat mentally challenged, or "half a bubble off," and can have amusing ways. Someone once said, "the health of a community may be judged by the number of eccentrics it tolerates."

Sarah Singleton tells amusing stories on a community fiddler who also "wasn't very smart" and went by the nickname "Howard Hoot." Once when Howard Hoot was at an outdoor gathering with his fiddle, someone asked him to play "Soldier's Joy." He reflectively looked up the road one way, pensively looked down the other way, and announced, "I can't play 'Soldier's Joy' on a cold day." I have heard this quote repeated at many square dances by Braxton County fiddlers about to play "Soldier's Joy."

Another time, Howard Hoot was helping with a hay harvest when the workers were called to the house for dinner. Howard happened to sit down at the end of the table in front of a large cake. After a prayer of thanks was given, he began to gorge himself on the cake. Somebody asked if he didn't want some beans and cornbread first, and he said no, the cake would "do just fine."

Because of the notion that old-time fiddle music is of the devil, church life, it seems, was an alternative to the dance floor for pent-up energy and frustrations. For some young men the church offered an opportunity to see and walk a girlfriend home once a week. Much courting was done on the way to and from church in the days when walking was the norm and farm work took up other available time. Camp meetings also were referred to as "mating grounds" for prospective eligible singles.

Phoeba Parsons remembered the way the church was organized in the relatively unsettled backcountry areas about 1924 and how much it represented social activity:

> I was converted when I was sixteen years old. We'd go to church to one another's houses. It's so far away in the woods, we didn't have no way of gettin' in and out hardly, only just little paths, you know. We'd just have meeting here tonight, and the next Saturday night up there, and down here to the next neighbor's house. I led the singing. It was Baptist. My mother and father both was Baptist. They had preachers come through here just every now and then. We'd have what you call prayer meeting. One'd read the Bible, and we'd sing, and they'd talk and get down and pray.
>
> We went to Sunday school about every Sunday. Four miles and back if we could. And in the wintertime, there's a round church house out here on Sand Ridge. Now that was our church we went to. Up to there and over to these woods, now. Plum up. I've took a-many a boyfriend and went over to church. I didn't run around. There wasn't nowhere to go to, only to a dance or something like that, [or] Sunday school. There wasn't nowhere to go.[43]

Religion also played a role in the development of singing style in West Virginia folk tradition. Shape-note singing today is a folk expression with a religious context still found in rural settings. The shape-note tradition in central West Virginia involves the seven-note system introduced in 1832 in Pennsylvania through *The Norristown New and Much Improved Music Reader*. In 1846, Philadelphian Jesse B. Aiken published the *Christian Minstrel*, which used the seven-note system. This book went far in replacing the older four-note system, or the so-called "fa so la" sys–tem, that had been used since sixteenth-century England.[44]

Clyde Case, a banjo player, ballad singer, basket maker, and shape-note singer recalled congregational singing in his parents' day:

> Back when I was a kid, my Dad and Mother, they sung. Back then they didn't have songbooks. They went to church, and the preacher lined out a song, what I mean, he went over the words of the songs, then him and the congregation would sing. They didn't have no books [with] notes and everything in 'em.
>
> Back in my day, people would come around and they'd make up a singin' school. If they could make up thirty or forty dollars, they'd teach ten lessons of singing. There used to be a man named Curt Vaughn, was a teacher, and Okie Cart and Emory Rollyson—different people. They'd come around, and there wasn't no church around here, but they had a schoolhouse down there open. Well, my dad he was always interested in things like that. He'd always give 'em money. Get enough money you know so they could have a singin' school. Well, I went to singin' schools ever since I was six or seven years old.[45]

Case complained that he cannot find good seven-note-system books anymore. It may be that what Clyde is missing are the older "minor-scale" tunes that accompanied the oldest songs. These older tunes, such as "Come Thou Fount of Every Blessing," one of Case's favorites, are closer to older folk tradition than newer compositions, or gospel hymns, in general use in hymnals today.

Religious singing tradition in central West Virginia also was influ-enced by the books of Joseph Funk of Singer's Glen in the Shenandoah Valley. Records list his first important book, *Genuine Church Music*, as being sold widely in central West Virginia.[46] In 1851, Joseph Funk's book *Harmonia Sacra* (sometimes jokingly called "Hominy Soaker") intro-duced the seven-note system to his followers. It appears that in the cen-tral counties of western Virginia this also helped bring on the change of notation systems. Most shape-note hymnals found today, such as the *New Cokesbury Hymnal*, published by the Methodist Episcopal church in 1928, use the seven-note system. They also abandoned the older "mi-nor" music, and in its stead use the more modern composed tunes and poetry. Even though such books as the "Cokesbury" have abandoned the oldest music, this particular hymnal includes and names six "Negro spirituals," which are folk-derived pieces.

One sect in West Virginia that has held to its traditional musical roots is the Primitive Baptists. The most conservative of all the Baptist sects, these "Hardshell" Baptists maintain old traditions through many aspects of their doctrine. The books used by the Primitives use only poetry, as no musical instruments are used in worship. The tunes themselves are maintained, remembered, and passed on through oral tradition. A free style of vocalizing words within the Primitive Baptist singing tradition brings to my mind the *sean nos* singing style of Irish tradition.

The "lined out" method of singing, mentioned by Clyde Case, is tenaciously held to by the "Old Regular Baptists" of eastern Kentucky. An African American choir at a Baptist church in Beckley in southern West Virginia performed shape-note singing but also "lined out" some of their pieces because choir leader Etta Persinger had learned the style from her father.[47]

Shape-note singing has survived without dependence on any formal monetary or institutional support. As the few remaining old shape-note teachers near their deaths, however, interest is on the wane. As those who have learned through the rural singing school tradition pass on, so will go the practice.

Religious singing and music traditions continue as a powerful force in the regional music of West Virginia, and every folk musician who plays secular music plays at least some spiritual music as well.

6

Poor Little Omie Wise

I'll tell you a story about little Naomi Wise
Of how she was flattered by John Lewis' lies.
Verse from Randolph County, West Virginia[1]

The process by which actual events, music, and legend intermingle is a fascinating facet of West Virginia folklore. Factual origins of music, song, and tales are extraneous to the role stories play in the minds of the folk. Inquiries are made, facts are discovered, memories are shared. These elements come together in some logical way for each person, often fulfilling a psychological need such as affirmation of values. Each person then passes his or her account of the story along to others, and the chronicled history of an event is altered to concur with existent variants of the song or tale. This is the folk process.

In Louis Watson Chappell's important collection of West Virginia ballads and folk songs (collected from 1937 to 1947 and housed at West Virginia University's West Virginia and Regional History Collection) is a piece from Kate Toney of Logan County titled "Down by Adam's Spring."[2] This ballad is a version of "Naoma Wise," a folk song connected to rich, long-debated lore.

Although the ballad is considered "North Carolina's principal single contribution to American folk song,"[3] many claim the song originated and the tragic murder it describes took place in West Virginia. Some believe that history repeats itself, and these two similar events occurring years apart in North Carolina and West Virginia seem to bear that out.

The murder of Naoma Wise is well documented through North Carolina court records and early texts. In 1808 Naoma Wise was murdered in Randolph County, North Carolina, probably by a young man named John Lewis. The incident took place after a meeting at Adam's

Spring, where Naoma had gone to meet Lewis, her lover. He is thought to have drowned her in the Deep River near a place known today as Naoma's Ford. Lewis escaped to Kentucky but was later captured and brought back to North Carolina where he stood trial for the crime. The jury acquitted him, but Lewis is said to have confessed to the murder a few years afterward on his deathbed.

The story of Naoma Wise has been immortalized through a folk song tradition that has spread far and wide. In 1817 an "eyewitness" to the events surrounding Naoma's death, wrote an account.[4] This became the source for another version, *The Story of Naomie Wise, or The Wrongs of a Beautiful Girl*, published in a pamphlet in 1874 by "Charlie Vernon." This was the pen name for Rev. Braxton Craven, who became president of Trinity College in Randolph County, North Carolina. Born in 1822, Craven may have heard first-hand accounts of the 1808 incident. His account includes the following poem, "Poor Naomi," on which most variants and recordings of the Omie Wise folk song appear to be based:

> Come all good people, I'd have you draw near,
> A sorrowful story you quickly shall hear;
> A story I'll tell you about N'omi Wise,
> How she was deluded by Lewis' lies.
>
> He promised to marry and use me quite well;
> But conduct contrary I sadly must tell,
> He promised to meet me at Adam's Spring;
> He promised me marriage and many fine things.
>
> Still nothing he gave, but yet flattered the case.
> He says we'll be married and have no disgrace,
> Come get up behind me, we'll go into town.
> And there we'll be married, in union be bound.
>
> I got up behind him and straightway did go
> To the bank of Deep River where the water did flow;
> He says now Naomi, I'll tell you my mind,
> I intend here to drown you and leave you behind.
>
> O pity your infant and spare me my life;
> Let me go rejected and not be your wife;
> No pity, no pity, this monster did cry;
> In Deep River's bottom your body shall lie.
>
> The wretch did then choke her, as we understand,
> And threw her in the river, below the milldam;
> Be it murder or treason, O! what a great crime,
> To drown poor Naomi and leave her behind.
>
> Naomi was missing they all did well know,

And hunting for her to the river did go;
And there found her floating on the water so deep,
Which caused all the people to sigh and to weep.

The neighbors were sent for to see the great sight,
While she lay floating all that long night;
So early next morning the inquest was held;
The jury correctly the murder did tell.

Craven's 1874 poem was reprinted several times, the last being in 1952. By the early to mid twentieth century, the folk song about Omie Wise was widely known. Variants have turned up in poetry, prose, and song in numerous sources. Tragedies sung about a girl named variously Naoma, Naomi, Omie, Oma, Omi, Ona, Oni, Loni, etc., have been collected throughout the South. A similar song motif shows up in African American tradition and dialect in Kentucky.[5] Claims to the murdered girl in the incident that generated the song also have come from Indiana and Missouri.[6]

Randolph County, West Virginia, also claims the poor girl. By examining the processes through which the Naoma Wise song/story has been disseminated in West Virginia, I began to understand the irrelevance of factual origins as they relate to folk song variants and legends. Claims to Naoma and the song about her death are a projection of a basic human need to reaffirm social status and claim local ownership of an event of importance.

My interest in Naoma Wise began in 1976 when Leroy Wingfield (born 1906), a resident of Randolph County, West Virginia, mentioned to me that the poor little girl of ballad fame actually had been drowned in the Cheat River, the major watershed of north central West Virginia. I made a mental note but brushed off the possibility as a bit of misinformation. I knew the North Carolina song well and was aware of its origin in that state.

In 1992 an acquaintance told me she had found a solitary grave in the woods on a mountainside near Cheat River in Randolph County. The grave, she said, was marked "Naomi Wise." The marker stated that the stone had been set in 1968 by a group connected to the Randolph County Historical Society. How does a grave on a hillside in Randolph County, West Virginia, end up with the name Naomi Wise chiseled in granite? I found the mystery irresistible, and many were ready to offer explanations.

Subsequently, Leroy Wingfield recounted that during the Depression he was helping his father-in-law cut timber on family property near the Cheat River when he noticed some roses growing in a clump in the woods. On closer inspection, he made out what appeared to be a grave site. Curious, he asked local gristmiller Robert Channel who was buried in the grave. Channel gave Wingfield some startling news: "That lassie was kinfolks to you!" The woman buried in the grave was Wingfield's mother's half sister.

"Well, that made me have a little bit of interest," Wingfield said, "so I said, 'How come?' And he told me he remembered when there was quite a lot of excitement when they found her body up there along the [Cheat] river and he said—they had this mill down there, up there, a sawmill and a gristmill together. He said they took boards and made her grave—a coffin. And he said, 'I was there.'"[7]

Channel told Wingfield he had helped pull the drowned girl out of the millrace and bury her on the hill above the river. It was then that Leroy Wingfield began to suspect the dead girl was Naoma Wise of ballad fame. He had learned the ballad as a young man and believed the Randolph County named in the song placed the incident in his neighborhood. He came to the conclusion, therefore, that the young woman made famous by the ballad was his own aunt.

At that point Wingfield suspected ownership of the ballad, but he had to convince others to affirm his claim. For years Wingfield considered the circumstances of the tragedy. He had learned that North Carolina claimed Naoma Wise, but he was convinced from local tradition that she really was buried on the hillside above the Cheat River in West Virginia. In 1967 Wingfield heard that Charles Chapman and his wife, Odie, were documenting cemeteries and graves in the county. He walked into the Southern States farm supply store in Elkins, where Chapman worked, and asked if he might want to add a grave to his list. Chapman said he would if there was some proof of who was buried in it. Wingfield replied that it was his mother's half sister Naoma Wise, of ballad fame.

The Chapmans, with Wingfield's help, set about to prove the identity of the person in the grave by locating and talking to the oldest residents in the area. One of their first discoveries was that a man named Randolph Wise had lived in an old log house near the grave during the time of the mysterious death and burial. Wise's Confederate Civil War record verifies his existence. The Wise residence is also confirmed through Randolph County courthouse records. In fact, remnants of the house were still standing when I visited the site in 1992. Local sources said Wise was the foster father of the dead girl. Additionally, the solitary grave is only a hundred yards from a place known locally as Allender's Spring, a name teasingly close to "Adam's Spring," the lovers' rendezvous in the original ballad.

As word of the Chapmans' search spread through the community, other people came forward with information. The Chapmans were told the girl had not been buried in the public cemetery because she was pregnant out of wedlock. As with the original North Carolina incident, this fact plays into the murder motive. Although foul play was suspected in most accounts of the death, no legal action was taken to bring anyone to justice, perhaps affirming the girl's lowly station in society.

Channel's recollection of Leroy Wingfield's familial connection to the dead girl found in Cheat River has validity. A woman named Caroline Elza, Wingfield's maternal grandmother (born circa 1838), was the mother of a girl who died mysteriously. Local tradition had it that one of several children born to Elza out of wedlock was called Naomi and was raised by Randolph Wise.

More local lore obtained by the Chapmans indicated that a man named John Lewis (same name as the suspected murderer of ballad fame), a logger from Scranton, Pennsylvania, was thought to have "left the country" after the girl's death to work for the Cherry River Boom and Lumber Company in Nicholas County, West Virginia. More oral tradition revealed he was fatally injured in a logging accident at Cheat Bridge, about thirty miles upstream from the grave. He was thought to have confessed the murder on his deathbed to a Reverend Grennels of Elkins, West Virginia.[8]

The Chapmans, lifelong residents of Randolph County, related well to their informants—neighbors who supplied the oral information and accounts. Their closeness to the community and affinity to its people helped them in their efforts and in all probability added to the conclusions they drew. After gathering the evidence, the Chapmans and Wingfield believed they had proved beyond any shadow of a doubt the identity of the poor soul in the lonesome grave along Cheat River. No one came forward to challenge their claim. Based on collaborating information from oral sources, the Randolph County Historical Society, then headed by the Chapmans, determined to mark the grave. With the help of a local church youth group, they built a gated enclosure around the grave and installed a marker: "NAOMI WISE KILLED IN THE LATE 1870'S."[9]

I believe the death of the girl occurred in 1887 and that she may have been involved with a man named John Kerns rather than John Lewis. There is no documentary proof that a John (or Jonathan) Lewis ever resided near Cheat River; however, a John Kerns, who was born in 1860 and was active in Randolph County during the late 1880s, in most other details fits the description of the villainous murderer the Chapmans learned about through local oral tradition. A native of the region, Kerns was probably the ill-famed logger who supposedly confessed on his deathbed.

Kerns was involved with many young women in the area during the mid to late 1880s. He may have been involved with a young woman named Ruhama, who was married in 1880 at age fifteen or sixteen to a

David Nelson. Ruhama lived in the area and was a daughter of Caroline Elza, Wingfield's mother's half sister. According to courthouse records, Ruhama died of "unknown cause" on November 21, 1887.

John Kerns frequented the area, seducing women on a regular basis, but seems to have overplayed his hand. Four "bastardy" cases were brought against Kerns in the late 1880s by neighborhood women.[10] One paternity suit was filed against Kerns on November 26, 1887, for a child born October 4, 1887. Another case was filed against him on November 28, 1887, by a different woman for a child born June 15, 1886. Kerns' world seems to have been crashing around him just days after Ruhama's death. In a confusing twist, the record also shows that Kerns obtained a license to marry a woman named Ruanna Nelson on November 25, 1887. Records show this to be a different person from Ruhama Nelson who died four days before.[11] The death of Ruhama Nelson and Kerns' plans to marry seem to have precipitated the rash of paternity suits from his other girlfriends.

John Kerns' love life is confusing at best. But we know that Ruhama Nelson, resident of the locale and daughter of Caroline Elza, died of "unknown cause" on November 21, 1887, in the midst of neighborhood scandal. Good evidence has the oldest local source saying she was pulled out of a millrace, with foul play suspected. According to Robert Channel, no one was tried for murder in the case, despite strong suspicion. All of the details surrounding this death point to Ruhama Nelson as the unfortunate soul found along Cheat River and buried in the solitary grave.

Ruhama's alleged link to Randolph Wise provides her with his last name. Statistics would put Wise's residence in the area at long odds, making this the most baffling coincidence of the whole affair. Records also indicate that Randolph Wise was somehow involved with Kerns, posting his bond on several occasions.

Although it may be impossible to know for certain, the traditional and circumstantial evidence points to the fact that Ruhama Nelson, lover of backwoods Casanova John Kerns, was the pregnant woman who died of unknown cause and was found in a millrace along Cheat River. Even her name, pronounced Ruhami in local dialect, is similar to Naoma (pronounced Naomi).[12] She may well be the West Virginia Omie Wise, reinforcing the belief that history repeats itself.

About thirty-six years after the death of Ruhama Nelson, the song about Omie Wise became widely accessible through commercial 78 rpm recordings. Carson J. Robison composed an original text and tune based on the Naoma Wise incident.[13] Other singers recorded Robison's version as the country music recording industry took off in the late 1920s.

Two basic Naoma Wise song types became common in oral circulation and have been published in numerous sources. One was based on the theme spread via the Braxton Craven pamphlet.[14] The other, which Carson Robison claims to have penned, is thematically true to the incident but introduces new words and music. Both songs are found in West Virginia in oral tradition. The Robison text includes the verse "in Randolph County now her body lies," causing the confusion that helped instigate the Randolph County, West Virginia, claim.[15]

Commercial recordings advanced both texts. In 1926 Al Craver recorded a version based on the Robison song (Columbia 15153-D). A similar version was released by Paul Mile's Red Fox Chasers in 1929 (Gennet 6945, rereleased on County 510). There was a ragtime version recorded by "Aunt Idy" Harper with the Coon Creek Girls (Vocalion 04354). In 1927 G.B. Grayson released "Ommie Wise," with solo fiddle, based on the Craven text (Victor 21625). Grayson's is easily the most gripping early recorded rendering of the song. Another version based on the Craven text was released in 1929 by Clarence "Tom" Ashley with banjo (Columbia 15522). The Grayson and Ashley tune melodies, both of folk origin, far surpass the commonplace music heard behind the versions based on the Robison text. A spine-tingling 1973 solo performance by Maggie Hammons Parker (Library of Congress L-65) is based on the older text, but with an unusual variation in its "minor" folk tune. The more standard tune (of folk origin) is heard on more recent performances by Doc Watson (Vanguard VRS 9152) and Roscoe Holcomb (Folkways FA 2368). I collected and produced a recording of another West Virginia tune and text, similar to Maggie Hammons Parker's, from Fayette County ballad singer Holley Hundly (Augusta AHR-009). The song has been widely recorded in recent years by other traditional singers and folk revivalists.

Variants of the song collected in West Virginia include the important verse stating "in Randolph County now her body lies." The following version, collected from Amanda Ellen Eddy of Rivesville, West Virginia, fits oral tradition as provided by Wingfield.

> Oh come all you young people, a story I will tell
> About a maid they called Naomi Wise.
> Her face was fair and handsome: She was loved by everyone;
> In Randolph County now her body lies.
>
> They say she had a lover, young Lewis was his name;
> Each evening he would have her by his side;
> She learned to love and trust him and she believed his word.
> He told her she was doomed to be his bride.
>
> One summer night he met her and took her for a ride;
> She thought that she was going to be wed.

They came down old Cheat River, and so the story goes,
"You have met your doom," these words the villain said.

She begged him just to spare her; the villain only laughed.
They say he was heartless to the core.
In the stream he threw her, below the old mill dam,
And sweet Naomi's smile was seen no more.

Next day they found her body, floating down the stream,
And all the folks for miles around did cry.
Young Lewis left the country; they brought him back again,
But could not prove that he had her to die.

They say that on his deathbed young Lewis did confess;
He said that he had killed Naomi Wise.
So now we know her spirit still lingers round the place
To save some girl from some villain's lies.

Young people, oh take warning and listen while I say,
You must take care before it's too late.
Don't listen to the story some villain tongue may tell,
Or you are sure to meet Naomi's fate.[16]

Eddy's text indicates a variant similar to other versions that stem from the Robison commercial recording. But by the time Eddy's text was collected and published in 1957, it had gained words that subscribe to the West Virginia incident.[17] Randolph County, the Cheat River, the presence of a mill, and the deathbed confession all subscribe to local tradition.

About ten years after the tale of Omie Wise reentered oral tradition by way of commercial recordings, Leroy Wingfield deduced that little Omie Wise was the young woman buried on the banks of Cheat River and began his investigation to prove it. When Wingfield inquired about the suspected grave, he located an eyewitness to a young girl being pulled out of the Cheat River, and discovered he was related to the victim, immediately the song, the murder, the grave, the place, and the participants logically came together in his mind and validated his claim to a piece of history—the folk process revealed!

In reality, an event in 1808 entered oral tradition; a text (Woody, 1817) and a pamphlet (Craven, 1824) were published, distributed, and re-published numerous times; and, more than one hundred years later, a song version of the story was commercially recorded by various artists and reentered oral tradition in West Virginia. The song was collected and deemed a West Virginia folk song in 1941 by Marie Boette. Boette made a field recording of Hazel Karickhoff singing her version of the song and published it in 1971. The Chapmans then read the account in Boette's book, *Singa Hipsy Doodle and Other Folksongs of West*

Naomi Wise's grave near the Cheat River, 1995. (Photograph by the author.)

Virginia, and told Leroy Wingfield about it.[18] From there the story got to Jim Comstock, the celebrated newspaper editor and publisher of *The West Virginia Hillbilly*, who put the new myth into the *West Virginia Songbag* and the *West Virginia Heritage Encyclopedia* (1974, 1976), consecrating Naoma Wise as a "bonafide" West Virginian.[19]

Through the folk process, historic reality evolved and changed to concur with oral tradition or the text of the recorded song. Members of the Randolph County (West Virginia) Historical Society approached the investigation of the song's origin using an unscientific method. They started with the conclusion (the song text) and sought evidence to support that theme, rather than starting with the basic question: who is buried in the solitary grave on the hillside above the Cheat River in West Virginia? Much of the evidence, then, was collected from oral sources and tradition that had been processed and filtered through folk minds that desired a certain conclusion.

Oral traditions have meaning and purpose. People need folk heroes, heroines, and villains, and poor little Naoma was ripe for the claiming. In early texts, she quickly became a beautiful trusting girl who was violated and murdered by a dark and sinister ne'er-do-well. She was viewed as a folk heroine of noted beauty and innocence, despite living in an age when her actual deeds were beyond the respectable social choices available to women. Accordingly, she was immortalized through folk song and narrative.

Along with a need to create and adopt such a heroine, my West Virginia informants and regional published sources maintain a sense of native pride bolstered by provincial ownership. Knowing of, or in Wingfield's case believing to be related to, the immortalized heroine of a backcountry tragedy provides the motive to find a way to claim ownership. Local "historians" commemorated the event, the memory, and the ownership rights by placing a stone wall around the spot where the old rose bush has about expired. Accounts are published describing how this girl belongs to West Virginia, despite the claims of other states. Occasionally someone stumbles onto the grave, reads the historical marker there, and the "true facts" of the case get reaffirmed in a local newspaper or other publication.[20]

The Naoma Wise story has bounced in and out of the written record, popular culture, recorded and unrecorded song, oral story and legend, regional traditions, racial groups, and geography for 185 years. No doubt it will continue. The "murdered girl" motif will crop up again in another time and another place, and Naoma's song may get recycled yet again. Through it all, may the poor little victims, whoever they are, rest in peace.

7

Oral Traditions

. . . The tree of life hath a richer foliage than can be traced through the bald branches of a pedigree.
Andrew Picken, 1833[1]

Just as the Naomi Wise legend in West Virginia is a product of a robust oral tradition, oral and aural traditions support and help create the region's rich body of spoken lore. Because of oral tradition there is endless lore surrounding fiddle tunes. William Byrne described a chance meeting with "Old Sol" Nelson during a fishing trip on Elk River, circa 1880. He gives us an account of nineteenth-century old-time fiddling in Clay and Braxton Counties, along with fiddle tune names that even then had gathered associated lore and speculation.

> After supper and while we were waiting for good dark, Sol brought down his fiddle and played for us his full repertory of fiddle "chunes" for which he was famous throughout the Elk Valley from Clay Courthouse to Sutton where he was known as "Old Sol Nelson, the Fiddler of the Wilderness." He played "Flat-Foot-in-the-Ashes," "Horneo," "Sugar in the Gourd," "Sourwood Mountains," "Wild Goose," "Cumberland Gap," and "Forked Deer" (Fauquier being the baptismal name of that tune, corrupted by years of mispronunciation and misapprehension), to my uneducated ear all sounding very much alike, but doubtless markedly different to the musician.[2]

Byrne's seemingly authoritative comment about the Forked Deer name comes home to roost in that he mistakenly labels the "Horneo" by spelling it as pronounced, doing a little corrupting of his own. The tune is the Horny Ewe. West Virginia dialect uses the old Scottish pronunciation, where ewe rhymes with row, thus:

I split my shin, and I broke my toe;
And I run a little race with the horny ewe.[3]

Where and how Byrne arrives at his Forked Deer name-origin theory
he does not say. Like Omie Wise, various states lay claim to the tune,
including Tennessee, where the Forked Deer River is thought to be significant. Byrne's "Fauquier" name comes from a county in northern
Virginia. Currence Hammonds learned the tune (with words) from "Old
Pete" Hammons, his great uncle. He says Pete made the tune of "Forked
Deer" after an incident where someone killed a deer on the Middle Fork
of Williams River:

> That Forked Deer was started, Pete told me—now that's my uncle—
> that was started from the Middle Fork of Williams River, up there at
> Big Beechy. A preacher had hunted for—I forget how long, four or five
> year—and he killed that forked horn deer and he made a song up on
> it. He said:
>
>> I've been a-hunting,
>> For five or six years;
>> And all that I killed,
>> Was a forked horn deer.
>
> . . . He made the song up when they's up there camped out. And I
> know it was right. I'm telling the truth about that unless Pete lied. For
> he come right into Pete's and down the Middle Fork and stopped at
> Pete's. Stayed all night at Pete's, and told Pete that he killed that deer
> that day and brought it in. And he told Pete, he said, "I made a song
> up on myself and the deer."
> Pete said, "I want to hear it." And he sung it for Uncle Pete. Him
> and Aunt Emily both told me. Then Pete went to playing it on the
> fiddle. . . . He sung the song about where he was camped on Big
> Beechy at the fork of Big Beechy under a rock. He'd camped under a
> rock, you know, a big rock put out. That's where he camped. He had it
> all figured out. He had a good song. There was no question to it. Now
> Pete said, "That's really true." That's the first ever I heard of it. Then
> they all went to playing it. Edden, he went to playing it on the fiddle.
> Pete, Old Man Pete, they all went to playing it.[4]

Currence carefully introduced a disclaimer here, "unless Pete lied,"
as most traditional storytellers do. No doubt that Uncle Pete played
and sang words to the tune, but the tune may be traced to the eighteenth century. Resourceful imaginations that render new-sprung in-
terpretations of historic fact should not be discounted on this basis.
Their importance rests in what it reveals to us about the tellers and
listeners of such tales. These tales, which gather accompanying lore
and variation through time, were not told for historians. Though often

Currence and Minnie Hammonds, 1980. (Photograph by the author.)

based on fact and strongly implying truth, their purpose was performance geared toward vivid impression and creative expression. A wonderful definition of folklore of this sort is "artistic communication within small groups."[5]

Currence told another deer hunting story whereby a fellow named Floyd Blankenship thought he had killed a deer, but "rode" the quarry down the mountain and into Williams River when it revived. It is a motif right out of Irish mythology that also turns up in the stories of the Pocahontas County Hammons family.[6]

The "Fauquier Deer" to "Forked Deer" name transformation presents an example of enunciation in local speech. Currence Hammonds pronounced it the "Fork-ed D-yere," making two syllables out of both words and adding an old dialectic y sound into the word Deer. Only occasionally found in the speech of older Appalachian residents today, this rising diphthong traces back to Middle English speech.[7]

Phoeba Parsons also carries ancient speech patterns and traditional ways into the late twentieth century. She would also say "d-yere."[8] Some would say this old form of speech invokes "hillbilly" connotations. Stereotypes associate the dialect of "hillbillies" with anything but the stalwart pedigree the word hillbilly has. It should be redefined for what it is: Hill (mountain) and billie (fellow or friend) are both Scottish words. A hillbilly is nothing more than a hill fellow or hill friend, a positive title of antiquity. However the compound is used as a pejorative, showing up in print for the first time in 1902.[9]

Another particularly ancient word is sometimes used for a tooth. In one tale, Edden Hammons complained that every time he played his fiddle, his wife would get on him to go to work. Finally, one day she left. Edden talked someone into taking him to try and get her back. They went to the wife's sister's house to inquire as to her whereabouts. When his wife's sister answered the door, Edden (meeting her for the first time) looked her up and down and asked her to turn around once. She did, whereupon Edden reportedly said in his drawn out way, "Now, upon my honor, that is Betty up and down, if it wasn't for that damn grupper tush (crippled or crooked tooth)."[10]

Although people in West Virginia soon "forgot" from whence they came regarding their ethnicity, telltale folkways and language indicate their background. I'm reminded of a story from rural Pendleton County in which a teacher, trying to illustrate fractions to her class, cut an apple in half. She asked the class what she had: They responded with, "Halves." Then she cut it in quarters and received the correct "Quarters" response. She further cut the quarters into eighths, but in answer to her question as to what she now had, a boy answered, "Snitz," the German word for cut-up and dried apples. Although most Pennsylvania German families came to Pendleton County in the late-eighteenth and early-nineteenth centuries, there are still many old-timers there who use and understand "Dutch" words.

A tremendous amount of oral folklore among country fiddlers concerns the fiddle instrument itself. This is especially true concerning lore about Stradivari, the Italian master. Many think they own genuine Stradivarius violins because of the fake tags the inexpensive copies invariably contain. Every fiddle repairer in the state has had to inform customers that no, their fiddle isn't a genuine Stradivarius.

Stradivari lore confused Ernie Carpenter. He once told me that Stradivarius made ninety violins, and that all but six were in known places. I was told by a Webster County fiddler that "Old Mr. Strad built twenty-one of those 'Dolphin' fiddles, and I was lucky enough to get one of 'em." "Old Mr. Strad" only made one "Dolphin" violin, an instrument of large reputation that today would sell for a fortune. He built approximately 660 instruments during his fifty-five years of work.[11] One Braxton fiddler told me that she owned the seventeenth one Stradivarius made, that it said so right on the tag, referring to the standard "factory" tag that, leaving room for a date, has printing that reads: Antonio Stradivarius 17__. A Braxton County musician told me that "according to the history" Stradivarius first made dulcimers when "he was just a little boy there running around in his father's carpenter shop." He went on to say that he started making fiddles after that.

Most often the stories are the hard luck type, such as "Uncle Bud" Sandy, who had a good fiddle one time that he traded away. He tried to recall the name. He said, "It was a S—Sada, what do you call it—Sadavarius? It was a thoroughbred!"[12] One woman told me that her father had a good fiddle made in "Stradivarius, Pennsylvania."

Pronunciation of foreign words and names present problems leading to variations when placed in oral traditions. Although words of colorful speech may reach back to ancient times, it seems that new colorful names for creatures are continually being invented. When I moved to Randolph County in 1975, I got to know a couple of interesting neighbors. One day I was out on the porch about to get water from a hand pump when I noticed a "lizard" (actually a salamander) in a bucket that was sitting on the well cap. I wondered aloud about how that thing ever got into the bucket of water. One fellow in all seriousness said, "Sometimes it rains down those things."

I asked this fellow if he ever saw any bluebirds around, and he said, "Oh yes, we got blue birds and red birds and yaller birds." It was not the answer I had expected, but it got me to thinking about the more colorful, colloquial names for "critters" (creatures), which I collect. Fishes are some of my favorites. Rivers and streams contain "silver sides," "goggleyes," "horney heads," "mud cats," "'baccer cans," "bull heads," "shovel heads," "blue pike," "red horse," and "water dogs." Waterdogs technically are not fish but reptiles also commonly known as "hellbenders." Salamanders are called lizards. True lizards are called "scorpions" or "hell hogs." Wasps are "waspers." There are also "good-a-logs," "tumblebugs," "jarflies," "newsbees," "cullbates," and "sawyers" (all insects).

The following song, verses of which I have collected from several West Virginia traditional singers, gives colloquial names for many birds of the region:

Quack said the crane as he set on a log,
Once I caught me a big bullfrog,
He kicked and he struggled and he got away,
I ain't had no dinner all this long day.

Well said the blackbird to the crow,
What makes white folks hate us so;
It's been our turn, ever since we were born,
To go out in the fields and pull up corn.

Well said the shitepoke to the crow,
Now don't you wish that it would snow;
The creek's all muddy and the pond's all dry,
If it wasn't for the tadpoles we'd all die.

Well said the crawfish, crawling along,
If I was a young man, I'd court strong;
I'd do just like the old folks say,
Court all night and sleep all day.

Well said the woodpecker peckin' on a tree,
Once I courted a fair lady;
She proved false and from me fled,
Ever since my head's been red.

Well said the owl with his head so white,
It's a very dark and a dreary night,
I've off'times heard the old folks say,
Court all night and sleep next day.

Well said the hummingbird sitting on a flower,
I never loved a pretty girl above a half an hour;
She never comes to hear me sing,
My voice is enough to charm a king.[13]

These verses, called the "Bird Song," include a crawfish here. Craw-fish may be called "crawdads" or "crawdabs." A "crane" is a great blue heron. A "shit-e-poke" is a green heron, which earned its descriptive appellation through its curious habit of defecating whenever taking to wing. A friend claims he heard a fundamentalist radio preacher warn his flock about "atheistic, intellectual, shitepokes!"

The third verse of this rhyme turns up in black tradition,[14] and the theme of animals engaging in dialogue is common in black tradition. Although not as common in white tradition, there are ancient examples of this. McNeil claims the "Bird Song" comes from "The Three Ravens," Child ballad #26, first printed in 1611.[15] The racial overtones of the second verse may be a minstrel period addition. One line in the third verse, "The creek's all muddy and the pond's all dry," is a title Burl Hammons uses for a fiddle tune.[16] Traditional songs are excellent vehicles on which ancient speech and colloquial names may ride through time.

I am amused by various terms for something that is angled or curved instead of straight or square. A farmer on Birch River, whom I used to help put up hay, would say that the hill "went sidling" (got angled or precipitous) when it was too steep on which to drive a tractor. "Tipling" means the same thing. Things might be "catywampers" or "squalled" (out of square), "creeled" (curved or bent), "whopper-jawed" or "sigogglin'" (angled or crooked), "hooved up" (bent up or out), or "stoved" or "stoved in" (jammed together or bent in). Ernie Carpenter, narrating a story about having to ford Elk River on a horse while the water was up and raging, said the ford did not go straight across, it went "slaunchways."

The Hammons family have practiced traditional Scots-Irish naming ways for generations.[17] Because of repetitive names, nicknames abound within the family. "Old Uncle Pete" differs from "Young Pete," who differs from "Wide Mouth Pete," also known as "Big Mouth Pete." In Randolph County there was a "Mountain Bob" Hammonds, a "Little Bob" Hammonds, and a "Drunken Bob" or "Moonshine Bob" Hammonds who also went by "Dry Run Bob." There are many Jesses, including "Juggie Jesse," who had a son, "Fightin' John," the one killed on Cranberry Ridge. There was also an "Old John" Hammonds, "Crooked Neck John," "Trampin' John," and a "Little John," who was mentioned in chapter four and who lived in Nicholas County.

Most nicknames are descriptive but they may derive through other thought processes. Braxton County fiddler "Howard Hoot" had a father nicknamed "Hoot" Riffle, so they called his son "Howard Hoot." This is an example of nicknaming whereby an Anglicized form of the old Gaelic patronym survives in West Virginia.[18] This form is also found in black tradition. A well-liked ex-slave in Braxton County named Molly married a man named "Gabe" (Gabriel) Johnson. After that she became known as Molly Gabe. A similar German tradition in West Virginia puts the man's name in front of the woman's, so if a man named Homer marries a woman named Rhoda, she becomes "Homer Rhoda."

Nicknames are a long-standing tradition in rural West Virginia culture, just as they were in the clan system of the English/Scottish border country.[19] A central West Virginia parallel would be the Hamrick family of Webster County. The Hamricks, of Scots-Irish stock, all descended from Benjamin Hamrick, an early settler in Webster County. Today, a large percentage of the county's population can trace their ancestry to this man.[20] Because of traditional naming ways, as above, name duplications abound and nicknames are necessary. The family has "Bearskin

Bill" Hamrick, "Trigger Ben" Hamrick, "Kelly Ben" Hamrick, "Curly Jim" Hamrick, "Curly Dave" Hamrick, "Frizzly John" Hamrick, "Bearshit" Hamrick, "Happy" Hamrick, "Applejack" Hamrick, and "Rimfire" Hamrick. There was also "Uncle Burn" Hamrick, "Sampy" Hamrick, "Hans" Hamrick, and "Retus" Hamrick, all fiddlers in the Webster Springs area. Dewey Hamrick (often pronounced "Jewey") and his son, Murrell, along with Bob Hamrick, carried the family's fiddling traditions to Randolph County.[21]

Nicknaming can be an oral tradition used to belittle or spite people. "Daddy" Blake had fathered a child out of wedlock, and paid the price of a ridiculing nickname throughout his lifetime. Another common type describes personal habits or activities. It could be "Fiddlin' John," "Soldier Jack," or "Squirrelly Bill" (who liked to hunt squirrels). Nicknames are apt to change. In Randolph County "Mountain Bob" Hammonds became "Preacher Bob" once he took up the occupation.

I knew of people nicknamed "Pigfoot," "Cowfoot," "Ramcat," "Dog–butt," "Mudcat" "Horsehead," "Jarfly," "Potatohead," "Highpockets," and "Drylegs" in the area. I've heard of a "Bigfoot" McElwain, from that musical family in Webster County whose last name was shortened down to "Wain" by some, whereby fiddler Lewis Johnson McElwain became "Uncle Jack Wain." Uncle and Aunt titles are terms of endearment, and do not necessarily denote any blood relation. Most older folks on Birch River had uncle and aunt titles permanently affixed to their names by everyone on the river. Nicknamed people there included an extremely inactive fellow who went by the nickname of "Loot." A local tale indicated that once, when he was being chided for his laziness, he retorted, "I live by the word of God where he says, 'Thou shalt not work on the Sabbath nor six days thereafter'!"

Another common oral tradition in West Virginia is the byword. Most tale tellers mimic the actual speaking voice of the story's characters, including the identifying byword(s) interjected throughout the tale. For instance, Edden Hammons's byword was "Upon my honor," with which he apparently started almost every sentence. In most tellings, this gets shortened to just "'Pon my honor," or, "My honor."

Maggie Hammons Parker remembered an old-timer whose bywords were "I'll eat hell." A common one is preceding a sentence with "I hope I may die," which comes out "hope-ma-die" and is shortened from "I hope I may die if this isn't the truth." It's like another one, "I'd take a dying oath" (that such and such is true, etc.), used by a man in Braxton County.

Currence Hammonds told me about old "Lyse" (Elias) Sanson. His byword was "this old head," and he would start almost every sentence with "This old head is going to" do this or that, or "This old head" thinks this or that. Lyse Sanson was remembered as one of the last great hunters in Webster County, along with Jesse Hammons and Tunis McElwain.[22] He was also a fiddler and a tireless long-distance walker. According to Currence, he could "out walk a dog" and thought nothing of walking thirty or forty miles to go somewhere at the drop of a hat. "He'd say, 'Now this old head of mine, I can walk her. I can go her. That old head,' he'd say. Poor—— well sir, he was a funny old fellow, old Lyse Sanson was. 'That old head of mine,' he'd say. He could play [a fiddle]."[23]

Old Randolph County banjo player Fred Hedrick uses bywords that come at the end of every sentence. He ends every sentence with the phrase "so it is," or "so she does," or whatever tense suits the preceding sentence: "It's getting mighty cold out there today, so it is." Or, "I've worked in the lumber camps most of my life, so I did."

I'm intrigued by these examples used by old folks to speak of themselves in the third person. It's fairly common, and I'm sure it is an old tradition. I knew Lou White when I lived in Tygart's Valley in 1975. Lou was an old-time mechanic who maintained a small junkyard and a one-stall garage that was so cluttered with tools, car parts, old mufflers, worn out tires, buckets of used antifreeze, and oily rags that he would literally have to scrape junk out of the way to be able to pull a car in next to the warmth of a pot-bellied stove to work on it. One time, when the transmission on my 1957 pickup went out, I limped into Lou's place with one forward gear. He greeted me with, "By crackie, Lou'll fix you right up," his byword, followed by his reference to himself in the third person. In no more than forty-five minutes Lou pulled an old transmission out of an old truck, pulled my bad one out, put in the new (old) one, and had me on my way. The cost was twenty-five dollars.

One time a friend of mine arrived at Lou's place on a Saturday morning needing to have a fuel pump replaced. He knocked at the door to Lou's house, which was placed squarely in the middle of the junkyard. When Lou came to the door and my friend made his needs known, he answered in the third person by saying, "By crackie, Lou's drunk today, you'll have to come back about Tuesday!"

8

Black George

Ought to ought, figure to figure;
All for Jack, and none for the nigger.
   Braxton County rhyme[1]

We call ourselves a melting pot, and yet we resist the melting
with all our strength. Here we are, millions of us, from every
country in the world, almost, and certainly all races, united in
political principle and yet resisting union in all other ways.
   "What Are We," Pearl Buck (native of Pocahontas County)

The old-time string music of the South has been influenced by the African American race since the Colonial period. African Americans in the South played fiddles in significant numbers even as or possibly before whites in America took it up as a folk instrument.[2] As the frontier was shaping up in western Virginia, the Lewis and Clark expedition to the West included three fiddlers, including an African American ex-slave, who mollified the Native Americans with their music.[3] Alan Jabbour noted that the entire history of fiddling in the upper South has been an intercultural experience.[4]

   African Americans escaping the bondage of slavery by fleeing up the Ohio River spread their fiddling traditions to points north and south on the waterway. Tom Collins, a nineteenth-century Ohio River flatboatman and fiddler, learned to play from blacks and heard varied forms of music played by different ethnic and racial groups during his twenty-four years of working on the "western waters."[5] Many runaway slaves advertised in the *Virginia Gazette* between 1738 and 1779 were identified as fiddlers, and African Americans were in great demand to fiddle at social functions in the antebellum era.

   West Virginia's first settlers with agricultural aspirations brought African American slaves with them to all of the major river valleys that drain the state. As was the case in other areas, the evolution of folk music in Braxton, Randolph, Pocahontas, and Greenbrier Counties, which all had slave populations, was a multiracial experience. Widely acclaimed West Virginia musician Frank George said his grandfather, whom he credits as his strongest musical influence, learned to dance and play banjo directly from the ex-slaves who practically raised him.[6]

Many older white musicians in central West Virginia attribute fiddle and banjo tunes to African American sources and talk about being influenced in some way by black musicians. These musicians influenced well-known white musical families such as the Hammonses, Wines, and Carpenters. Kentucky fiddler Doc Roberts, whose commercial recordings made him widely influential, traced most of his best tunes to African American fiddler Owen Walker. These included "Waynesboro," a tune that found favor with West Virginia fiddlers. Roberts is regarded as an important conduit, bringing black fiddling traditions to white audiences.[7]

Documentation of the Hammons family recognizes particularly strong white mountain music traditions. However, Grafton Lacy (identified in the Library of Congress Hammons Family recording project as Lacy Grafton) was an African American man who taught Hammons family members some tunes.[8] So while the Hammonses' old-world traditions were preserved and Burl Hammons played age-old fiddle tunes of British and Irish origin, his repertoire contained many fiddle tunes influenced by African American and minstrel tradition.[9] Most banjo players in the family also played tunes of black origin. Around 1920 Currence Hammonds learned tunes and songs directly from African American banjo players near his home at Huttonsville.[10]

The legacy of black influence on early old-time string music is considerable. African Americans turned the Anglo/Celtic reels into hoedowns and added the "hot" element to southern fiddling.[11] They put the syncopation into fiddle bowing that is the trademark of southern fiddling style.[12] This caused the jigs, hornpipes, clogs, and other old-world rhythmic dance tunes to evolve into the breakdowns that became the signature of southern old-time fiddle music. The word "breakdown" is an African American dance term that comes from the corn shucking frolics that were traditional to blacks throughout the South.[13] Blacks added the new steps and body movement to European clogs, jigs, hornpipes, and reels that changed these dances into American step dance forms.[14]

The down stroke on the banjo also demonstrates African American influence. In *Negro Folk Rhymes*, Talley points out that the many versions of "Liza Jane," "Shortening Bread," "Cotton Eyed Joe," "Here Rattler Here," and scores of other fiddle tunes now widespread in white tradition were common in African American tradition. Tunes with verses

where animals talk to each other, as in African folktales, make up a
sizable portion of material. Other standard tunes credited to African
American origin and/or the minstrel stage are "Boatsman," "Cindy,"
"Whoa Mule," "Lynchburg Town," "The Year of Jubilo," "Golden Slip-
pers,"[15] and "Jump Jim Crow."[16]

Many white fiddlers in West Virginia use "cross tunings," in which
they refer to the low strings as the "bass" and "counter" and the high
strings as the "triplum" and "fine." Fiddlers of Scottish extraction in
the Maritime Provinces of Canada use these terms, and the "high bass"
tuning is found among Scots-Irish fiddlers of Pennsylvania[17] and Irish
fiddlers,[18] assuring the claim of European origin. However, a sizable
body of the lyrics of tunes played in cross tunings show up in African
American tradition.[19]

Bud Sandy, an old-time banjo player and dancer, recalled that ex-
slave Milt Perkins played fiddle in the Burnsville area. Perkins almost
always had a fiddle with him, even when riding his horse. He kept it in
an old wooden case with a wire wrapped around it. Perkins would stop
anywhere "right beside the road and fiddle you a tune."[20] Another area
musician noted that Perkins would "tickle people to death" with his
fiddling.[21]

Perkins taught a white fiddler, Tyson Moss, how to play in the old
cross tunings of (high to low) EAEA, C#AEA, and DADD. Moss went on
to teach these tunings and tunes to fiddlers in the western part of the
county.[22] Here is an example of an African American teaching whites
old-time music. Aspects of the music, including the instrument, tunings,
and probably many of the melodies, are of European origin, but Perkins
communicated a fiddle style greatly influenced by African rhythm and
syncopation.

Ex-slaves who settled in the hollows of Old Woman's Run and along
Granny's Creek in Braxton County, West Virginia, probably fared better
than other post–Civil War African Americans in the South (where "de-
plorable conditions" were rampant[23]) because of their music traditions.
Of course the iron fist of slavery had a crushing effect on the African
spirit in antebellum Braxton County, as it did elsewhere, but folk expression, through music, lingered and bloomed in the descendants of
slaves. There was interchange and sharing of cultural traditions and a
shared acceptance of music traditions. Braxton County residents have
fond memories of the many former slaves who lived in the area.

"Black George," Milt Perkins, Jilly Grace, Grafton Lacy, Cal Lucky,
and many more African American fiddlers influenced central West Virginia music tradition. The white old-time musicians discussed in this
book speak of these musicians. I have documented blacks playing fiddles
and banjos in Hardy, Pendleton, Randolph, Pocahontas, Greenbrier,

Braxton, and Harrison Counties. Many talk about particular characters, some of whom in the first half of the twentieth century were of the rambling hobo variety. In lean times they used music as a means of obtaining food and lodging. Some stayed for long periods of time at first one house and then the next, "working out" their board.

About 1930, an African American banjo player stopped at the home of the Grant Samples family near the mouth of Tate Creek on Elk River. He wanted something to eat and said he would play the banjo he was carrying in exchange for food. He impressed the family not only with his music but with all manner of tricks as he played, such as twirling the banjo without missing a lick.

A fairly well known African American banjo player named Bill Gamp lived at Gilmer Station, near the Braxton/Gilmer County line, and influenced musicians in that area.

Melvin Wine and others remember an old black itinerant who went only by the name of "Lost John." Wine said Lost John could play two French harps (harmonicas) at once, one with his mouth and one with his nose. Maynard Blake, an old musician from the Exchange area, recalled lyrics to a song Lost John played in the 1930s:

I don't know what his real name was, but he called himself Lost John. He sung a song about hisself, he said someplace in the song, "I heard a noise down under the ground; the devil was a-draggin' Lost John around."

He was as comical as he could be. One time down on the railroad track—Uncle Ben Riffle was in the bunch—they met and was a-talkin' and somebody else come along and they stopped and seen that Lost John had a guitar, and that fellow said, he said, "Do you play that thing?"

"Well," he said, "I try."

He said, "Well, sing us a song and play it."

He started and come to that there part playin' Lost John and he said, "I heard a noise down under the ground, the devil was a-draggin' Lost John around." Old Uncle Ben Riffle, it tickled him so, and he was standing in the middle of the track. He started to back up a-laughing and he caught his heel on the railroad rail and he slid right down over the cinders and briers.[24]

Several mulatto families in northern Braxton County have spawned musicians through several generations. Jilly Grace was a mulatto fiddler in the Burnsville area who sometimes played for old-style horse-drawn merry-go-rounds. Melvin Wine remembered that Grace played a tune called "Tippy Get Your Hair Cut" for his father. Bob Wine could not even bribe Grace to play the tune a second time, but he managed to learn it anyway.[25]

"There was one colored fellow used to come to our house. He could pick the guitar or banjo, either one," recalled Bud Sandy. "Jesus Christ, he could pick a banjo though. We always called him 'Hunter.' He was an awful fellow to hunt. He had two or three old hounds. He lived out [at] McKay. He kindly knocked it—thumped it. By the way, he could play it though. Once in a while he'd sing a little. He's the one learnt me to play John Henry."[26]

African Americans came as slaves with the early settlers to all the major river valleys in the state. Additionally, large numbers were brought as early as 1808 to work in the salt mines of Kanawha County. By 1850 there were 3,140 blacks there.[27] It follows that numerous white musicians would experience black culture at that Kanawha County river juncture, if not having done so at home. Be assured that this group was playing music, singing, and dancing in rhythms associated with their race. One study of runaway slaves in the South found 627 whose descriptions (in advertisements by their owners) listed them as being players of the fiddle or violin.[28]

In Hale's classic work, *Trans-Allegheny Pioneers,* he mentions that a fiddle and banjo were necessities for the long September hunting expeditions of his youth (ca. 1830). According to Hale, "family servants" were present at these hunting camps, and nighttime activities included music playing by the family and the black slaves. Hale's maternal Scots-Irish grandparents were the first white couple to be married west of the Alleghenies. This incident provides an intriguing account of musical interactions between blacks and whites with fiddles and banjos present, and before the minstrel era. This scene simulates the virtual birth of a musical genre (old-time string music) in the American backcountry.[29]

During a period of industrialization in the mid to late nineteenth century, new waves of African Americans migrated to West Virginia to provide labor in the coal mines, for railroad construction, and for railroad operation. These movements left a legacy easily observed in the John Henry, John Hardy, New River, and C&O railroad songs.[30] This added to, rather than began, the African American string music legacy. How much the minstrel-era influenced old-time music and how much traditional African American folk music influenced minstrel music is open for debate. Conway argues that minstrel banjo music, including playing style and repertoire, derived directly from African American folk tradition.[31] Evidence shows blackface minstrels drew heavily from black folk tradition, and all of West Virginia's musical families play tunes from the minstrel stage. This makes them part of a biracial evolution.

White banjo players in the Hammons family and in the Tygart Valley play versions of "Johnny Booker," a tune from the minstrel era. Most

Fiddle and banjo music, the basis of the traditional string-band sound, represents a uniting of rhythmic and melodic influences from separate cultural,
racial, and continental origins. Shown here are John and Robert Samples of
Braxton County. (Date and photographer unknown; author's collection.)

West Virginia banjo players play minstrel favorite "Walkin' in the Parlor," which is sometimes called "Tude Evans" after a West Virginia woman who played it.[32] One version of this tune has some topical verses that comment on the nature of John D. Rockefeller.[33] Melvin Wine still plays the tune "Jump Jim Crow," which traces to African American folk tradition and became prominent in blackface minstrelsy. The tune lent its sentiments to the "Jim Crow" era of later social meaning.[34]

Hundreds of white and black West Virginians sought work when the coal mines were booming at Widen in Clay County. Many whites had their first meaningful encounters with African Americans and other ethnic groups while working there. While African Americans made up 6.6 percent of West Virginia's population in 1930, they accounted for 21.8 percent of the state's mining force.[35]

Brooks Hardway, an old-time banjo player who grew up dancing to fiddle music, met black musicians at Widen and in other communities where they lived. He learned a number of tunes from one black man known, because of his size, as "Hugie."

I met some guitar pickers that was out of this world. They played them blues, and I learned a lot of their tunes, and I did love them too. I learned some good tunes off a colored man in Widen. And, I learned more tunes off a white man who had learned them from colored men.

I met Raymond Knight in the year of 1932. He's dead and gone— drunk hisself to death. Whiskey took him to his grave. But my guitar pickin' was learned from him and one of them niggers that was in Widen. Old "Backwater Blues" and I don't know how many— Raymond Knight introduced me to them negroes in Widen. Raymond liked my style, and I liked his style. We was right down each other's alley in turn and disposition and the music blood that was in our veins. . . .

Raymond Knight and I used to go to Granny's Crick and visit a man. Raymond Knight was acquainted with them Granny's Crick folks, and there was a white man that had married a colored woman, and he lived in amongst these people—they had a little territory of their own. That woman could fix up a meal in the best shape—she was the best cook I ever eat after. And so clever, there was nothing in the way of cleverness that these people didn't have. Payton Burns was the man's name. Raymond Knight used to go to his house and stay a week. He made whiskey. Had the best moonshine you ever tasted. We'd go there to get to drink that whiskey and play music. He'd set there and listen as long as you stayed up and played, day or night. We used to take a man with us named Grafton Lacy. Grafton Lacy was from Flatwoods. He was a colored man, but he lived in the white section. Raymond Knight knew Grafton Lacy, and he was a guitar player. We would visit Payton Burns and stay a week at a time.[36]

Fiddler Jack of
Harper's Ferry,
West Virginia, 1903.
(Photograph by
John H. Tarbell.)

His stories indicate an enormous interchange of musical technique and style and social activity. Music is the ticket here. The common fascination with music, along with some liquid refreshment, enabled and induced these folks to transcend established mores and enjoy and share music in a social situation. Musicians and other artists, respecting each other's talents, traditionally have created common ground for breaking down such barriers.

"Black George" was another itinerant musician and ex-slave fondly remembered by area musicians for his talents and personality. Melvin Wine proudly showed off an old homemade fiddle that belonged to Black George:[37]

> It was an old black fellow owned it, and he played all over this country. They called him Black George. Wherever you seen him he usually had that fiddle under his arm. He wasn't a loud fiddler, but he just played good—real good. He was a good honest feller and he's gone, so I'll try to take care of his fiddle.
>
> He scared me very bad when I was a little fellow. I hadn't seen no black people, and we lived up a holler, and he came down where me and my sister was a-gettin' water from a spring. He said to us, he said, "Where does Bob Wine live?" That was my father. We didn't tell him yea or nay. We just broke and run to the house. We run to the house

and told Dad and them about it, so Dad come out and he knew him.
He hollered for him to come on up to the house. So he stayed there,
maybe all night, I don't remember. We learned to like the old fellow."[38]

Fiddle played by "Black George."
(Photograph by the author; courtesy
of Augusta Heritage Center.)

The Blakes, a large family of musicians, also welcomed Black George into their house for long periods of time. Everett White, who was raised in Braxton County, was a great grandson to the man who owned Black George as a slave and is related to the musical Wine family. He recalled a racial incident concerning Black George, his grandfather, and an acquaintance:

> His name was John McNemar, he was a fiddle player. I'll tell you something kind of funny that happened. He was at my grandfather Wine's house one time. A bunch of musicians was there, singers and people that played instruments. Black George was there—He didn't like old Black George, old John didn't. And after while he said, "Mister Nelson Wines, unless I change my mind, I'll never set my foot in your house no more." Grandpa set there a little bit and said, "Unless I change my mind, I don't give a damn."
>   . . . He was a good violin player, Black George was. I think his name was Morris—I think. When he got his freedom from Grandpa Johnny, that was my great grandfather, he told him he was free. He was free to get married and have a family of his own, or whatever he wanted to do. He told Grandpa he was as free as he wanted to be. He'd been treated right and he was as free as he wanted to be. Dad said he laid down across the bed and cried when Grandpa told him he had his freedom.[39]

George Morris died in 1919 on Old Woman's Run at the home of another ex-slave. The rats ate off his toes before they got him buried, which was in the African American cemetery on Camden Hill on the divide between Granny's Creek and Old Woman's Run near the town of Sutton. A rough field stone with a faint, hand-chiseled "G M" marks his grave.

Among other African American fiddlers in the county in the early to mid twentieth century were George Bailes, who lived on Benny's Run before the land was taken for the Burnsville Dam,[40] and Jessie Rhea, a woman who lived on Old Woman's Run.[41] Considering the small size of the African American community in the county, a considerable group of African American fiddlers are remembered for their musical talent.

Despite obvious black influence on old-time music, not only in West Virginia but throughout the South, very little African American string music found its way onto commercial recordings. New directions in the recording industry in the early 1920s segregated old-time music into white and black categories called "hillbilly" and "race" records. Record producer Ralph Peer coined these terms and the marketing strategy behind them. Producers and promoters did not use the term "hillbilly music" at first because they thought it to be disparaging. "Old-time" or "mountain music" were terms ascribed to the domain of white players around the time of the first radio performance in 1922 and the first old-time music recording in 1923.[42] Companies promoted blues music as the music of the African American race. Blacks certainly played and developed the blues as a musical genre, but they also played and were influential to the string-band music that was evolving through the period. Beginning with vaudeville and jazz-oriented blues recordings of African Americans in 1920, by 1926 blues music was presented and promoted in a more folk-rooted, "downhome" style.[43]

This effort by the record companies, whether conscious or unconscious, altered the natural course of folk music evolution within the African American and white communities. Recordings vied with radio as the principal vehicle through which regional folk music became popularized and thus widespread. Having established racial categories, the companies eventually geared their promotional efforts to the white market. Whereas promotional materials for old-time music recordings pictured responsible-looking whites playing, dancing, and being jolly in more dignified settings, throughout the latter half of the nineteenth century materials depicting African American musicians were caricatured stereotypes. Watermelon patches and lazy African Americans lounging about, sometimes with banjos and in humorous situations, were often shown. Based on early minstrel images (where blacks were mocked by whites in blackface), these images continued into late nineteenth century magazine illustrations and Currier and Ives lithographs. As early as 1891, on cylinder records, the recording companies had "novelty" categories with humorous, mocking recordings in their offerings. These often were performed by whites and promoted to whites, at the expense of African Americans or other ethnicities.[44] This may have instigated the beginning of the end for African American old-time string music. The one-two punch of derisive media and the promotion of race records took effect. Blues was the musical expression of blacks, and old-time music became an expression of whites.

The genre of old-time string music among African Americans is practically unknown today. Almost all of the generation of black people who played old-time string music on fiddles and banjos have died. In recent years, a few blacks in West Virginia who grew up with the older string music tradition continued to play it through their lifetimes. Uncle Homer Walker of Mercer County, Clarence Tross of Hardy, and several Pendleton County musicians were final examples of black banjo players in the state. Today, just a few African American old-timers and a few younger revivalists are found nationwide.

In the late 1920s, recorded blues as played by African Americans became commercially recorded and distributed by white country music performers like Jimmy Rodgers. The recording industry, which before this had promoted blues as the music of African American people through race records, was now accepting and promoting white performers who were playing African American-founded blues music. In West Virginia, white crossover artists such as Dick Justice and Frank Hutchinson played black music that was issued on country labels for white audiences. Hutchinson, a native of Raleigh County, became known as the "pride of West Virginia." The bluesy style of Hutchinson's music is carried on today in the music of southern West Virginia's Carl Rutherford.[45]

Our old-time music is a mixture of music from many sources. The folk music of African American people in the South, going back to the Colonial era, was old-time music that utilized fiddles and banjos.[46] Today it is recognized as traditional mountain music. While whites still struggle to overcome the pejorative "hillbilly," "cracker," or "clodhopper" stereotypical images in the media, the music is promoted widely in a positive way as "old-time music."[47]

While many West Virginia musicians did not directly experience old-time string music played by African Americans in the nineteenth century, new avenues of cross-cultural movement were brewing. By the 1920s, musical influences on most of West Virginia's old-time musicians included that which came from new commercial media. The "hot" music of the Georgia fiddle bands and acclaimed southern fiddlers, like John Carson for instance, were now influencing rural fiddlers throughout the region. This music, in large part shaped by black instrumental and vocal tradition, was gaining wide acceptance. People started singing with stringed instruments, having only recently gained access to guitars (a difficult instrument to make at home) through mail order catalogs. The older traditional fiddlers, those born in the mid-nineteenth century in the more isolated parts of West Virginia, were not as affected. At the same time, the next generation of younger musicians was eating it up. New repertoires were blossoming, and tunes called rags and blues as well as breakdowns, all forms of African American–influenced music and dance, were gaining popularity among fiddlers. More and more of the tunes of old-time musicians in the state came from these new sources and were quickly accepted in folk tradition. Music originally introduced on the minstrel stage as well as hot new music from southern folk tradition, heard through these new media sources, was gaining wide acceptance. These new influences, widespread through commercial association, became part of folk tradition. The old repertoires, largely based on European music, would never be the same.

9

Dancin' and Fightin'

Do the dances still rage? . . . Is the war over down in that
neighborhood?
Postscript to a letter written by M.W. Humphreys from
Lexington, Virginia, to his brothers in Braxton County,
dated 10 April 1866.[1]

An early instance of folk music and dance in central West Virginia was
recorded by "Rattlesnake Bill" Dodrill. It occurred at the first meeting
of the Free Masons in the region, which took place on Gauley River,
now Webster County, at the home of Col. Isaac Gregory, in the year
1800. Accounts of music and dance on the western Virginia frontier are
scarce, as most historians of the day were taken with chronicling the
Indian Wars and gave little thought to social customs. He noted: "After
the meeting the women and children were invited in and all joined in a
regular 'Old Virginia hoedown.' To the music of two violins playing such
lively tunes as 'Leather Britches' and 'Flat Foot in the Ashes' they danced
until daylight."[2]

In May of 1988 I attended a public square dance at Flatwoods in
Braxton County. It was not all that different from the pioneer dance
mentioned above. For instance, the same tunes were played. These
modern dances always begin at eight o'clock sharp, so about twenty till
eight, people started rolling in. Promptness is not only observed but
seems to be a passion with these country folks. When I arrived, Cy
McQuain, who usually sets up his sound system for these affairs, came
to me in his affable way, shaking my hand, laughing, and asking, "Where's
your fiddle?" This night, the music will include Cy's wife, Zita, on guitar, Sarah Singleton on fiddle, Mary Squires also on guitar and singing
between sets, and Carl Davis playing a banjo-mandolin.

Although this is the hired band for the evening, the pay is only ten

Sarah Singleton, 1990.
(Photograph by the
author.)

dollars each and normally several others are asked to fiddle or perhaps
sing a song or two between sets. I am sometimes asked to play banjo, if
I have brought one along, and to fiddle a few. There is never a designated caller at these affairs, but it is presumed that several will show up
and share the duty throughout the evening.

Things get rolling when Sarah Singleton saws out four beats and
the rest join her for a rousing version of "Hell among the Yearlings."
Here a ritual begins: about two-thirds of the crowd, whose number might
total fifty or more, get up and start hoedowning (flatfooting or clog-
ging) on the floor. Cy meanders around with an ear to adjusting the
sound, which usually means reacting to bystanders' helpful hints to
"bring the fiddle up some."

One fellow does a sort of backwards skipping flatfoot dance while
shuffling around the hall, back first. All the while he claps his hands
and shouts at the top of his voice, "square dance, square dance," in an
effort to get a caller to the microphone and get things going. Another

man, perhaps the best flatfoot dancer there, has arrived with a reddish cast to his face, without even having made the first of several runs to the car to visit with John Barleycorn. Although primarily a teetotaling crowd, a fact to which the group owes its longevity as a dancing community, they tolerate this guy because of his dancing skills.

After five minutes of unstructured revelry with the band getting in the groove and the dancers showing their stuff, the music stops and a caller gets on the microphone. "Okay, square 'em up," he shouts in a distorted voice, much too loud over the system. Cy makes a dive for the controls as couples pair up and form circles of four couples on the dance floor. With the caller simply making a pitch to the crowd to get on the floor, the dancers know what sort of formation to take. A few callers will have everyone in a large circle to dance "The Railroad Track," "Adam and Eve," or maybe "Old Dan Tucker."

In Braxton County, the head couple may be anywhere in the set regardless of orientation to the caller or band. The fiddlers play the same tune throughout each dance, and no medleys are used. For now the dancers have arranged themselves in five neat squares of four couples. Sarah Singleton saws four beats in the key of D and takes off on "Raggedy Ann." Caller Jack Mayse starts out:

> Honor your partner,
> Honor your corner,[3]

Mayse continues:

> All join hands and make that wheel,
> The more you dance the better you feel.
> Other way back in an Indian line,
> The ladies in the front and the gents behind.

This second call is the lead-off call for most all the dances and all the callers. When the circle has roughly returned to its original place, the caller commands:

> Allemande left your corner,
> Grand right and left.
> Meet your partner and promenade home.

Everyone knows out of habit that the promenade starts the second time a couple meets, that is, after everyone has made a complete circle of the set.

From the prerequisite "All join hands" beginning, the caller might put the dancers through any number of figures that are local favorites. A large repertoire of figures comes into play at dances. They are frac-

tionally divided among the callers, of which four or five might be expected to call a few figures at any given dance.

The lead-off caller, Jack Mayse, decides on "Chase the Rabbit." This
typically titles the dance and indicates the lead figure:

> Chase that rabbit,
> Chase that squirrel,
> Chase that pretty girl round the world.

Through this figure, the lead couple takes off to dance with the second
couple, the one to their right. Any couple within the set may be designated as the lead couple. Sometimes it is whoever responds most quickly
to the caller's instruction to lead out to the right. More often, an experienced dancer designates with a point and a nod just before the dance
starts that a certain couple should lead. "Chase the Rabbit" has the
woman going between the members of the second couple and the man
following, first around the other woman, then around the man. This
repeats with the other couples. The next call goes:

> Chase that rabbit,
> Chase that coon,
> Chase that hairy old baboon.

At which time the lead couple switches places, and the woman chases
the man. In Braxton County the interim figure most often called that
goes between the couples who lead the signature figures of the dance is:

> Left hand lady with the right hand around,
> Partner by the left;
> You swing mine, and I'll swing yours,
> Give me back mine, I'll give you back yours.

When all couples dance the main figure and chorus and everybody is
back home swinging their partners, the caller usually chants:

> Step right back and watch her smile,
> Step right up and swing her awhile,
> Step right back and watch her grin,
> Step right up and do it again.

Followed by:

> Allemande left your corner, grand right and left.
> Promenade all.

When all couples have completed the figure and promenaded for the last time, they haphazardly drift off the floor. At this point the musicians notice the dance is ending, Singleton fiddles a tag like "shave and a haircut, two bits," the music ends, and the dancers applaud the band.

Once or twice during an evening's dance when the music has gotten pretty good and the dancers are charged up, the music will continue after the dance ends. Everyone stays out on the floor and "hoedowns" for a few minutes.

If other fiddlers have shown up at the dance, the protocol is to ask them to fiddle for a dance or two. At this dance Carl Davis, the banjo-mandolin player, spelled Singleton for a dance. Dance regulars asked a fiddler from nearby Upshur County to play one tune. They also dutifully asked Ernie Carpenter to play. There seems to be an unspoken reverence for Carpenter because of age and fiddling skill.

Between square dances, slow or "round" dancing like waltzes or two-steps are done to country songs. Mary Squires sings these while playing her guitar, and others may play along on whatever instruments they choose. Announcements about future dances are made during the interim, and cards are signed for sick or hospitalized members of the dance community. Anyone is welcome to make any sort of relevant announcement.

There is a mix of married people with their spouses and married people without their spouses dancing at these affairs. All men dance with all women, wives or otherwise. Men always ask the women to dance, never the other way around. Only men do the calling. The average age is about 55, with a few children younger than ten years old present and one man older than eighty present and dancing. Only a few teenagers show up, and they are related to the dance regulars. Newcomers are welcomed, but no form of instruction takes place. Newcomers get pushed through by well meaning and helpful regulars, who take them as partners.

The public dance described above is an outgrowth of "house dances" that took place earlier in Braxton County. House dances were prevalent well into the twentieth century in most rural communities.

"Everybody'd move out all the furniture, and there'd only be about one room, one set," said Jack Mayse, recalling house dances in his home. "Most generally had a fiddle and a guitar player. My dad was the figure caller. There was no figure callers in the country but him. Maybe we'd go to have an apple peeling, to make apple butter. We'd go there and peel enough apples to make a big kettle of apple butter, and we'd have a square dance after that."[4]

There was no homogeneous style of dancing among rural communities in central West Virginia. House dances, and the limited space and numbers implied in their practice, were the norm. Currence Hammonds of Webster County knew circles and reels but had never seen a square set until he saw people from outside the region do it.[5]

Over time house dances gave way to more public affairs, and platform dances became popular. Jack Mayse remembered dances on a platform built by Shelt Carpenter at the Braxton County fairgrounds:

> They'd have [dances] at houses, different houses. Here, there, and yonder. Then they started the old fairground over here at Sutton. Ernie Carpenter was learnin' how to play, and his brother and his sister, and Ernie's dad, Shelt. There'd be a bunch there at the fair, and they'd say, "John go down and get your crowd, these big shots wants to watch you square dance." They would. Shelt'd go down in the crowd and get my dad and bring him up there. John'd call figures, and he'd have his own dancers. Pick dancers. It was just like Grand Old Opry.

[Later] they'd have a square dance every Saturday night down at the Armory at Gassaway. My dad would call figures at one end, and I started to call figures down at the lower end. I had all the young ones down there, you see, 'cause I didn't care whether those boys would throw those girls down or what they did with them. My dad wasn't that a-way. He'd call you down.[6]

The popularity of outdoor wooden platforms for dancing in the late nineteenth and early twentieth centuries brought dances out of private homes and made them more public affairs. With the advent of the steam-powered band mill, lumber for such platforms was for the first time cheap and accessible to common people. Before that, a board was a prized possession that took great effort to produce. Water-powered mills were not common, and whip-sawed or pit-sawed boards took much manpower to produce.

Enterprising people earned money from dances. In the 1920s, an African American banjo player, Bill Gamp, held dances at his house. The dancers compensated the musicians, Gamp included, in some small way, but it was Gamp's sale of his home brew that made the enterprise a successful venture. By the 1930s, dances were moving outside (in good weather), and most cost dancers ten cents per couple per set.[7] Musicians divided this money among themselves and the platform owner. Like Bill Gamp, the owners often sold homemade spirits on the side for extra cash. At a community in Randolph County, near Huttonsville, moonshiners built a platform and sold their wares at dances. This channeled more income to the musicians but also caused problems. Rowdiness and fighting closed down many a dance there. Eventually larger community buildings like the Armory in Gassaway became available for community dancing.

A dance in Randolph County, circa 1870. (Sketch by Porte Crayon; from *Harper's New Monthly Magazine,* September 1872.)

"My Dad, I've never seen him drunk in my life," said Jack Mayse, recalling his father's days of calling dances during Prohibition. "Now, he'd take a little jigger of whiskey anytime. He'd call it a little schnapps. But that was it. He'd go to a square dance, and my cousin was a bootlegger, bring some of that old white lightning, and I'd take him and a gallon jug to Gassaway, which I didn't care you know. I had a '26 Ford. Pop would pour a little bit of whiskey out in a bottle. Medicine bottle. He didn't give a damn if the law was standin' there or not, he'd just take a little nip of it. Calling figures, you know what I mean. That was it, but after that square dance, he was ready to go home."[8]

Cakewalks, which are popular today in West Virginia, also are an aspect of old-time dances. Nowadays cakewalks occur during breaks between sets at community square dances. In fact some fund-raising events consist solely of cakewalks, where cakewalkers vie for as many as forty cakes in an evening. The object is to win a cake through a lottery process from a sponsoring community organization which provides the cakes and collects the money. Typically the band plays a tune while "walkers" circle about the dance floor. In Braxton County, they dance around in couples, and most do a clog, hoedown, or skipping step to the music. When the music stops, officials determine who has ended up on or is closest to a predetermined spot on the dance floor. In another, older form, a broom is dropped by a blindfolded person when the music stops. Whoever it hits "takes the cake."

I attended a dance where cakes were walked off in Jackson County in 1994. Walkers formed a ring and moved in a counterclockwise direction. When the music stopped, dancers remained in position while a man went to the center of the ring to spin a bowling pin. It spun for as long as a minute, creating heightened apprehension about where it would stop. When it eventually did, the spinner determined which couple was in the position pointed out by the pin, and they took the cake.

Cakewalks as observed in late-twentieth-century West Virginia are a far cry from the origins of the practice. Although the origin of the modern cakewalk is not clear, cakewalks belong to an Afro-American genesis and originated in Southern antebellum plantation life.[9] The cakewalk was a strutting step performed by couples in a ring and early on involved efforts by slaves to parody the formal dances of their high-society masters. Cotillions were dances used at the end of an evening's program in which the host and hostess danced around the room in a circle in various ways and were mimicked and followed by the guests. Cakewalks among the African American initiators of the form, in turn, were mimicking these performances by their white masters.

Early performances seem to have little to do, however, with cakes. The introduction of cakes may be the result of a name transformation. There is an old Southern expression, "the cock of the walk," which indicates the "dominant bully or master spirit."[10] I wonder if that expression, which fits the performance of the master during an evening-ending walk-around,[11] evolved from "cock of the walk" to "cakewalk."

On the minstrel stages, beginning about 1840, the cakewalk, with its name secured, continued on an interesting path. Here, whites in blackface mimicked the African American dance, which was in its own time a way that African Americans had mocked whites. The minstrel form soon began using African Americans, also in blackface,[12] as well as whites to perform cakewalks. The scenario comes full circle when, in the 1890s, cakewalks swept white high society in a popular craze. Thus, during the late nineteenth century, socialites unwittingly mimicked themselves in a dance form that had been processed through a succession of social strata, folk traditions, and popular entertainment forms, all the while playing back and forth between groups with mocking racial overtones.[13] Special music, composed for the practice, then found its way into folk repertoires. For example, a piece titled "Eli Green's

Cake Walk" published in 1896, shows up in Nebraska fiddling tradition.[14] Schoolhouses were popular places to have box socials or pie socials, and these often were followed by cakewalks.[15]

Old-timers I talked to reminisced about some great dancers at the events in their pasts.

"My daddy was the best double shuffle backstep man I ever saw," said Brooks Hardway. "They had an old backstep called the double shuffle backstep. Dad had it natural. I've saw him get on the old sled of a morning to go up to the cornfield or wheatfield. He'd get on that old sled with that old board bottom in it, and he hit a few licks of the most beautiful double shuffle I ever saw in my life."[16]

People in Randolph County and surrounding counties remember a man named Gander Digman as the best hoedown dancer around. Digman danced around beer joints, county fairs, and public events for drinks and tips. At one time he danced in blackface with a trio of musicians, suggesting a vestige of the minstrel era in the twentieth century. Robert Hamrick, Blackie Cool, and Jennings "Jinks" Morris provided the music. Digman had a pair of hickory-soled shoes specially made for dancing and was remembered to have danced in his sleep.[17] Some describe how he could make a chair dance by holding onto its posts and tapping out the rhythm with the chair legs as part of his routine.

Banjo player Russell Higgins, another Randolph Countian, danced around lumber camps with his brother, Ernest.[18] Russell's favorite step is the "Dry Fork Shackleback." He also does some hambone and recites patter as he dances:

> Granny will your dog bite,
> Your hen peck, your rooster fight;
> Your turkey walk a fence rail?
> No, child, no.

Jim Flint of Braxton County started calling figures in beer joints at age fifteen. He was hustled into the kitchen when "the law" came around, as he was too young to legally be there. Jim listed dances, by their main figure, that were in his repertoire:

> Swing your maw and then your paw
> Around that couple, take a little peep
> Around that couple, swing in the rear
> Elbow swing
> The star
> Chase the rabbit, chase the squirrel
> Balance four
> Around that couple and through that couple

> Cheat or swing
> Figure eight
> Whirligig her in and whirligig her out
> Butterfly whirl
> Birdie in the cage
> Bail the ocean, bail the sea
> Elevate the hall
> Ladies go gee, gents go haw
> Swing 'em on the right and corners on the left
> Shoot that pretty girl through to me
> Outside under-inside over,
> Right hand across, left hand back
> Ladies bow and the gents know how

Larger circle dances included:

> Old Dan Tucker
> Nine pin
> Railroad track

Some standard patter, reserved for choruses at Braxton County dances, is:

> Swing the quarter, then the half

Or:

> Swing the one that stole the sheep,
> Then the one that ate the meat;
> Then the one that gnawed the bone,
> Then the one who carried it home.

For promenading:

> Sweep the hall
> Sweep her clean
> The dirtiest old hall, I ever seen.

For swinging:

> Swing your partner, pat her on the head,
> If she don't like biscuits, feed her cornbread.

For ending:

> Up the river and around the bend,
> That's all there is, this is the end.

The dances of olden days were not always the civil events that the present-day Braxton County square dance (described earlier) is. Fighting and feuding are also parts of traditional folk life, and fighting at square dances has been a nemesis to continuing dance traditions. Some folks, however, say they have gone through a whole lifetime without seeing trouble at a dance.

Ott Scott was an old rounder who grew up back in the country around Little Otter in Braxton County. He made no bones about being an instigator of fights:

> We had a good one there at Belfont one time. Had a feller there by the name of Flem Burbidge. He was pickin' a banjo. He couldn't pick much. Some of 'em made it up: one was to hit me, and I was to fall over through among the dancers, and when I got up I would be over where Burbidge was, and I's to hit him. Boy, we did. I laid it to him, and they caught me up and throwed me off of a high porch out into the yard. I lit in the yard and when I lit, the fellow jumped right on my back. He was a-chuggin' me down. Some woman come along, a [local girl]. She stuck a knife in his back. He had me down there, slammin' my head in the ground, she stuck a knife in his back. That loosened him. She cut five different people there that night. She cut one feller down across the shoulder, and they asked me when they had us up for trial how he got that done, and I told 'em I didn't know, that I saw him crawlin' under the house, a-tryin' to get out an old sythe snath [handle] to fight with an' I said, "I think he done it on a nail." I had the knife for a long time. Somebody knocked it out of her hand, and I found it. I kept the knife. [The court] couldn't get nothin' out of nobody.
>
> The worst I ever seen was back over here on Fall Run. That was the Browns and the Bulls [who] fought in there one night at the dance. A feller there had on a pair of gum boots by the name of Denver Barnhouse. When they got done fightin' in there, well, a bunch of 'em, why they had to pull his boots off him and shake the glass out of 'em where they'd hit one another over the head with pint whiskey bottles.[19]

Fighting was a way of dealing with problems beyond the mental resolve of the fighters. However there seems to be ample evidence for another kind of fighting, not with the usual motives that lead to violence. This kind of fighting has more to do with wanting an invigorating physical and psychological experience. Independence and self-reliance are traits we recognize and respect in old-time people. It's been said that in ancient cultures people didn't think out their problems so much as they danced them out, a physical way of affecting the course of events, if only in a psychological sense. They also hunted them out, fiddled them out, and fought them out. Scott described a fight of this kind:

Sunday come, and we hadn't got to fight any through the weekdays, we'd walk five miles to get to have a good fight on Sunday somewhere. We'd just get out and see who was the best man. Nobody was mad. We'd have black eyes, nose mashed, one thing and another. Just seein' who was the best man—toughest. We's pretty rough back there in them younger days.[20]

At one Braxton County dance in the early twentieth century, a fight brewed because the local boys were jealous of others who had come from a surrounding community and danced with the local girls. "On the dining room table there was a pitcher of water, some glasses and a bowl of sugar. Jesse went to the table, took a tumbler and poured some water into it, and added a generous helping of sugar. He was wearing leather knee boots so he produced a bottle of whiskey from one boot and added a slug of that to the drink. He then took a long-barreled Colt revolver from the other boot, poked it into the glass and stirred the mixture. After taking a drink he looked around the room at an attentive audience and remarked, 'If anyone wants to have trouble this would be a good time to start.' As if on cue the fiddler struck up a tune, and the dance began."[21]

Maynard Blake, a cousin to a family of musicians from the Salt Lick area, witnessed and related one of the worst fights ever at a dance in Braxton County. The hatred evident in the fight caused Blake to re-think his involvement with music and dancing:

The roughest I ever saw at a square dance, it was the last one I went to. I imagine my brother and Uncle Jack, they was the one's that was playin' the music. . . . I thought everybody was a-havin' a good time, and after while somebody came in and said there was a fight outside. Said somebody's getting cut all to pieces. . . . It was a grudge. Been going on for years. Dewey Singleton and Basil, they was Sedge's boys. They was pretty mouthy. Tom Singleton, that was the older of the bunch, now I don't know what he carried, but he carried a blackjack or something he called "Old Major." One of them boys walked up and asked him, "Is Old Major here tonight?" He said, "Why don't you try to find out." Basil took a swing at him and that's what started it. Dewey Singleton hit Pat Singleton. Had a pair of steel knucks on his hand. It just cut that down through there and just peeled it right back to his ear. So Tom Singleton and Dewey's brother, they went into it, and Tom stabbed him about six or seven times in the back. Tom Singleton cut Dewey Singleton's muscle of his arm right through there till it just gapped open about like that-there. There was about two or three fist fights a-goin' on in the yard at the same time. I don't know who all was into it.

When they started to leave, why, they takin' the boys to get taken care of by the doctor. They told Pat and Tom, that was a son and father, to leave, but the dance was over. They still wanted to hang around and get into an argument. . . . So [a fellow] said, "Yea Tom, you're ready to leave." He said, "You and Pat can go now." And he just reached in, and that was all he said. Just reached in his shirt and got that gun in his hand. He said, "Yea Tom, you're ready to leave."

As he went out at the gate to leave, somebody threw a rock at him and missed him and just stripped the tops of three or four of the palings. Just broke 'em off right close to his head.

They got them started out of there, that boy and his dad, and as they went by, they was a-walkin'. Somebody started shootin' at 'em and shot the boy right down in the calf of the leg and the bullet went down and out right above his ankle. That was enough for me. I said, "No more."[22]

Fights in which vengeance, grudges, ill will, and hatred are involved, are negative experiences with both parties angered. Some fights, however, are remembered as positive experiences and appear to be impersonal events. In some instances, fights are remembered as having a sort of dignity. Some fights are legendary within families and communities. The Cottrells were a frontier family that had a reputation, even in the eighteenth century, of being fond of such fights. Phoeba Cottrell Parsons remembers a fight of this type her father told her about, involving an ancestor, "Whiggy" Cottrell:

[Whiggy] he's a-settin' behind the table and up come a stranger. . . .

He said, "Is this where Whiggy Cottrell lives, the bully? I's told he lives here."

He said, "Yes sir, come right on in and have a chair and get you something to eat." He said, "We have cornbread to eat and stuff like 'at, but if we can live on it, you can eat one mess."

He said, "Okay, thank you." He come in and sit down. Ate his dinner. When he eat his dinner, he said, "Now I come to whip you."

He said, "Now you might do it and you might not, but we will see."

He said, "Well, step out here."

Well, they said the ground was kind of like this, up and down, where they started a-fightin', and he was gettin' the best of Whiggy. Some of 'em said, "Oh, Whiggy's a-goin' to get whupped this time." They said, "No, he won't." They said, "He ain't never been whupped yet." "Well this time he's a-gettin' her now."

And he run and jumped a little gutter, you know, there's a little crick run down out there from the house, they said. He jumped that gutter, and he sunk down to his knees, and here come that fellow. He jumped it too. And said, when he raised he broke his jaw in three pieces, and that stopped that. They carried him out of there and got him to a doctor, and that was that.[23]

Feuds are another type of fracas that were prevalent and could involve whole families. The Hammons family arrived in West Virginia after being involved in a feud of sorts on the Kentucky border, but the family did not leave feuding and fighting in Kentucky (see Chapter 4). A feud of sorts took place between the Hammonses and the Fletchers on Cranberry Ridge in Nicholas County.

The trouble began in 1915 over a vague incident involving a stolen saddle. Ellen Hammons, a sister to the Hammons brothers, threatened a Fletcher woman and warned she would get her brothers to settle the matter. Various events followed, and it was agreed upon that the concerned parties would "have it out" at a certain time at the Powers Schoolhouse on Cranberry Ridge. According to a 1914 news article in the *Nicholas Chronicle*, however, the two groups met by accident.[24] "Nan" Mullins Hammons,[25] mother to Fightin' John, was said to have carried rocks for the men of the family to use in the fight.

The two Hammons brothers, John and Maston, stood side by side near the school when Joe Fletcher approached. John Hammons, who was carrying a shotgun, got into an argument with Fletcher, hit him, and knocked him down. Fletcher pulled out a pistol and shot John Hammons twice. Before John fell, Maston Hammons, who was standing to his left, got a hold of the shotgun, which was under John's left arm, and shot Fletcher at close range, killing him. A son-in-law of Fletcher's, hidden in ambush, then shot Maston Hammons twice but only wounded him.[26]

Maston Hammons would not implicate anyone at his trial, even though he knew who had shot him. He apparently preferred to think the dispute had been settled honorably and, accordingly, was not any business of the law's. Hammons was found guilty of voluntary manslaughter at the Summersville court trial.[27] A motion was made by Hammons' court-appointed lawyer to set aside the verdict because of "refusal of testimony by the defendant and objection to [that] by the state."[28] This was to no avail.[29]

Fiddler and banjo player John Christian,[30] who lived in the area and knew the parties involved, remembered that a double funeral was held for the dead men. Maston Hammons served two years in Moundsville. Other people "came up missing" on Cranberry Ridge during that period. While being questioned about the whereabouts of a missing man during one investigation, Nan Hammons was not cooperative. She is quoted as saying that she "could light her pipe and walk to his bones before it went out."

People have observed that the old-time Cranberry Ridge families were high-strung people who "all enjoyed a good fight." They were not alone. The freedom to settle an argument without interference was thought of as a right that was held to tenaciously by some of West Virginia's old-time people. Some note that this is a cultural trait.[31]

The following fight (about 1900), narrated by Currence Hammonds, happened on Williams River near the incident above after several residents had gone to vote in an election. It exhibits the willingness of old-timers to "get into it" whether they had any stake or not:

"There was my Dad and Abe Cobb, Bill Faye, Andy Rose, Bill Mahaffey, Uncle Pete, oh, I don't know, there was a bunch [at his father's house]. . . . This Norman Cogar was there. They got him to playin' the banjo. . . . They was all a-drinkin', aw, just every one of them was a-drinkin'.

Well, they got kindly in an argument. . . . One word brought on another, and the next thing Pete and Bill Mahaffey got into a fight. Bill Mahaffey called Uncle Pete a liar, and Uncle Pete just smacked him, right in the house. Well, the old man, when he hit him, the old man told Pete, he said, "Now you fellows get out of the house. I don't want it in here."

Pete said, "Come on out." Well, Bill Mahaffey would go now, he didn't care. Agin' he got out to where Pete was, Pete had got a pair of knucks out of his pocket. . . . It was getting, oh, it was dark enough that you could just see a little bit. Well, Uncle Paris was out on the porch, standing there. Uncle Pete, he laid it on to Mahaffey with them knucks. Now he hit him three licks right in the face, and he never knocked him down. Now, that's a fact. . . . He was a big man, about a hundred and ninety pounds, and I mean to tell you he was all man there. He wasn't big paunched nor nothing, he was just built. He had muscles on him.

Well, somebody pulled their coat off and hung it on a nail, you know they had a post set up—round posts, made out of poplar—but they'd hung their coat on this nail and just took their hat off and hung on the nail. And Uncle Paris was just standing there. But somebody staggered over agin' Uncle Paris. Oh, by that time, there was four or five of them into the fight. There was Bill Faye and Andy Rose and Conley Cobb. They was all about into it. Well, somebody knocked somebody over agin' Uncle Paris and pushed him off the porch, and he thought they hit him. He jumped back upon the porch and there stood that man right there in his face. He thought it was a man and he just ka-bang, he took that post and he hit it, he just knocked it down. He knocked it clear out in the yard and there it laid, the post did.

Uncle Paris stood and looked at it and said, "If I ain't killed him I'll be damned." By that time the old man [Currence's father], he'd come out. Grandpap was there. Grandpap Hammonds. He come out,

Grandpap did, and when he come out, well Grandpap, oh he was pretty old then, he grabbed a stick, Grandpap did. And he said, when he grabbed the stick, he said, "Now, I'm the wheel horse." And he landed it down on the porch, you know, and it just cracked when he hit the old porch.

Well, I was a kid. I was standing over in the corner watching it. Well, this Abe Cobb, he run at the old man's Daddy. That's Grandpap. He went in to catch him you know. He was figuring on hitting him is what he was figuring on doin'. And he didn't more than get up there to take a holt, well the old man hit him on the side of the head. Now he laid him down.

And here come Andy Rose and Bill Faye a-fightin'. They come out there and they fought. I never seen nothing like that. Old Bill he jumped up, you know, or Andy, and said, "I ain't afraid of hell nor high waters."

And Bill Faye said, "By God, I'm not nuther [sic]." I'm a-telling you, when they parted them now there was blood a-flyin'. . . . Norman [Cogar] was standing picking the banjo, and while they's a-fightin', Norman went to picking the banjo just as hard as he could play. He really was laying it on it now, and he broke a string on the banjo while he was picking it standing there. And he broke that string and he just went on picking on the rest of them.

Well, by that time, somebody got Bill Mahaffey off of Pete,—and got him back and was talkin' to him. . . . Gooch White, oh, he was a big square built fellow, boy, and he thought there was nobody could bother him or touch him. . . . He thought he was a bully. He just jumped out and throwed his coat off in the yard and dared any man to fight him. Now, he'd just come there [when the fight was about over]. I'm a son-of-a-gun if old Bill Mahaffey didn't make a dive at him. Now, he fought him. I'll bet you the first lick he hit him he went further out there than that yard. And when he hit the ground Bill Mahaffey was there. Boy you could hear those licks just ka-bang, ka-spat. They got him off him. Now old Gooch White went home. He didn't brag on the next one. Gosh, it was, oh I forget how long that he couldn't shut his mouth. He hit him in the jaw. Broke his jaw. Oh, they used to have a lot of fun!"[32]

10

Hard Times and Jo-Heads

Poor people have poor ways.
Webster County proverb

Memories of West Virginia's old-timers abound with stories about the hard times created by the Great Depression. Phoeba Parsons once said it is perfectly okay to be poor, "but it's awful unhandy sometimes." Hard times brought ingenuity, however, and didn't keep musicians from their craft.

When I moved in 1975 to an abandoned farm in Randolph County, I was struck by the simple living conditions of some neighbors. Of particular interest was a family that lived on a farm just around a small hill and up a hollow. The family consisted of a seventy-year-old man and wife and two grown boys, twins. (These fellows had the unsettling habit of silently and mysteriously showing up to see what was happening at a neighbor's place. Approaching quietly from the rear, they would announce their presence by making an offhand comment about what the neighbor was doing.) The family lived simply in an old two-story "Yankee frame" farmhouse of good proportion, well built with local lumber, sealed on the inside with tongue-and-groove lumber and on the outside with wooden "German siding." The living room had the usual King-O-Heat stove and was where everyone gathered during cold weather. The overwhelming starkness of the home proclaimed hard times. Although very clean, there was not one thing, not one curiosity of any kind, on a shelf or hanging on a wall. There were no books. The only article of either intellectual or artistic interest in sight was a "brownie calendar." These calendars list the signs of the zodiac and phases of the moon for planting. It was on the wall above the kitchen table, right under the only other wall ornament, the clock.

Hard times by today's standards, however, do not come close to the hard times of the Great Depression. The Depression was rough on musicians, and some hit the road with the idea of finding better times. Most came back poorer and hungrier than when they left.

Blackie Cool[1] and his Webster County/Randolph County string band, which included "Jinx" Morris and Dewey Hamrick, played on the road quite a bit in the 1930s. Times were tough, so they supplemented their music income with counterfeit coins. Morris seems to have been the artisan who made the molds. They used zinc from canning jar lids and ground glass, among other ingredients, for the material in their phony coins. They spent their counterfeit money in every state that touches West Virginia, but not in-state, until Blackie Cool took a counterfeit quarter into a local store and bought a two-cent pencil, anticipating twenty-three cents of "good" change. According to fiddler Woody Simmons, the clerk looked the coin over and tapped it on the counter. Blackie asked, "Is there something wrong with it?" The clerk said, "It looks all right but doesn't sound quite right." Blackie then took out a counterfeit fifty-cent piece and paid for it with that, getting forty-eight cents in real change.

The law finally caught up with the trio, and Jinx Morris served seven years in the penitentiary for the crime. No evidence was turned up against Blackie, but he confided to a friend that while being questioned by authorities about the crime, the coin molds were under his bed in the next room. Hamrick's father apparently knew and had influence with a "Judge Baker" of Elkins, and Hamrick, for whatever reason, only received seven years of probation. For a musician, the probationary terms were particularly cruel. Besides staying out of trouble and having to "attend church every Sunday," Hamrick was forbidden to play his fiddle for the seven years![2]

Blackie Cool's antics did not end there. It may be about this time that he joined a circus and took a timely trip to Mexico. He met some musicians while there and learned a few Spanish pieces. Blackie eventually returned, like most West Virginians who leave, and stayed active playing music in the area until his death in 1988.

Sometime in the 1940s, Clayton McMitchen and his Georgia Wildcats performed in Webster Springs. Through some unknown turn of events, Blackie sat in for a sick or absent guitar player and played a few shows. Impressed, McMitchen invited Blackie to join the band on the spot and be part of its touring show. After a talk with his persuasive girlfriend, Blackie declined the offer.

Blackie found ways to spend his share of time in jail, mostly through his habit of drinking and fighting. He escaped from several cells, once chipping a hole through a concrete floor and digging out of confinement and another time coating himself with jail-food butter and slipping between the bars. A newspaper headline of the time proclaimed that no jail could hold him.[3]

In his later years, Blackie was a warm, friendly guy, who was extremely generous with his considerable musical talents. I knocked on Blackie's door in 1976, after being told about him by a man from Valley Head. When I introduced myself and told him I heard he could play a guitar, Blackie invited me in but said he had not played for twenty or so years. When he brought out his guitar from a back room, it was in perfect tune!

During the Depression, Melvin Wine, his brother Clarence, and Brooks Hardway went to Fairmont to make their fortunes playing music. They auditioned at WMMN and were invited to play daily on live radio. However, the pay would not have covered their living expenses and would have conflicted with better-paying jobs they could get playing for square dances. They decided to play music on the streets during the day and get square dance jobs at night.

Clarence provided the humor the band needed in its busking activities. He ad-libbed verses as they played, insulted occasional onlookers, and did whatever needed to be done, other than play music, to hold a crowd. In one instance, Clarence held Hardway's feet while Hardway walked on his hands. Clarence pretended to drive him with a whip like a horse through the streets. After they attracted some attention, Melvin, toting the instruments, would catch up to them and they would keep the crowd entertained with music, breaking occasionally to pass a hat.

During this stint, Clarence's wit and biting humor got the band in imminent danger. Some Italian Americans invited them to their club one evening for a dance. Apparently the band's "hillbilly" repertoire was not sitting too well with the Italians, who wanted to dance couple or "round" dances rather than the square dances for which the band usually played. One fellow told the band he and the others could not dance to "their kind of music." He then glared at Clarence the next time he danced past the bandstand. Clarence whispered to Melvin that the next time the man looked at him that way, he would make him a collar and necktie out of his banjo. The inevitable happened. Clarence jumped up and was raising his banjo to fulfill his intent when Melvin tackled him. There was a lot of excitement, but they managed to escape unscathed.

The Depression couldn't stop the old-time musicians from fiddling, and stories of how they got access to instruments during those hard times are interesting. Braxton County fiddler, Kenton Sears, seemed determined to beat the odds against him and learn to play an instrument. He went to great lengths to get something on which to play. His is a typical story of how a traditional fiddler gets started against the ever-present backdrop of hard times:

I decided I wanted to play [Dad's] fiddle—he had a beautiful fiddle. He didn't want me to tear it up or dismantle it in any way, so he told me to stay away from it unless he told me. But, when he'd be gone I'd get it out of the case. I'd always shine her back up and put it back in as near as I could. One time I broke a string on it! He knew that I did it. It was a prize possession back in them days. It wasn't that he didn't want me to do it, but he didn't want me to destroy his good fiddle. You could understand that.

I learnt to play on a fiddle that was made out of a cigar box with a fiddle neck in it. Back them days, cigars would come out in wooden boxes. I got this cigar box and cut square holes in the side of it so I could get my bow in there and glued it up and took some pins and pinned it. I'll never forget the first set of strings I bought—I ordered from Sears Roebuck. Paid seventeen cents for 'em. They was Silvertones.[4]

Many traditional musicians have had tough times until recently. French Carpenter, who sometimes traveled and played with old-time banjo player Jenes Cottrell, had to turn down music jobs because he didn't have the ways or means to get there before being paid.[5] Most of the oldest banjo players I questioned, those born around the turn of the century, started out on homemade instruments. Most of these banjos were fretless. Sometimes, getting a factory-made rim provided the impetus to build the rest of the instrument. Dena Johnston Knicely remembered such a case when she was a young girl in Greenbrier County:

My brother, he whittled out a neck, you know, they had a piece of wood, and he found an old banjo . . . rim and some . . . hooks. He put that all together, and he got an old cat. He killed this old cat and tanned the hide, you know, fixed it, stretched it over that banjo. Put it on that neck and that's what I learned to play on. Then, when I got a banjo with the frets on there, I didn't know what to do with them things. With them things on there, I didn't know where to go 'cause I had to go by the sound. That's what I learned to play on when I was just a kid at home pecking around on the thing. Every time it'd come a little rain or dampness, that old head, you know, would get soft. You couldn't get a racket out of it. Get it heated up and stretched out there, why it'd play pretty good.[6]

Clyde Case remembered having a store-bought model from a pawn shop and restoring it to playing shape several times:

That banjo was bought in a pawn shop down in Georgia in 1917 by a man by the name of Lanty Jones. He's dead now. His brother's name was Buck. Buck Jones. He could clawhammer it and give it that double shuffle with his thumb.

I made the bridge out of apple wood . . . it's either apple wood or beech. That's a calfskin head. It come from Sears Roebuck I'd say in . . . sometime in the 1930s. It had a flour-sack head, made out of . . . a 25-pound flour sack, when I got it. Didn't sound bad either. I put a groundhog-hide head in it. I tanned a groundhog hide and put it in first, and it got wet and drew up and split, so I ordered this calfskin head. That there [bracket on the truss rod] was made out of the whistle of a steam engine locomotive that went in Elk River sometime in the early nineteen hundreds. . . . The tailpiece, I made that out of the same piece of brass. That there [a metal piece on the truss rod] is the nut that holds the speedometer cable of a 1926-model Star automobile. That there nut up there that the strings goes across is the end off a three-year-old heifer's horn we dehorned one time [it also has some brass frets made from an old flashlight case].[7]

Fiddler Mose Coffman described to me that in one of his first musical experiences as a child, an old African American woman, probably an ex-slave, sat on the kitchen floor of his house playing the tune "Greenbrier River" on an old fretless banjo. In sharp contrast, *Harper's Magazine* in 1888 characterized a scene that gave an inkling of how members of the upper class spent their leisure time. In the scene a young man lounges about with his dainty wife at the Greenbrier Hotel in White Sulpher Springs (only twenty miles from where Dena Knicely's brother tanned a cat hide for his homemade banjo and even fewer from Coffman's home). The man has a mint julep, and his wife lies on a hammock with a finely crafted banjo.[8] The paradox leaves one wondering about time and space.

Fretless banjos made in eastern cities as early as the 1840s, as the minstrel era began, derived from homemade or "folk-made" banjos. "Factory" banjos, made by William Boucher, a German drum maker of Baltimore, popularized the bracket and hook, or drum-head configuration, for banjos in the 1840s. Based on folk design, these early banjos supplied the minstrel stages, which greatly affected the banjo's popularity.

As more and more whites took up the banjo, the instruments started changing from homemade folk instruments to mass-produced, refined representations of folk instruments. The instrument in the Greenbrier Hotel scenario is an evolved result of this process. Older-style fretless instruments, originally copied by the new banjo manufacturers, gave way to fretted instruments by the late 1870s and 1880s. Early companies kept pace with speedy manufacturing processes as the country industrialized, and patents for new innovations were rampant. To accommodate a fad that was sweeping the middle and upper classes of the country, both the looks and concept of the instrument underwent radical changes. The banjo was leaving the plantation, the stereotypical watermelon

Jenes Cottrell with homemade banjo.
(Courtesy of the Comstock Collection,
Booth Library, Davis & Elkins College.)

patches, and the minstrel stage and appearing in more refined settings such as the Greenbrier, fashionable homes, collegiate functions, and within banjo "orchestras" and fraternities.[9]

As these new popular instruments emerged, evolved, and gained wider circulation, the folk artisans took cues from the manufacturers and incorporated the innovations into their own instruments. They added frets and changed the rims to replicate factory-made models. Folk instruments typically had wooden rims, which the manufacturers changed to spun metal (over wood). Later, manufacturers used laminated wood rims with metal (sometimes brass) tone rings. A wide array of rims, from solid wood to solid metal, are found among homemade banjos made in this century. Jenes Cottrell, using the traditional make-do philosophy, created his banjo rims from suitable parts found in the transmissions of 1956 Buicks.[10] I also have seen "lard can" banjos (lard cans are used for the heads) and greased flour sacks substituted for skin heads. The older-style banjos, with small skin heads pressed between wooden rims and fretless necks, did hang on in some isolated areas of the southern Appalachians. This type of banjo is found in West Virginia, but is no longer made except as a reproduction. Charlie Blevins, of Mingo County, plays an old one and owns several. Frank George plays an old, fretless instrument with a small skin head set within a larger wooden body. An old fretless instrument of this type from Boone County has a slate-covered fingerboard.[11]

Some older banjo makers, while using the new rim and bracket configurations, were reluctant to add frets, which dictated a revolutionary shift in playing style (as noted by Dena Knicely). Most players eventually made the change to fretted banjos, but some new banjos probably had their frets removed to make them playable. Most of the older banjo players I have recorded in central West Virginia began playing on fretless instruments.[12]

Woody Simmons, a Tygart Valley fiddle and banjo player, described how his father made a banjo for him. The process appears to indicate an amalgamation of the older folk-derived banjo style and newer popular models. Simmons' father made the rim out of white oak that he boiled and then bent. The brackets were hand forged. He forged the stretcher rim from a buggy rake tooth, and the banjo had five frets made from fence wire. He "raveled" his first set of strings out of a screen door, and Simmons used these until he could afford a store-bought set of Sunrise strings. Although cats and groundhogs provided the hides of choice for banjo heads, calfskin heads (as used on the "factory" banjos) eventually were put on most existing older folk-made banjos.

Newfound popularity greatly affected the looks of banjos in the mid to late nineteenth century and through the twentieth century. Some of the most ornate five-string banjos were built near the turn of the century in Boston by the Fairbanks, and later, Cole and Fairbanks companies.[13] The Stewart Company in Philadelphia and Dobson Company in Baltimore produced finely crafted models. The folk artisans made an effort to simulate this new fancy ornamentation with rhinestones, buttons, brass tacks, and a variety of other materials inlaid into the headstocks and fingerboards. Jenes Cottrell decorated his by slicing small disks of plastic knitting needles and inlaying them into his necks in wild geometric patterns. In a more reserved tradition, ribbons were tied around the headstock for decoration.

Turn-of-the-century mail-order catalogs made instruments accessible everywhere. An interior photo of a store in Sutton, West Virginia, in 1902, shows a dozen or so banjos lining the walls. County seats like

Sutton, Richwood, Elkins, and Marlinton sold factory-made banjos at these early dates and probably until the Depression, when money to buy one was hard to come by.

The banjo, of course, has African roots, and the oldest way of playing, that attributed to African origin, is the down-stroke style.[14] The down-stroke method is known as "rapping," "clawhammering," "frailing," "flailing," "thumping," and "beating."

An old song, of African American and/or minstrel origin, describes "beating" a banjo:

> Stay a little longer and don't keep a noise
> While old Massa and Missus is sleeping.
> We'll go to the barnyard and wake up the boys
> And have a little banjo beating.[15]

In the seventeenth and eighteenth centuries, terms used for banjos in the hands of Africans in the New World include strum-strum, merrywang, banjie, bangil, banja, bandora, bangelo, banjah, banjar, banjer, banjor, banshaw, bantu, and banza[16] among others. The Senegalese in Africa still have a lute they call a "bania."[17] Our name for the instrument, banjo, appears to be an Anglicized version of an African word. It is still often called a "banjer" in West Virginia, as it was by some early slaves. Some West Virginia players, Currence Hammonds and Carl Davis to name a couple, refer to banjos as jo-heads, and bluegrass pickers commonly call them five-strings.

As the looks of the instrument changed, a new style of playing developed. The style of up-picking with the fingers in what had been the "guitar" or "parlor style" was affecting rural West Virginia players. Almost all of central West Virginia's old-time players have pieces in their repertoires played with this style of up-picking, often with just forefinger and thumb. A few players in rural West Virginia went so far as to order books of playing methods. Jinx Morris grew up in the early twentieth century learning the clawhammer style but ordered a banjo-playing-method book to learn how to pick. His curiosity was piqued after hearing recordings of Fred Van Eps, who played in the classical style.[18] Even the Hammons family, well known for its backwoods ways, played many such "parlor" pieces. These tunes and playing styles continued in popularity into the twentieth century, getting a boost from the recording industry.

Segregation along racial lines, however strongly in place in nineteenth-century West Virginia, did not halt the spread of folk music between the races. The white race eagerly accepted the banjo as a folk instrument. Repertoires and playing style easily crossed racial and class lines. The model of white melodies played to black rhythms, however, may be an oversimplification. For instance, a sizable portion of lyrics in mountain music show up in black collections.[19] It is also true that much European melody transferred to the banjo just as easily. Even the Child ballads adapted well to banjo accompaniment. Variations of the tune "Old Christmas Morning," associated with the "Old Christmas" tradition (see chapter one), remain as banjo tunes in West Virginia.[20] "Pete" Humphreys of Kanawha County played a version in the clawhammer style. In this instance we have European music, played on an African-derived folk instrument, that evolved through influence of an upper-class popular movement, played in an African playing style, by a white traditional Appalachian musician. Like the cakewalk, it has passed through many stages of development. It presents another scenario of how traditional music intertwines race and class, as well as popular and folk tradition.

11

Hog Harps, Waterswivels, and Fence Scorpions

His voice as the sound of the dulcimer sweet,
Is heard through the shadows of death. . . .
"Samanthra," Shape note hymn[1]

As a fiddler, I admit to at one time subscribing to a bias regarding fretted dulcimers. Although I was aware of dulcimer traditions noted in the literature, I had not witnessed the instruments in traditional settings, as I had fiddles and banjos. The dulcimers I saw were played by younger people who had learned tunes in books from libraries. I had not seen them played by older people, like the fiddlers and banjo players I knew, who had "come by it honest."

One night in 1977 a couple of fellows I knew in Braxton County came to the farm to play a few tunes. During the visit, one fellow mentioned an old guy who lived up the hollow from him who played a dulcimer. I memorized his name and where he lived, but I could not quite picture it. Why would someone fool around with one of those things? I could not resolve my curiosity, and within days I headed for Raccoon Creek to find the dulcimer-playing Carl Davis.

When I arrived at Davis' place, he was just finishing planting potatoes. He was a mechanic and a welder—a well-rounded farmer. He had "cobbled up" a pretty ingenious attachment for his old International tractor to plow, furrow, plant, and hill potatoes in one pass. He was standing by his tractor when I pulled into his yard. I asked if he was Carl Davis, and he replied, "What's left of him."

It turned out Davis was a fiddler, a square dance caller, fox chaser (with the best hounds around), tale teller, blacksmith, clock fixer, and more. To me, he was a fascinating fellow. After chatting awhile, I asked

Carl Davis working on an instrument in his Braxton County shop, 1998. (Photograph by the author.)

about his dulcimer. Davis brought out an old "delcimer" (as he and many West Virginians call it) and said it was his father's. Until then, I had never inspected an *old* dulcimer. This one, I later deduced, was a nineteenth-century instrument. When I asked if he would play for me, he brought out one he had made himself. Using a cow-horn pick and a hickory-stick noter, Davis blazed away at tunes like "Sugar in the Gourd" and "Mississippi Sawyers."

Davis was serious about the music he played on his dulcimer, and he played some serious old-time music. This visit led to more and then visits with other area dulcimer players, including Davis' older brother,

John. Before long I realized I had stumbled onto a den of dulcimer-playing families who took their music as seriously as the fiddle-playing families I knew.

Before hearing Carl Davis and the others play, I shared the sentiments of some fiddlers who consider dulcimer music inferior to fiddle and banjo music. Disparaging remarks I heard about the instrument included: "I wouldn't cross the road to hear one"; "I wouldn't swat a dog across the ass with one of those things"; and "You take and tune it up real good, then you tie a ribbon around the peghead, hang it up on the wall, get down your banjo, and play some real music."[2] Fiddler Melvin Wine remembered that his family always kept a dulcimer in their home, but it did not rank with the fiddle. Even Carl Davis, who comes from a family of dulcimer players and makers, seldom plays the dulcimer away from home although he plays the fiddle and banjo-mandolin at monthly community dances.

After my exposure to Davis, however, it was time for some reconsideration. Several older people whose musical opinions I sought and respected told me the dulcimer-fiddle music they grew up with was "the best music there is" and "couldn't be beat."[3] Many have given the instrument respect, including it in string ensembles that play dance music. I have found two instances where people played dulcimers in gospel groups and half a dozen where people played them for square dance music. Hobart Blake and Sarah Blake Singleton, members of the musical Braxton County family of Bragg Run, remember dances where the only music was that of a dulcimer and a guitar.

In 1988 I began an effort to document traditional (as opposed to revival) dulcimers and dulcimer makers in Braxton County. I found many. Although unnoticed by those involved with the national revival of the fretted dulcimer, portions of southern and central West Virginia, I am convinced, have a stronger dulcimer tradition than any area in the country. A region that includes Braxton County and parts of Clay and Nicholas Counties was a hotbed. Jesse James, an eighty-plus-year-old resident of Frametown in Braxton County, told me that at one time (speaking of ca. 1920) "everybody thought they had to have one of those things!" There was a sort of dulcimer craze going on in Braxton County. I have located numerous examples of instruments made in the period of 1917 to 1935. I also have documented older activity in the county from the nineteenth century. Thus, during the early twentieth century there may have been a small-scale localized revival that was entirely separate from the large-scale national revival of years later. Without benefit of media influence, this was a true folk revival.

Before investigating the dulcimer tradition in West Virginia, I will discuss the various names for the instrument. The fretted dulcimer also is known as the mountain, Kentucky, Appalachian, or lap dulcimer. Hobart Blake, born in 1900, and Lola Blake Cutlip, his sister, remembered the instrument being called a waterswivel.[4] The waterswivel name is a puzzler. One possibility is that it comes from the German "vater's fiedel" (father's fiddle) and is simply an Anglicized form of the words. Lola's married name, Cutlip, is Anglicized from Gottlieb, proving that German to English transformations have a precedent. Other names I have heard for dulcimers in central West Virginia are hog harp, hog fiddle, feather harp, and church dulcimer (which was used to describe a large six-stringed dulcimer in Nicholas County). One old Braxton Countian remembered an old man calling it a "fence scorpion." This is a colloquial name for a type of lizard or skink seen on rail fences. Junior Lloyd, a Braxton County player, simply calls his dulcimer a scorpion. In central West Virginia, especially Clay and Nicholas Counties, the name hog fiddle is a more common name for the instrument than dulcimer. All of these name variations point to the fact that the fretted dulcimer developed within a folk culture and did not have the favor of a popular movement with which to solidify a common name for the instrument.

Differing accounts of the dulcimer's origin exist as well. Some wrongly believe it is the instrument mentioned in the Bible.[5] According to Homer Blake of Walkersville, his grandfather, Braxton Countian Stewart Blake, told him two things were crucial to making a good-sounding dulcimer. These were to hollow out the fingerboard and leave the back unfinished. In his book *A Catalog of Pre-Revival Appalachian Dulcimers*, L. Allen Smith pictured and/or described thirty-eight fretted zithers, many from the early German settlements of southeastern Pennsylvania.[6] In his descriptions, Smith noted that many of the earliest examples of these instruments had unfinished backs. The backs of these instruments simply never had a finish such as varnish or paint applied.[7] To make the connection between Stewart Blake's statement and the descriptions in Smith's book, one has to accept the fact that fretted dulcimers evolved from the family of European instruments characterized by the German fretted zither or sheitholt.[8] However there has been debate and no shortage of misinformation concerning the origins of mountain dulcimers.

Dr. Patrick Gainer taught more than twelve thousand students (by his own count) at West Virginia University. In his teaching and writing he insisted the mountain dulcimer descended from the rebec, an instrument he said came to this country from the British Isles. He published this in numerous places in West Virginia including his book *Folk Songs From The West Virginia Hills*.[9]

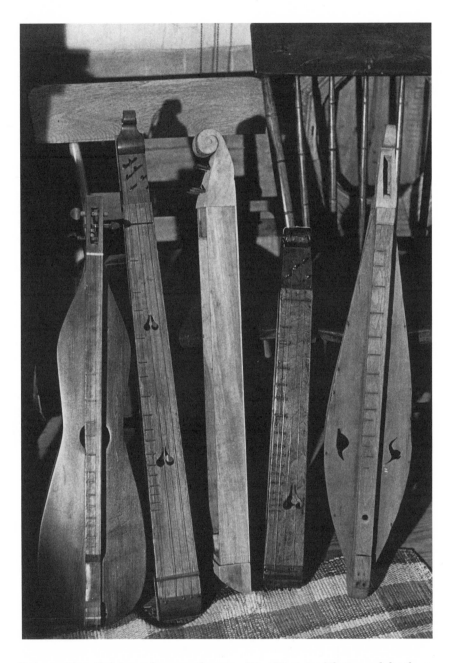

Various zithers/dulcimers from southeastern West Virginia. (Photograph by the author; courtesy of the Jim Costa Collection.)

Gainer's influence was so prevalent that the seeds of his theory were sown even among some older traditional players I have met.[10] Basil Blake, a Braxton Countian who started making dulcimers in the 1920s having learned from his older brothers, had dealings with Gainer from playing at the West Virginia State Folk Festival, which Gainer organized in 1950. Blake was the youngest member of a large family of dulcimer makers and players and probably the only older Braxton County maker to have had much exposure to the modern revival. Apparently having been told by Gainer that the instrument he had made and always known as a "delcimer" was actually a rebec, Blake spread the word to his family members. During an interview in 1988, Blake's sister Sarah told me Blake had said the old name for the dulcimer was a "laybeck." The folk process of phonetic transformation already was at work, proving the word rebec had scant reference and little meaning to these musicians.

Gainer was not alone in his theory. John Jacob Niles, of Kentucky, had similar notions. Gainer and Niles seemed to recognize only those elements of Appalachian folk culture that have roots in the Anglo-Celtic world.[11] If dulcimers evolved from rebecs, there would be some evidence to support the claim.

Although Gainer cites no examples of the rebec name being applied by Appalachians to what we know as a dulcimer, several examples exist of dulcimers or dulcimer-like instruments being referred to as zithers (actually "cithers") by folks in the Valley of Virginia. These references allude to German origins. Additionally, all of the old fretted zithers from Pennsylvania and Virginia as well as examples I have seen in Greenbrier, Hardy, Randolph, and Summers Counties in West Virginia, have diatonic fret intervals. Virtually all of the old (and new) Appalachian dulcimers known to exist use this fret system. Rebecs, on the other hand, were only "sometimes fretted," had necks, and, when fretted, had chromatic intervals.[12] There has never been a diatonically fretted folk instrument in the British Isles.[13] In the preface to Cecil Sharp's *English Folksongs from the Southern Appalachians*, 1932, Maud Karpeles noted the possibility of the dulcimer being descended from a German zither housed in the Metropolitan Museum of Art. As early as 1937 Allen Eaton also suggested a German provenance.[14] In 1957 Charles Seeger published information regarding the true background of the instrument.[15]

The use of a bow was apparently common to both rebecs and fretted German zithers (the true antecedents of the Appalachian dulcimers) and may have led to the erroneous conclusion. Early Pennsylvania examples of fretted zithers were bowed, and some of those instruments still have bows with them.[16] Summers County instrument collector Jim Costa acquired two old fretted zithers at a farm sale, where older family members referred to the instruments as dulcimers. This gives a direct oral link from the fretted zithers, which we know are of German (via Pennsylvania) origin, and cross-checks with examples of dulcimers or dulcimer-like instruments being called zithers.[17]

Dulcimers were played with a bow in some cases in West Virginia. Dena Knicely (1910-1994), a dulcimer player in Greenbrier County, described the fashion in which her father, Samuel Johnston (born in 1866), played. He used a feather to play dance tunes but used a bow to play hymns. The instrument her father played, still in Greenbrier County, is an Appalachian dulcimer and is one of many noted that have small feet on the bottom. This suggests it could lay on a table to be played. Knicely said her father would sit in front of a window with the dulcimer headstock propped up on the sill when he played it with a bow.[18]

A man named David Baughman, who made dulcimers in Webster County, was a fiddler of Pennsylvania German stock and the first settler on the Gauley River in the late 1830s.[19] In 1822 David Baughman's family established a homestead at the mouth of Skyles Creek in what is now Webster County. I lived for fourteen years on Skyles Creek, a mile and a half above the old Baughman homestead where David was raised. There was memory of a dulcimer tradition in that neighborhood. The Fowlers, who had intermarried with the Baughmans, remembered owning an "old one" that, by their account, fits the description of a straight-sided, fretted zither. If David Baughman learned about dulcimers here, it would almost have to have been from his father, Christopher Baughman, born in 1788 in Botetorte County, Virginia. There were only a few other settlers in the area. They seemed to have no ties to musical traditions,[20] and one had come from Greenbrier County with the Baughmans. It seems, then, that Christopher, a settler in a virtual wilderness,[21] was the bearer of a dulcimer-making tradition. Christopher's family were German immigrants who arrived on the frontier of Virginia in the 1750s. If this hypothesis is correct, we have a dulcimer tradition, in the Appalachians, among people who came from Germany, stayed briefly in Pennsylvania, and came to the Virginia frontier. This presents the genesis of the Appalachian dulcimer.

The Bostic family, who were also Pennsylvania Germans, came to Summers County and left as a legacy two old fretted zithers (which they called dulcimers, above).[22] In Hardy County, an interesting old instrument with features of both old fretted zithers and more evolved dulcimers is at the old homeplace of the Dasher family. The Dasher family, from the Palitine region of Germany, immigrated to Pennsylvania in 1757 and then moved to the Virginia frontier in the South Branch Valley that same year.[23] The instrument has been in the family as long as oldest family members can remember.

Lewis Hinkle of Volga in Upshur County made dulcimers in or before the 1880s. His family can be traced from Germany to Pennsylvania, to North Carolina, then to (West) Virginia in the eighteenth century. A Milton Townsend of Upshur County, influenced by Hinkle, made dulcimers in the early twentieth century.[24] Evidence shows that the areas where Pennsylvania Germans settled in significant numbers in the eighteenth century are where the old-world zither-type instruments are most often found. The Greenbrier and South Branch Valleys have fretted zither/dulcimer traditions. There is some proof that one existed in Randolph County.[25] More central counties that were settled a bit later such as Braxton have a more recent association with the instrument.

The unanswered questions are when, why, and where did the instrument change from the German zither type to the "mountain" style. In *The Story of the Dulcimer*, Ralph Smith promotes a theory that the older fretted zithers simply became the hollow fingerboard of the mountain dulcimer. One thing that can be proved is that both instrument types existed side by side in West Virginia. Many instruments, including some very old examples, have turned up in northern West Virginia within a family collection.[26]

By the time the dulcimer hit its peak in central West Virginia, as found in Braxton County, German ties to the instrument had completely dissolved and its identity had become regional. The instrument in central West Virginia, although associated with a time period, more importantly is now part of a regional tradition. This presents the difference between a popular movement and a folk tradition.

Regardless of the instrument's origins, a rich tradition of dulcimer making and playing exists in southern and central West Virginia. I identified eighteen traditional builders who made and played dulcimers in Braxton County (see table 1). All but one came before the earliest revival date, placed by L. Allen Smith at 1940. Some of these makers made only a few instruments. The widespread recent revival of the instrument had little effect on Braxton County until well after 1960. As late as the mid 1970s, people whose only influences were older traditional makers in their family or neighborhood made dulcimers. Basil Blake made and helped make dulcimers from the 1920s until his death in the mid 1980s.

Lola Blake Cutlip remembered her Uncle Henry Gerwig (1866-1938), a dulcimer maker of the late nineteenth and early twentieth centuries. She owned a dulcimer he made for "Aunt Maude," his spouse. Cutlip described how Aunt Maude played her dulcimer with a goose quill.[27] Henry Gerwig became a fine wood worker and an industrious and respected member of the "German" community on Steer Creek in Braxton County. Other German families in the community were Engels, Whitsels,

Table 1. Pre-Revival Braxton County Dulcimer Makers.

Basil Blake, Bragg Run
Hillary Blake, Clover Fork
Lora Blake, Bragg Run
Reuben Blake, Bragg Run
Stewart Blake, Clover Fork
Wayne Conrad, Salt Lick
Carl Davis, Raccoon Creek
John Davis, Sugar Creek
Herbert Frame, Little Otter
Henry Gerwig, Steer Creek
Sylvan James, Lower Mill Creek
Jack Keith, Salt Lick
Edwin H. "Preacher" LaFon, Sugar Creek
Junior Lloyd, Buffington Run
Ivan Posey, Sutton
Isaac Shaver, Scott Fork
Glen Singleton, Lower Mill Creek
Amity White, Falls Mill

Ellisons, and Schmidts (later changed to Smith). They all had emigrated together on the same ship from Europe.[28] Henry Gerwig's father, Christian Gerwig (1826-1903), immigrated as a young boy from Neusatz in the Kingdom of Wurtemburg around 1830, settling on Steer Creek in 1840.[29] Henry Gerwig's house and workshop burned down, but his fine barn still stands. It appears to be the only Pennsylvania-style bank barn in the area. This style of barn exists in areas of West Virginia such as Pendleton County where concentrations of Pennsylvania Germans settled, but in Gerwig's case the family came straight from Germany.

The Gerwig family apparently encountered the dulcimer and its music in this country. Here, a first-generation German American may have become reunited with an evolved tradition of his ancestors. A Greenbrier County family, the Coffmans, produced at least one dulcimer maker, Henry Coffman, who was active in the 1880s. The Coffmans (or Kaufmans) came to Greenbrier County in a Conestoga wagon in the eighteenth century, from Lancaster County, Pennsylvania, where a fretted zither tradition existed.

Henry Gerwig's dulcimer resembled the "Huntington pattern."[30] A shop in Huntington, West Virginia, operated by Charles Prichard, produced numbers of instruments sometime after 1850.[31] These models are of the hourglass shape and are thought to have influenced many makers over a wide area. Examples have turned up in Greenbrier County, Mannington, Morgantown, various Ohio locations, and even as far away as Missouri. Assuming that many of these Huntington dulcimers have been in these locations for a long period of time, it is probable that they were patterns for many pre-revival makers.

Junior Lloyd of Napier in Braxton County made a dulcimer about 1951 that he patterned after one made by Basil Blake. Lloyd grew up with dulcimers, having learned to play one as a child in the 1930s. As far as I can tell, he had no outside influence in making his own dulcimer in the fifties. He is still an active player and has taught some tunes to his granddaughter, who also does not seem to have been influenced by any national revival of the instrument.[32]

Members of the Jack Blake family remembered that brother Lora (pronounced Lory) brought home a dulcimer pattern when he returned from World War I. The story differs among siblings, with the most popular being that he got the pattern in France or Germany. Another, the more probable version, has him getting it from a fellow soldier. Hobart Blake said it was an actual dulcimer his brother brought home and that he "took a pattern from it." Hobart also remembered that dulcimers were in the area long before Lora went away to the war, and it is easy to document pre-World War I instruments in the area. Jack Keith made a dulcimer that was brought to Beatrice Metheny's farm by her mother on horseback, in 1899.[33]

The youngest member of the Blake family of Bragg Run was Basil, who, as previously mentioned, started making dulcimers in the 1920s. Sometime in the early fifties Basil rejected the family pattern for a smaller version to make an instrument for a niece.[34] He then continued to make all his dulcimers on the smaller pattern, an event noted frequently by family members. His niece, Reva Fincham,[35] still owns and plays the first "little one" he made. Reva has been playing dulcimer since she was a child. She has four or five uncles who made or helped make dulcimers, more than a dozen relatives who could play, and she married into a dulcimer-playing family.

Hobart Blake was born in 1900 and is now the oldest living Blake family member. He remembered how the old dulcimers were made by family members in the teens and twenties:

> [Lora] brung that dulcimer up there, and he laid it down on a paper and marked around it. About a month or two after that, he went into it, and I helped him plane the boards, and he made one. Somebody brung it [the first one he saw] in here from way off. Some of John Dean's people, I can't think of who it was brung it in there. I can remember seeing it. Just exactly like that one. It was put together mighty poorly, had it pinned together with pins. It didn't sound good. When we got this pattern here and made these, they cut down in the

edge of them and set the rim down in it. Lora was a good carpenter.
He heated them bands and put them in the press. When they got dry,
they just set down in there and just fit exactly. He made several of
them. Reva's got one. Basil made several of them at Cedarville. As
soon as he was big enough to go to work [Basil started making them].

Jack Keith was a stave mill man. I worked for him there. Reuben
[another brother] and Lora made some dulcimers. They made one for
Jack Keith. They made one for a man over on Cedar Creek. Oh, my
God they made lots of them. . . . We made lots of them, but I never
cared nothing about them. I helped make them, but when they's made
I was done with them. I helped sand the stuff down and helped glue
them together. Make clamps to hold them together till they dried.
Make wooden clamps out of a board. Them necks is made hollow.
First they made—they made 'em solid. Didn't sound right. They took
the neck out of it, and I helped them with a backin' chisel. Cut it out
inside and made it thin on each side of the neck. It sounded good.

They made 'em out of chestnut before the chestnut trees got too
bad and got those worm holes in 'em. Chestnut wood used to be nice
wood—made awful good lumber. It was light. After it dried it was
perfectly light. . . .

Back at that time you couldn't hardly get boards thin enough to
make a dulcimer. The first ones we made, we sawed an inch board
open with a crosscut saw. Fix a place to hold it, and one got up above
and one sawed it under. Then, planed it as thin as we could get it. I've
worked hours planing them things for it.[36]

The Blakes of Bragg Run were distantly related to another family of
Blakes who lived on Clover Fork, near Orlando on the northern edge of
Braxton County. A colorful family, many of the members go by nicknames. Hillary, or "Hilly," Blake was born on Clover Fork in 1911. He
was a dulcimer and fiddle maker. He recalled that his uncle, Stewart
Blake, "hewed a dulcimer out of a fence rail." "Bunk" Blake either "made
or helped to make" dulcimers. Amos or "Daddy" Blake, also became
involved with making dulcimers. "Tater" Blake has an old chestnut one
made by Stewart with an elaborately carved peghead. Hilly remembered that in hard times, Stewart made his strings out of old broom
wire. I asked Audra Van Noy, who had an old dulcimer made by Stewart
and Bunk Blake, if the instrument had any writing on the inside. She
said, "No, neither one of them could read or write."

Carl Davis' brother John Davis (1914-1989), of Sugar Creek, made
and played dulcimers and talked about his family's music:

> My Dad, he played the dulcimer. They called it a hog harp, some
> people did, who didn't know what the name of it was. . . . He brought
> [the dulcimer] home, and he said, "The first one learns to play that

can have it when I'm done with it." Well, I got me a piece of cow's
horn for a pick and a match stick or a pencil or whatever it was. So I
learned to play it, first one. Well, my mother remembered that, and all
the kids remembered it. After he passed away, they said, "That's your
dulcimer. Dad give you that when you's ten years old." I've had it ever
since. It's been played on, I'll tell you that. I made one off the pattern
of that one.[37]

Carl Davis also recalled the family music:

My father had one. He played like "Old Dan Tucker," and he played
one called "Gal with the Blue Dress On," . . . "Old Joe Clark," stuff like
that. My mother would let me get up in the bed and pound around on
it, and I got so I could play several pieces on it. I made two or three
small ones out of poplar. They sounded real good, and I sold one or
two. Scattered them around over the country. The first I made, I just
made three strings. They used to make these old barrels—kegs, out of
beech, and I made them sides out of beech [staves], and I made the
tops out of yellow poplar. It's easy to work.[38]

Carl Davis also played publicly at an early age. When he was in the
fourth grade, some friends talked about his dulcimer playing and piqued
the curiosity of Davis' teacher. The teacher asked Davis to play the instrument at the last-day-of-school festivities.

In 1952, while working as a blacksmith and boarding away from
home at the mines at Widen in neighboring Clay County, Davis made
the dulcimer he now plays. With some time on his hands, he set out to
make a dulcimer, causing quite a stir around the mining camp. A fiddler, Davis plays at the local dances, but he also is asked occasionally to
play the dulcimer during the breaks between sets.

Davis uses a different tuning than most. "The old timers used to
tune [the strings] all alike," Davis said. "I always thought they sounded
a little better with these two down and your bass." In this tuning, for a
three-stringed instrument, the first two or "fine" strings are tuned to D.
The bass or "coarse" string may be tuned to either A or G.[39]

A fine Nicholas County dulcimer player and maker, Walter Miller
(1914-1994) got his first dulcimer by trading a shotgun in 1928.[40] Miller
tuned the first three strings alike to G and his bass string down to C.

Materials used to make dulcimers as well as the dulcimers themselves varied among old-time dulcimer makers and players. Most of Walter
Miller's dulcimers had four strings, but back in the thirties he made several six-stringed instruments. A player named Freeman McKinney, from
a dulcimer-making and -playing family in Clay County, plays an old four-
string "hog fiddle" his brother helped make about 1920. General Custer

Walter Miller, circa 1932. (Author's collection.)

Nicholas (his actual name) played a similar looking instrument. Most players use guitar or banjo strings on their dulcimers.[41]

Most of the Blakes preferred cow-horn picks and hickory noters. Other players use various combinations of materials to make picks including quills, tobacco cans, old felt hats, and, lately, plastic milk jugs.

Freeman McKinney claimed the best picks come from the whale-bone stays in women's corsets. I have not encountered anyone in Braxton County who frets a dulcimer with his or her fingers, but Walter Miller used his fingers to make chords.

"Preacher" LaFon played and made dulcimers years ago. He lived near the mouth of Sugar Creek in Braxton County. The instrument of his I saw, made of cherry with a walnut neck, appears to be similar to those made by old Nicholas County maker Henry Bryant.

Herbert Frame from Little Otter, who moved to Atwater, Ohio, began making dulcimers in Braxton County in 1932. When he started making dulcimers, he used broom wire for frets, a comb for the nut, and a hickory noter with a notch and a straight pick for playing. He apparently made dulcimers to sell for income.

Amity White spent an appreciable amount of time in Braxton County and left at least two dulcimers there. He also made fiddles and later engaged in coffin making in Wirt County. White's dulcimer-playing nephew Hubert Duvall remembered a neighbor who played a dulcimer made from an old fruit box.

To date, central West Virginia is not considered significant regarding its pre-revival association with the dulcimer.[42] Certainly the dulcimer was never as popular here as the fiddle or banjo. While I have identified 179 twentieth-century old-time fiddlers in Braxton County and numerous fiddle makers, I would estimate there have been 50 dulcimer players in the county in the same period. However, the information I collected in Braxton County supports evidence of a strong tradition of dulcimer activity that goes back well into the nineteenth century.

12

The Magic String

There are those who touch the magic string,
And noisy fame is proud to win them;
Alas! for those who never sing,
But die with all their music in them.
    John Bowyer Calwell, Lewisburg, West Virginia, 1839

The old photograph on the cover of the Library of Congress study of the Hammons family demonstrates turn-of-the-century cultural values deep in the West Virginia hills. Pete Hammons holds a fiddle, an important cultural marker. Paris Hammons holds a gun, significant to self-reliant family ways. Neal Hammonds holds a wind-up phonograph, exploding a myth about cultural isolation in the Appalachian Mountains.

Several Appalachian music collectors nod to the allegory that early seclusion and isolation are the reasons for the music's existence. Sharp's *Folksongs from the Southern Appalachians*, published in 1932, is a classic example. Before Sharp's collection was published, Kephart's 1922 volume, *Our Southern Highlanders*, romanticized the isolation of southern Appalachia as well as the ethnic makeup of its inhabitants (perhaps influencing Sharp).[1] Isolation is one part of the equation, but it tends to oversimplify a more complex situation. Is it not possible that people hang on to their folk music because it has intrinsic value and artistic merit that affords identity, rather than for the simple reason that they had no other choice?

The photograph was taken by a Braxton County photographer, circa 1906, at Cornelius (Neal) Hammonds' home on Williams River at the mouth of the Mill Branch. The three brothers seem to be making a calculated statement by holding items of importance and usefulness. However, the photograph belies any argument that this family was musically isolated from the rest of the world. Before 1922, there was not even a category in the commercial recording industry for rural,

The Hammons Family, circa 1906. (Author's collection.)

southern, mountain, country, hillbilly, or anything remotely resembling the family's folk music. Just what kind of music played on this machine in the home of these "isolated" mountain people? Most likely it was a hodgepodge of minstrel-era takeoffs, comedies in dialect based on racial or ethnic stereotypes, vaudeville and show tunes, sentimental ballads, and possibly operatic delights.[2] Occasionally a common American fiddle tune with humorous dialogue like "Arkansas Traveler" was available. Some classical banjo pieces also were available, but the commercial recordings represented the popular sounds of the day. The same recorded disks listened to by phonograph owners in New York City were available and listened to by phonograph owners on the remote Williams River in Webster County, West Virginia.[3]

Neal Hammonds was married to the former Elizabeth Baughman, a dulcimer player. Yet Liz and the fretted dulcimer she played were not chosen to be a part of the photograph. When this photograph was taken, Liz's dulcimer was out of sight but just paces away inside the log wall of the old house. Her son, Currence, said the dulcimer and the rest of the family were present when the photo was taken. The photo affirms a value system, a pecking order, in which the dulcimer, the woman, and the children took second place to the men, the fiddle, the gun, and the phonograph. Hammons women took the traditional backseat to their men, just as the dulcimer played second best to the fiddle.

The presence of the phonograph in this photo reveals an interest in and awareness of popular cultural forms. It also helps explain aspects of this generation's musical legacy as found in the repertoires of their children. Numerous tunes, such as "Walkin' in the Parlor" and "Boatsman," are once-popular tunes from minstrel show and stage that turn up in many traditional repertoires. Burl Hammons, son and nephew of the depicted men, fiddled a tune, "Darky's Dream," having learned it from African American musician Grafton Lacy. George Lansing, a white Boston banjo player in the 1880s, composed the tune.[4] So this tune, of white origin, was composed to sound like an African American melody (or what the composer thought was African based on performances of the popular stage), and in roughly forty years the tune reentered a rural African American tradition and was passed back to a white Appalachian fiddler. By that time it was firmly entrenched in folk tradition, yet it was born of popular culture and advanced by new popular media. On Burl's fiddle recording,[5] "Darky's Dream" is positioned in sequence next to the fiddled melody of the song "Red Buck" (often called the "Vance Song.")[6] The "Red Buck" piece concerns regional events one would expect to find in the folklore and repertoire of the Hammons family. Did Burl pause long enough to differentiate between the varied sources of these and other tunes in his repertoire? As a fine musician, he surely noticed the melodic and rhythmic variation. I am sure Burl also thought of tunes in varying ways, such as light-hearted, once-popular ditties or cherished family gems representing the traditions of his ancestors.

The Hammons family was operating on the Big Sandy River from 1790 until the 1850s. An Ohio riverman, Tom Collins, who based in the Parkersburg area and operated on the river between 1849 and 1873, was a fiddler. Tom encountered a wide variety of music on his excursions from the deep South to the Northwest. Most of his work (on flatboats) was along the Ohio River between (West) Virginia and Ohio. Collins encountered men who operated on the Big Sandy and the Kanawha. He fiddled for "dances," "frolics," "balls," and "cotillions," as far inland as Jackson and Roane Counties in (West) Virginia. On his travels, he noted German fiddlers and African American fiddle and banjo players. He heard and observed flute music, bagpipe music, minstrel shows, clog dancing, fiddling, and fiddling with dancing in a Union Army camp. Collins reported numerous instances of both African Americans and whites singing, dancing, and playing music in and around Ohio River towns and on the boats that plied the river.[7] This eclectic mix of folk and popular fare was transported along the waterways at surprising speeds. It surely affected people like the Hammonses, who worked on the Big Sandy, and the Cottrells, who traveled the West Fork of the Little Kanawha to Ohio River trading venues. Phoeba Parsons related that the early pioneer Cottrells would take a certain animal bone that was used as a measure of currency when Cottrell family members would go down the West Fork to reach the Ohio River and Indian trading venues.[8] The Carpenters also transcended the Elk and Kanawha Rivers and even made and traded "barge gunwales" directly to Ohio rivermen.

Producers of recordings of traditional music, including me, make editorial decisions about what material to present to the public when it cannot all be presented. Recently penned and/or commercially popularized ditties may not make the cut in deference to folk music with an older pedigree. The whole question of promoting the "authentic" aspects of a folk artist's repertoire, regardless of his or her preference, is in question.[9] However, the entire repertoire should be examined and considered if we are going to base analysis of social history on that repertoire. We should wonder how many songs were passed over by Cecil Sharp because they did not fit into the parameters of his *English Folksongs from the Southern Appalachians*. He did not hesitate to write about the geographical and social isolation of his subjects and how that related to the ancient repertoire he was collecting from them, but I would bet his singers had a much wider repertoire than the one he presents. The Hammons family, at the time the photograph was taken (well before Sharp's collecting activity), lived in extremely geographically isolated surroundings on the edge of what is now designated the Cranberry Wilderness Area of the Monongahela National Forest. Maggie Hammons, Burl's sister, sang some of the rarest of old-world ballads such as "Hindhorn" (Child #17), but she also sang ditties from the pen of Stephen Foster like "Uncle Ned."

There is a movement afoot to classify today's southern whites as representative of Celtic culture. This is accompanied by further efforts to classify Appalachians as specific bearers of Celtic heritage.[10] More recently, white southern Appalachian musicians are represented as "Celtic-Americans,"[11] which crosses boundaries of reason. In the most recent West Virginia census, more people claimed Germanic heritage than any other ethnicity.[12] More people may be conscious of a German surname, and thus heritage, than an Anglo or Celtic surname. Still, names alone do not tell the whole story: many a German Schmidt became a Smith in America, for example.[13] The marriage of Neal Hammons (right in photo) and Liz Baughman represents a significant ethnic alliance. It is a historic model that repeats a long history of such unions since the eighteenth-century frontier. The Baughman family is typical of Pennsylvania German pioneers who came to the Appalachian frontier in the eighteenth century. The Hammons family, if traditional family history is correct, were Scots-Irish immigrants who proceeded to this same frontier, in the same period, and for much the same reasons.

A glance at the Pocahontas County Hammons family tree reveals that four of the seven siblings who are children of Paris Hammons (center in photo) took mates with Anglo/Celtic surnames (one Fowler, one Riddle, and two Roberts). Four of their mates (Edden married twice) had Germanic surnames (one Shaffer, one Baughman, two Cogars).[14] Genealogical studies prove this blending of ethnicities to be a normal situation documented since the pioneer period. The Cogars descend from a Pennsylvania German pioneer, Johann Conrad Gauger (later Cowger or Cogar).[15] Many Cogars were fine musicians.[16] Likewise, the Baughmans are noted as fine ballad singers, some were dulcimer makers and players, and some were gifted fiddlers.[17]

By the beginning of the twentieth century, ethnicities had genetically dissipated among those descended from the older stock of pioneer inhabitants in West Virginia. The exception is African Americans. Though they often became mulattos and were thus also of European lineage, they are classified as a homogeneous group and visually categorized. A regional or, more often, state identity (Virginia) quickly replaced the European and African identities. Beginning with World War I and continuing through World War II and beyond, things German were out of favor. This helped the regional identity take a firm hold and caused German ethnicity to disappear. Still, we cannot reshape musical history to match patriotic or cultural ideals. Moreover, we cannot accept that a significant cultural influence simply bowed to others and retreated into obscurity.

If Appalachians of Celtic, Anglo, and Germanic heritage play music of Celtic origin (but also in ways that show African, Anglo, and German influence), does that make them Celtic-Americans? If they play music of African American instigation (most play a few blues tunes, for instance), are they African Americans? The facts remain that Germanic and Anglo people settled in the southern Appalachians in substantial numbers early on and Africans made up a small but musically influential minority. Much popular music and art music from the Germanic areas of Europe, and of German composition, entered folk tradition and is widely found in the repertoires of musicians of the southern mountains as well as in the repertoires of most American fiddlers.[18]

The fretted dulcimer tradition in the Appalachians is maligned by some who refute its Germanic origins.[19] It also is proposed that dulcimer traditions in "the mountains" are the product of misinformation expounded by outsiders, who promulgated the dulcimer as the quaint entertainment of Appalachian people.[20] This "cultural intervention" is factually supported in a few specific areas, but "the mountains" in West Virginia also harbor a legitimate, long-standing, and unaffected dulcimer heritage. The tradition here is uninfluenced by any outside interests prior to the mid-twentieth-century national revival. Direct links can be made, through rightful tradition bearers, between the evolved fretted dulcimer in central West Virginia and the fretted zithers of Pennsylvania and Europe. These continuous links now approach a three-hundred-year span in America.

The number of traditional dulcimer makers and players in Braxton County may indicate that area to have the strongest pre-revival dulcimer tradition in the Appalachians. I believe it is entirely possible, and highly probable, that other concentrations of makers exist(ed). Broader field research is needed to achieve a wider understanding of these traditions in the state.

Like Germanic heritage, African influence, rooted in the American South, needs to be accorded its rightful place among the basic elements responsible for the development of old-time music. I have heard this fact questioned by traditional music enthusiasts. This is probably because it has had such little public exposure, but there are also onerous signs of racism being a factor. Work by Blaustein (1975), Epstein (1977), Winans (1979), Titon (1979), Tallmadge (1984), Abrahams (1992), Jabbour (1993), Conway (1995), and others has opened the door. Now, at the end of the twentieth century, it demands wider understanding and recognition. Banjos, lyrics, tune structure, syncopated bowing of fiddle breakdowns, and more than three hundred years of fiddle and banjo performance style all point to a strong African American presence. However, it is too simple to generalize that African rhythm met European melody and the result is American music. White music structure, style, and repertoire is present in African American music, and the reverse contributions made through African melody and European rhythm are still unclear. Only now are people beginning to wonder if African fiddle-like instruments, such as the kakoshis, goge, and kalandin were brought to America and/or made in America and have had an effect on American fiddling tradition.[21] John Minton has found evidence that slaves were playing West African fiddles in the South. He also documents the gourd fiddle as an African instrument. We should wonder if the gourd fiddles Edden Hammons in West Virginia and Eck Robertson in Texas learned on, and the numerous ones that are (accidentally) documented in print, were heirs to an African provenance.[22]

Malone said it has never been possible for this country to racially segregate its musical forms.[23] He pointed out that there is no real distinction between music in the lowlands of the rural South and the uplands of the southern Appalachians. The similarity, as he put it, goes "from the tidewater of Virginia to the pinelands of Texas." He sees the "mountain music" classification to be a romanticized term that really only means "southern music."[24] Conway used African American banjo artists of the North Carolina piedmont to illustrate "African Echoes" of the banjo "in Appalachia."[25] Whatever varied title is used for rural southern music, it has been played from Chicago to Atlanta, Mississippi to Richmond, Boston to Bakersfield, and Canada to Europe, among people of every stripe. But we still fantasize that if you travel to some remote hollow in the "isolated" Appalachians, you will find the hole in the rock from which all the music emanates! As with Jack, of folktale fame, who sets out to find the hole where the northwest wind comes out, this mindset continues to sidestep reason and act on lore about traditional music's origins. The mystique about place (the mountains) is romantic and pervasive, but it includes a sense of time (where time stands still); adds a cryptic rural setting (Sharp's "laurel country," Kephart's "laurel," or Price's "Last Forest"); and uses an idealized identity (Celtic-Americans or "contemporary ancestors") to keep the allegory alive.

Allen Batteau said, "Appalachia is a creature of the urban imagination."[26] Indeed, I have yet to meet an old-timer who subscribes to the notion of Appalachia as a region and himself or herself as an Appalachian. The informants in this work considered themselves West Virginians almost to a person (although some might call themselves "hillbillies" in a facetious way). If the idea of "Appalachia" is an urban myth, it was reaffirmed by a poor image of Appalachians imposed through the "War on Poverty" and supported by literary works such as those by Caudill and Weller.[27]

Religious conviction continues to affect popularity of traditional dancing in the mountain state because of the devil-fiddle-dancing synthesis.[28] This disposition is not new, although its popularity may be at an all time low. Now, however, new pressures have overwhelmingly replaced it and are taking their toll on traditional dance. Modernization is, in effect, doing what thousands of preachers over centuries have not been able to achieve. It is bringing about the discontinuance of traditional dancing to fiddle music. A nationwide dance resurgence with a strong following has scant resemblance to traditional rural community dancing in West Virginia. This vibrant new scene has grown from an urban movement and taken on structure and mores that are unfamiliar to many rural traditional dancers. Disparate traditional forms within this revival include relatively modern couples-dancing (to Cajun or Swing music) that often replaces the social or community group dancing with which the movement started. But this condition replicates similar events in the eighteenth century.[29] Beyond that, an overwhelming movement, from Atlanta to Seattle, toward New England, contra dancing often replaces square and circle dances that are traditional in the South and Midwest and from Pennsylvania to the Southwest. This movement leaves most old-time rural dancers out in the cold.

Most of the old-style fiddlers, who were so much a part of traditional instrumental music in the state just twenty-five years ago are gone. In their place remain some energetic younger bloods who are every bit as enthusiastic and talented as their predecessors. They are different, however, in that they have been exposed to and impressed by a wider array of music than their predecessors could imagine. Young musicians, who not so long ago would have had the chance to learn old-time music from local, community, or family sources, endure a barrage of musical genres and are often detoured by them. Musicians now travel across many county and/or state lines to their mentors and depend on recorded offerings to find desired material. Those who want to play the oldest styles of traditional music have made a conscious and intellectual decision to do so, rather than following a natural course of events. But as we have seen, the turn-of-the-century Hammons family made choices too. Some traditional music enthusiasts are fighting the popular music media blitz by actively promoting old-time music on the radio.[30]

Time marches on, and so does music. Folk music has been and always will be in a state of transformation. Changes have taken old-world music and given us American folk music. Changes have blended European and African music, perhaps spiced with a pinch of Native American and other seasonings, and given us old-time music. Popular fads in music and dance will come and go. The best will be retained, claimed, used, and then added to that which has passed the test of time through a natural selection process. Still, the amount and variety of material encountered by today's musicians surely dwarfs the past. The available body of recorded traditional fiddle music alone presents a dizzying array of choices.

I have faith that traditional folk music is alive and well in West Virginia as we enter the twenty-first century. Collective human experience and values will not be denied emergence as expressive sight and sound. Tradition depends on knowledge from the past influencing activities and situations in the present. We should not doubt that the process will continue. But we must recognize and sustain folk artists whose values and life's calling put them at risk and not forget to pay the fiddler.

Committees to select appropriate music for regional traditional music events maintain ever-growing lists. If there is any indication that traditional music in the region is waning, it is not readily evident. Is it changing? Yes, but values in old-time music will gradually change in accordance with the values of those who play it, as they have always done, although the process has quickened. Some values are timeless, however, and those who "play of a fiddle" and present aspects of music that bring about "chills of hilarity" will be appreciated for a long time to come.

Notes

Introduction

1. Burt Struthers, *Philadelphia: Holy Experiment* (New York: Doubleday, Doran & Company, 1945), 196.

2. *Seventh Day Baptist General Conference*, 1910, vol. 2.

3. Henry Glassie, *Pattern in the Material Folk Culture of the Eastern United States* (Philadelphia: Univ. of Pennsylvania Press, 1968), 76.

4. A general definition of the folklore profession today concludes that folk art represents an expression of values that are shared within folk communities.

5. In terms of fiddle music, Blaustein calls it a cross-cultural transfusion. See, Richard Jason Blaustein, "Rethinking Folk Revivalism: Grass-roots Preservationism and Folk Romanticism," in Neil V. Rosenberg, ed., *Transforming Tradition* (Urbana and Chicago: Univ. of Illinois Press, 1993), 259.

6. Jeff Todd Titon explains the blues revival in these terms. See "Reconstructing the Blues: Reflections on the 1960s Blues Revival," in Rosenberg, ed., 1993, 225.

Chapter 1. Chills of Hilarity

1. This appears in German over the door of a house in Helvetia, Randolph County. See Milnes, producer, *Helvetia: The Swiss of West Virginia* (AHR-93).

2. Brooks Hardway, interview, 17 September 1988, Augusta Collection. See Senate Cottrell, field recording by Fern Rollyson, in the Augusta Collection for a discussion of the tune "Piney Mountain."

3. Melvin Wine, interview by author, tape recording, 23 June 1988. Augusta Collection, Davis and Elkins College, Elkins, W.Va.

4. Linda C. Burman-Hall, "Southern American Folk Fiddling: Context and Style," (Ph.D. diss., Princeton Univ., 1974), 14. Burman-Hall reports that music throughout the Christian world has served to enhance worship through incantation, chant, and hymn.

5. Bob (R.J.) Stewart, *Where Is Saint George? Pagan Imagery in English Folksong.* (London: Blandford Press, 1977 and 1988), 22, notes: ". . . perhaps

the idea of racial memory of tradition would be a better means of explaining the survival of myths." D.K. Wilgus, *Anglo-American Folksong Scholarship Since 1898* (1959; reprint, Westport, Conn.: Greenwood Press, 1982), xiv, 4, in considering the origins of ballads, uses the term "collective soul," which seems related to this concept of "racial memory," but he warns against dependence on this concept, saying we have to accept the "individual" folk artist. See also, Wilgus, "An Introduction to the Study of Hillbilly Music," *Journal of American Folklore* 78, no. 309 (July-September 1965): 195.

6. In some of the Evangelical and Holiness churches of West Virginia, a decided difference may be observed in the amount of overt emotion shown in worship. Preachers, rather than being intellectual persuaders or convincers, turn to being emotional shouters and cryers. Congregations change from being restrained listeners to being active participants who pray out loud, reaffirm the preacher's points, and leave their inhibitions at home. Unstructured dancing during the service is common. Today, it's often electronic music with a heavy beat and amplified preaching that predominates at these affairs. In the past, when music for such purposes was necessarily acoustic, the sound of the music was the main ingredient to help in the transcending experience.

7. Donald Andrew Beisswenger, "Fiddling Way Out Yonder: Community and Style in the Music of Melvin Wine" (Ph.D. diss., Univ. of Memphis, 1997), reports this from Bob Wine, Melvin Wine's father.

8. Emma Bell Miles, *The Spirit of the Mountains* (1905; reprint, Knoxville: Univ. of Tennessee Press, 1975), 153.

9. Jon Butler, *Awash in a Sea of Faith: Christianizing the American People* (Cambridge and London: Harvard Univ. Press, 1990), 19. Halpert documents the widespread nature of these beliefs. See Halpert, in Abrahams, ed. 1995, 44-54. See also Milnes, *Fiddles, Snakes and Dogdays*, AHV-97.

10. Clyde Case, interview by author, tape recording, Duck, West Virginia, 17 November 1989, Augusta Collection.

11. Fleischhauer and Jabbour, eds., *The Hammons Family, A Study of a West Virginia Family's Traditions* (Washington, D.C.: Library of Congress, AFS L-65, L-66), recordings with booklet, 21. The EAEA tuning is seen in published form in England in 1685, and was noted in Scotland, but is found on the European continent even earlier (Burman-Hall 1974, 46).

12. Phyllis Marks, *Folksongs and Ballads, vol. 2*, (Augusta Heritage Recordings, AHR-008, 1991). See Currence and Minnie Hammonds "Jimmy Randall," field recording by author, Huttonsville, W.Va., 2 August 1983, Augusta Collection; and Hazel Stover, "Molly Bender," video recording by author, Clay, W.Va., 2 October 1995, Augusta Collection.

13. Deitz, Dennis, *The Greenbrier Ghost and Other Strange Stories* (Charleston, W.Va.: Mountain Memories Books, 1990), 2-24; and Thompson, Stith, *Motif-Index of Folk Literature* (Bloomington: Indiana Univ. Press), E231, E231.1, E324.

14. For a discussion of this relationship, in many cultures, see Halpert, "The Devil, the Fiddle and Dancing." See also Milnes, *Fiddles, Snakes and Dogdays*, AHV-97.

15. Currence Hammonds, interview by author, tape recording, Huttonsville, W.Va., 10 July 1979, Augusta Collection.

16. Carl Degler, interview by author, videotape recording, Crystal Springs, W.Va., 15 February 1995, Augusta Collection.

17. In *Charlotte Elizabeth's Personal Recollections* (London, 1847), she notes an Irish St. John's Eve celebration in which ritualistic music and dance was apparent: *The fire being kindled, a splendid blaze shot up; and for a while they stood contemplating it with faces strangely disfigured by the peculiar light first emitted when the bogwood was thrown on it. After a short pause, the ground was cleared in front of an old blind piper, the very "beau ideal" of energy, drollery, and shrewdness, who, seated on a low chair, with a well-plenished jug within his reach, screwed his pipes to the liveliest tunes, and the endless jig began.* Music and ritualistic dance at this "Christian celebration" perplexed the writer (Hislop, 1916). For a thorough discussion of religious attitude toward dance, see Ann Wagner, *Adversaries of Dance: From the Puritans to the Present* (Urbana and Chicago: Univ. of Illinois Press, 1997).

18. McElwain was at least tied once at a contest, see John A. Cuthbert and Alan Jabbour, eds., *Edden Hammons, His Life and Music*, booklet with recording (Morgantown: West Virginia Univ. Press, 1984). Typically, older fiddlers interviewed, speaking of Edden Hammons, would say: "He was right up there next to Jack Wain." See George Bright, interview by author, 30 March 1980, Augusta Collection.

19. Brooks Hardway, interview, 17 September 1988.

20. Pheoba Parsons, interview with author, tape recording, Calhoun County, 30 March 1989, Augusta Collection.

21. Brooks Hardway, interview, 17 September 1988.

22. Alan Jabbour, notes to recording *American Fiddle Tunes* (Washington, D.C., Library of Congress, AFS L-62, 1971), 2-5, cites eighty bibliographic and discographic references for the tune before 1955, beginning with McGlashan, Alexander, *A Collection of Scots Measures*, Edinburgh: Neil Stewart, (circa) 1781. Although Jabbour's writing here is concerned with American fiddling in general, it is appropriate for Appalachian fiddle music. Jabbour, an old-time fiddler himself, has collected in places like West Virginia and brings not only a resourceful academic background but a personal involvement with folk fiddlers to the examination of origins and influences on West Virginia's fiddle music.

23. Jabbour, Alan, "The Fiddle in the Blue Ridge," in Worley, Beth, and Vaughn Webb, eds., *Blue Ridge Folk Instruments and Their Makers*, a catalog from an exhibit of the same name (Ferrum, Va.: Ferrum College, 1993.)

24. Jabbour 1971, 1, and Burman-Hall 1974, 12.

25. See Jabbour (1971) and Bayard (1944, 1982) for a complete comparison of notes. In central West Virginia, this tune is most often titled "Round Town Gals."

26. Richard Jason Blaustein. "Traditional Music and Social Change: The Old Time Fiddlers Association Movement in the United States." (Ph.D. diss., Indiana Univ., 1975), 15-16.

27. This was recorded by Posey Rorrer (fiddle) of Charlie Poole's North Carolina Ramblers in 1926. Kenny Rorrer, *Rambling Blues: The Life and Times of Charlie Poole* (Danville, Va.: 1982), 99. Poole's band also released "Under the

Double Eagle," a tune written by an Austrian. Study of American fiddle tunes turns up considerable Germanic sources for the music.

28. Blaustein, 1975, 15.

29. The ancient Greeks ascribed certain "humours" to modal scales, and Wine seems to verbalize this in his description of the emotions he felt from his father's music.

30. Presently, the only published recorded source of Triplett's music is the tune "Little Cat" on the album *The Music Never Dies, A Vandalia Sampler, 1977-1987*, Elderberry Records, 1988, and Milnes, *Fiddles, Snakes and Dog Days* (video production), Augusta Heritage Center, 1997.

31. This tune by Carpenter may be heard on *Old-Time Fiddling of Braxton County, Volume 1*, AHR-012. Midwest variants are called "Yankee Squirrel Hunter" and "Squirrel Hunter." Also see a version by Rob Propst, field recording by Nick Royal, 4 November 1974, Augusta Collection.

32. See recording, Burl Hammons, AHR-017.

33. Robert Simmons, interview by author, 17 March 1992, Augusta Collection.

34. Margaret Bennett, *The Last Stronghold: Scottish Gaelic Traditions in Newfoundland* (St. Johns: Breakwater Press, 1989), 109-17.

35. Neil MacAlpine, *A Pronouncing English-Gaelic Dictionary* (Glasgow: Maclaren and Sons, 1957).

36. Christmas shifted by eleven days with the change from the Julian calendar to the Gregorian calendar, which Britain adopted in 1751. See Milnes 1995.

37. See recordings, Pete Humphreys, *Old-Time Banjo Anthology, Vol. 2*, Marimac AHS 5; Melvin Wine, Poplar LP1; French Carpenter, Folk Promotions (no catalog number or date).

38. Woody Simmons's fiddling may be heard on *All Smiles Tonight*, ER-002, and "Foggy Valley," AHR-020.

39. Brooks Hardway, interview, 17 September 1988.

40. Melvin's singing grandfather, Nelson Wine, didn't play, but whistled tunes that his father, Smith, played on the fiddle. He also whistled them for his son, Bob, to learn on the fiddle. Nelson Wine was collected by Lalah Lovett, see John Harrington Cox, *Folk-Songs of the South* (1925), 321. Singers and fiddlers had different talents that didn't mix. See also Beisswenger, *Fiddling Way Out Yonder* (1997), 92, and Artley, *The West Virginia Country Fiddler* (1955), 78.

41. Karpeles, see Cecil Sharp, *English Folk Songs from the Southern Appalachians* (London: Oxford Univ. Press, 1932). Singing with banjo was common in minstrel tradition (see Conway, Cecelia, *African Banjo Echoes in Appalachia: A Study of Folk Traditions* (Knoxville: Univ. of Tennessee Press, 1995), chapter 2.

42. Such venues are common in West Virginia. The "Sagebrush Roundup," near Fairmont, Marion County, is a prime example. There is a similar affair in Grant County, the "Mountain Opry," and one in Braxton County, at the community center in Chapel. These affairs, when they include more old-time or traditional music, such as one in Copen in Braxton County, or (more typically) in private homes, tend to be more participatory, and there is not a stage, or focal

point, from which to perform to an audience. The musicians are more likely to face each other in a circle.

Chapter 2. Choking the Goose

1. Omar Slaughter, interview by author, videotape recording, 20 April 1995, Augusta Collection.

2. W.E.R. Byrne, *Tale of the Elk* (Richwood, W.Va.: Mountain State Press, 1940), 78.

3. The McElwain family name is often shortened to simply Wayne or Wain in Webster County. The area where the family settled on Laurel Creek is known as Wainville.

4. Sampson Newton Miller, *Annals of Webster County, West Virginia, Before and Since Organization, 1863.* (Buckhannon, W.Va.: West Virginia Wesleyan College, 1969.) "Hard to crowd" is a regional expression meaning "standing out from," or "better than." Also see Milnes, "Uncle Jack McElwain (1856-1938)," 1993.

5. John A. Cuthbert, ed., *West Virginia Folk Music.* (Morgantown: West Virginia Univ. Press, 1982), 38.

6. Kenny Hamill, *West Virginia Place Names* (Piedmont, W.Va.: West Virginia Place Name Press, 1945,) 232.

7. Bud Sandy, interview by author, tape recording, Burnsville, W.Va., 5 November 1987, Augusta Collection.

8. Ernie Carpenter, interview by author, tape recording, Sutton, W.Va., 17 January 1986, Augusta Collection.

9. Ernie Carpenter, interview by author, tape recording, Sutton, W.Va., 5 June 1991, Augusta Collection. Tom Jack was close to seven feet tall. The Woods were a pioneer family who spawned several fiddlers and were early settlers on the head of Birch River. Arthur Woods, interview by author, field notes, 2 October 1996, Augusta Collection.

10. Cuthbert and Jabbour 1984, from newspaper article from Akron, Ohio, reprinted in the *Richwood News Leader*, 17 September 1969.

11. Ibid.

12. There was also a "joint" known as the "Pig's Ear" in neighboring Braxton County on Granny's Creek. In rhyming slang, the term has similar drinking connotations.

13. "Cross tuning" (see chapter 1, note 11) indicates fiddle tunings that vary from the normal or "natural" tuning of EADG (high to low). Most central West Virginia old-time fiddlers use more than one tuning, with EAEA being used most often. Most European and some Eastern countries use or used nonstandard tunings on the fiddle for their folk music. In North America, the strongest tradition of varied tunings persists in the southern Appalachians, with central West Virginia being a stronghold. These tunings are also found in Cape Breton. See Jody Stecher, "Cross Tuning Workshop," *Fiddler Magazine* 4, no. 2 (Summer 1997), 29.

14. Tunes recorded by Dillon on LWO 2471 on 26 July 1956 are "Old Joe

Clark," "Who's Been Here Since I've Been Gone," "Old Joe Clark" (again), "Arkansas Traveler," "Mockingbird," "Mississippi Sawyer," "Soldier's Joy," "Gunboat," "Girl I Left behind Me," "Old Sledge," "Washington's March," "Cumberland Gap," "Turkey in the Straw," "Sally Gooden," "Grey Eagle," "Boatsman," "Sourwood Mountain," "Old Dan Tucker," "Riffle (Cripple) Creek," "Liza Jane," "Log Cabin in the Lane (Nelly Grey)," "Fiddler's Dram."

15. These recordings are contained within the Rollyson Collection in the Augusta Collection at Davis and Elkins College.

16. Miller 1969, 253.

17. Cuthbert 1982.

18. Mose Coffman, interview by author, tape recording, Sweet Springs, W.Va., 23 February 1991, Augusta Collection.

19. William T. Price, *Historical Sketches of Pocahontas County, West Virginia* (1901; reprint, Marlinton, W.Va.: Price Brothers, 1963), 62. A typical Juba rhyme I've found in West Virginia from a white source is: "She sifts the meal, She gave me the husk. She baked the bread, She gave me the crust. She fried the meat, She gave me the bone. She kicked my tail, And sent me home. Whop o haw Juba. Juba this and Juba that, Juba skinned the yellow cat."

20. Bayard 1982 notes the practice of "cutting" (xxi) among "rough-and-tumble" old-time fiddlers in Pennsylvania (xvi). The term was used to describe the cutting short of a phrase in a tune and was "frowned upon" by the better fiddlers.

21. Harold Courlander, *Negro Folk Music, U.S.A.* (1963; reprint, New York: Columbia Univ. Press, 1991), 191-2. Also see Wolfe, ed., 1922; *Thomas W. Talley's Negro Folk Rhymes* (Knoxville: Univ. of Tennessee Press, 1991), 235, 254, and 269 for descriptions of juba rhymes and dances. The tradition comes from the African *giouba* dance, which resembled a jig with elaborate variation. The form was bolstered in early American minstrelsy by William Henry Lane, thought to be a free-born black, who performed as "Master Juba." His fame reached far and wide and he was touted as the "greatest dancer in the world." His ability to mock the best steps of all his competitors, then go on to wow audiences with his superior ability, proved him an exceptional dancer. See Marian Hannah Winter, "Juba and American Minstrelsy," in *Inside the Minstrel Mask: Readings in Nineteenth-Century Blackface Minstrelsy*, ed. Annemarie Bean, James V. Hatch, and Brooks McNamara (Hanover and London: Wesleyan Univ. Press, 1996).

22. Byrne 1940, 283.

23. Wilson Douglas, interview, 8 December 1988, Augusta Collection.

24. The murder in 1917 of Preston Tanner resulted in a mob that almost lynched two men. People thought Andrew Sampson and his son, Howard, to be guilty of killing Tanner, robbing him, and attempting to burn the corpse. A local attorney barely talked the mob out of completing a break-in at the unattended jail at Clay. The next day, Sampson told the attorney that the mob sounded about like "a barn dance in Booger Hole," equating the mob violence to the normalcy of life there. Previously, Howard Sampson had been tried for "fighting, cutting, and shooting in Booger Hole." This time, the jury found him guilty of the murder of Tanner and sentenced him to life. The court dropped the charges

against Andrew Sampson for lack of evidence. Upon his return home, the community served notice to Andrew to "get out of Booger Hole!" See Henry B. Davenport, *Tales of the Elk and Other Stories* (1943; reprint, Gauley Bridge: Thomas Imprints, 1992), 61-66. Harvey Sampson is recorded on AHR-004C. Homer Sampson may be heard singing "The House Carpenter," "Salem's Bright King," and "The Battle of Mill Springs" on *Folksongs and Ballads*, vol. 3, AHR-009.

25. "Nicut" (pronounced nye-cut) comes from nigh-cut, meaning near-cut or short cut, an old term still found in Northern Ireland, Michael J. Murphy, *Tyrone Folk Quest* (Belfast: Blackstaff Press, 1973), 58.

26. Col. D.S. Dewees, *Recollections of a Lifetime* (Calhoun County, W.Va.: Eden, 1904), 6. John Davison Sutton, *History of Braxton County and Central West Virginia* (Sutton, W.Va.: 1919), 85.

27. The ancestors of these people in Northern Ireland had practiced "pulling up ways," a term that describes the destruction of roads being built throughout the Ulster region, in an attempt to stop encroaching civilization (Fischer 1989, 631, cites Hughes, *North Country Life in the Eighteenth Century: The North East, 1700-1750* [London: 1952], 16).

28. Deweese 1904; Dodrill 1915; Sutton, 1919.

29. Virginia R. Carr, "Adam O'Brien." *Journal of the Braxton County Historical Society*, 11, no. 3 (25 September 1983), 61.

30. Sutton, 1919, 275.

31. Ernie Carpenter, interview by Amy Davis, Sutton, W.Va., 8 January 1983, Augusta Collection.

32. Field recordings of these musicians are in the Augusta Collection.

33. Malvin Newton Artley, "The West Virginia Country Fiddler: An Aspect of the Folk Music Tradition in the United States" (Ph.D. diss., Chicago Musical College, 1955).

34. Ward Jarvis, interview by author, 2 April 1988, Augusta Collection.

35. Ward Jarvis' fiddling may be heard on *Old-Time Fiddling of Braxton County*, vol. 1, AHR-012.

36. Ray McMillon, interview by author, Exchange, W.Va., 28 April 1988, Augusta Collection.

37. Avis and Jim Ross, interview by author, Flatwoods, W.Va., 26 June 1988, Augusta Collection.

38. Tribe 1984, 82, 97, 118, 126, 133-4.

39. The pen name of David Strauther.

40. Porte Crayon, "The Mountains," *Harper's New Monthly Magazine* 45 (1872): June to November, 514-16.

41. Wilson Douglas, interview by author, 8 December 1988.

42. I have recorded numerous old-world ballads and songs in the area including many that came with the early waves of settlers. See *Folksongs and Ballads*, vols. 1-4, Augusta Heritage Recordings, 1991-1992.

Chapter 3. The Carpenter Legacy.

1. Ernie Carpenter's music and stories are documented on *Elk River Blues*,

an LP of his music, AHR-003 with booklet, "Tales of the Elk River Country," also published in *Goldenseal* 12, no. 2, Gerald Milnes and Michael Kline, 1986.

2. See *Goldenseal* 12, no. 2 (above).

3. More than a century before the Carpenters arrived at their Elk River home on the western frontier, Andrew and James Cobb navigated the Elk. They were from Massachusetts. In 1675, they became lost on the northeastern waters of the Susquehanna River in Pennsylvania during the King Phillip's War. The brothers found their way to the Allegheny River and on to the Ohio. They traveled downstream to the mouth of the Great Kanawha and proceeded east to the mouth of Elk. Their accurate description of the Elk and its tributaries establishes them as the first white men on the river. They ran out of navigable water near what is now Webster Springs, about twenty miles upstream from the present Braxton County line. Here they abandoned their canoe and made their way back over the Alleghenies to waters flowing east and civilization. *Webster Echo*, 15 January 1904, from "Boston Public Record Archives."

4. Ernie Carpenter, interview by Amy Noel Davis, Sutton, W.Va., 8 January 1983, Augusta Collection.

5. Ernie Carpenter, interview by Michael Kline and author, tape recording, 12 February 1981, Augusta Collection. Lucullus Virgil McWhorter, *The Border Settlers of Northwestern Virginia, From 1768 to 1795* (Hamilton, Oh.: Republican Publishing Company, 1915), 205.

6. Artley confuses the two Sol Carpenters. Malvin Newton Artley, "The West Virginia Country Fiddler: An Aspect of the Folk Music Tradition in the United States," (Ph.D. diss., Chicago Musical College, 1955).

7. French Carpenter's version of the tune and the tale may be heard on Old-Time Songs and Tunes from Clay County, West Virginia, Folk Promotions, Charleston, W.Va., (no date).

8. Mamie Santy, interview by author, Chloe, W.Va., 29 April 1987, Augusta Collection.

9. Fleischhauer and Jabbour 1973, 21-22.

10. Sylvia O'Brien, interview by author, videotape recording, Big Otter, W.Va., 21 March 1995, relates the folklore about baby Solomon. Ken Davidson, notes to *Old-Time Songs and Tunes From Clay County, West Virginia*; Jenes Cottrell and David Frank (French) Carpenter, notes, no date. Notes to side two, #5, "Shelvin' Rock": "According to ancestors, this tune was made up after French's grandfather was born under a rock while his family was traveling downstream to a new settlement. This rock is located in Webster Co., W. Va." Davidson mistakenly identifies the Solomon Carpenter who was born under the Shelvin' Rock as French's grandfather, who was also named Solomon Carpenter. The Solomon of Civil War fame, also known as "Devil Sol," was born forty to fifty years later, though of the same lineage. Artley (1955) reports a tune, "Old Solly's Favorite," about the former, while another tune, "Little Solly's Favorite," commemorates the latter.

11. Melvin Wine plays a tune called "Shelvin Rock," learned from his father, which is an entirely different tune and is similar to what fiddler Henry Reed called "Billy in the Lowland."

12. Byrne 1940, 124-29. Republished, *Journal of the Braxton Historical Society* 1, no. 1 (1973).

13. Although Christmas trees were noted in Germany as early as the 1600s, they did not reach the British Isles until the mid nineteenth century. Richard Thonger, *A Calendar of German Customs* (Great Britain: Oswald Wolff Ltd., 1966), 110-11. Also see Josef Ruland, *Christmas in Germany* (Bonn: Hohwacht, 1978).

14. Daniel J. Foley, *The Christmas Tree* (Philadelphia and New York: Chilton, 1960), 68. Earlier, seventeenth-century Puritan Cotton Mather railed against any and all Christmas celebrating including "revelling, dicing, carding, masking, and mummering." The earliest documented Christmas trees in America occur among Pennsylvania Germans: Easton in 1816, Lancaster County in 1822, York in 1823, Philadelphia in 1825 and 1834, and Cincinnati, Ohio, in 1835. By the late 1840s they were becoming widespread. A German immigrant introduced one to Boston in 1832. The book *Kriss Kringle's Christmas Tree*, published in Philadelphia in 1845, was important to the widespread popularity of the practice of bringing a tree indoors as part of the Christmas observance. The pagan origins of Christmas trees had become Christianized in Scandinavia and Germany, had come to America through the German Reformed and Moravian sects, were popularized through mid nineteenth century publications, and re-entered family tradition and widespread custom. The Christmas tree rite reached nationwide proportion by the mid to late nineteenth century (Foley 1960, 67-86). One surprisingly early example does turn up in western Virginia, at Clarksburg, in 1829. See Haymond 1910, 261-2.

15. In *Crabb's Mythology*, published in London in 1854, it is stated that the pagan Celts worshipped the cross long before the crucifixion of Christ. Still another nineteenth century source notes that: ". . . the Druids in their groves were accustomed to select their most stately and beautiful tree as an emblem of the Deity they adored, and having cut the side branches, they affixed two of the largest of them to the highest part of the trunk, in such a manner that those branches extended on each side like the arms of a man, and, together with the body, presented the appearance of a huge cross" (Hislop 1916, 199). Bonwick writes: "The blazing or fiery cross . . . was well known in both Ireland and Scotland (among Celtic people)" (Bonwick 1894, 198).

16. "This salt is sent down Kenhawa (sic) River in boats to every part of the western country, and exchanged for articles of consumption." Anne Royal, "The Salt Works Of Kenhawa County," in *Stories and Verse of West Virginia*, ed. Ella May Turner (1923; reprint, Richwood, W.Va.: Comstock, 1974), 24.

17. True to the folk tale form, this story has taken on variants, even though it has appeared in print. Sutton reports that a man named Gibson was drowned in this incident, but that his last remark was that "God almighty had never made the water in which he could not swim." Sutton 1919, 30.

18. *Goldenseal* 12, no. 2 (Summer 1986).

19. Ibid.

20. Notes from *Elk River Blues*, AHR-003.

21. This would be a wooden and tin "pie safe," a mainstay piece of furniture in households of the period.

22. Ernie Carpenter, interview by Michael Kline and author, Sutton, W.Va., 12 February 1981, Augusta Collection.

23. Melvin Wine, interview by author, Copen, W.Va., 19 November 1988, Augusta Collection.

24. Wilson Douglas, interview by author, Clendenin, W.Va., 8 December 1988, Augusta Collection.

25. Most people within the folk culture of West Virginia speak in the relative terms of up (or above) and down (or below), meaning upstream or downstream, and not north or south.

26. Brooks Hardway, interview, 17 September 1988, Augusta Collection.

27. Wilson Douglas, interview, 8 December 1988.

Chapter 4. "Upon My Honor"

1. Diller's keen observation and identification led to the study by Carl Fleischhauer and Alan Jabbour, *The Hammons Family, A West Virginia Family's Traditions* (Washington, D.C.: Library of Congress, 1973).

2. For accounts of the Scots-Irish and North British movement into Appalachia, see Fischer 1989, Cunningham 1987, and Leyburn 1962. Most local West Virginia county histories identify early immigrants as having Scots-Irish roots. A study of southern fiddling influences reports that Scots, Irish, and North British influence is the greatest (Burman-Hall 1974).

3. Tyler Blethen and Curtis Wood Jr., *From Ulster to Carolina: The Migration of the Scotch-Irish to Southwestern North Carolina* (Cullowhee, N.C.: Western Carolina Univ., 1983), 27. See also Maldwyn Jones, *American Immigration* (Chicago, London: Univ. of Chicago Press, 1960), 21. Jones notes that encouragement from provincial authorities brought on this emigration from Northern Ireland to South Carolina.

4. Marion O'Brien, interview by author, Webster County, 21 August 1989, Augusta Collection, and Fleischhauer and Jabbour, eds., 1973, 4.

5. William Ely, *The Big Sandy Valley* (1887; reprint, Catlettsburg, Ky.: Heritage Books, 1987), 11, 104.

6. See recorded tale "The Yankee and Marcum," Fleischhauer and Jabbour, eds. (notes, 22), 1973.

7. See Ronald V. Hardway, "The Last Pioneers," *The Webster Independent* 9, no. 1 (Fall/Winter 1994-1995), 1-45.

8. Altina Waller, *Feud: Hatfields, McCoys, and Social Change in Appalachia, 1860-1900* (Chapel Hill: Univ. of North Carolina Press, 1988), describes a region where "poverty was almost unknown," of "a pre-modern life-style of hard work alleviated by seasonal rhythms," and where "Such formal institutions as county court and church provided institutional structures for social cohesion and shared cultural values."

9. Otis K. Rice, *The Allegheny Frontier, West Virginia Beginnings, 1730-1830* (Lexington: Univ. Press of Kentucky, 1970), 180, quoting W.P. Strickland, ed., *Biographical, Historical, and Miscellaneous, Illustrative of Pioneer Life* (Cincinnati, 1855).

10. Waller 1988, 40, states that the timber industry did not begin in the valley until after the Civil War, but in this case the Hammonses were employed in a wood products business several years before the war.

11. Fleischhauer and Jabbour, eds., 1973, 4.

12. These are wooden sticks, split from chestnut, that were used for the purpose of dying materials.

13. Marion O'Brien, interview by author, 21 August 1989, Augusta Collection.

14. Hardway 1994, 12-16. Information on the Clifton and Riddle families came from my Birch River neighbors.

15. Waller 1988, describes the Sandy/Tug Valley of the period where families of a dozen or more children were common, but parents of those children had little hope of providing arable land for their growing families. People were impoverished by the situation and either developed or worked in a newly developing timber market, or left. Waller sees these conditions as the real inducement for the famous Hatfield-McCoy feud.

16. Price 1906, as reported by Cuthbert and Jabbour, eds., 1984.

17. Douglas McNeil, *The Last Forest, Tales of the Allegheny Woods* (1940; reprint, Parsons, W.Va.: Pocahontas Communications Cooperative Corporation, 1990).

18. Stephen Vincent Benet, "The Mountain Whippoorwill, Or, How Hillbilly Jim Won the Great Fiddler's Prize," From *Selected Works of Stephen Vincent Benet*. Rinehart, 1925.

19. McNeil 1940.

20. Wiggins 1987, 85.

21. A small place on the edge of Marlinton, Pocahontas County.

22. Courtesy of Bob Bright, author unknown.

23. Millie Hammons, interview by author, Adolph, W.Va., 1 September 1993, Augusta Collection. See also Anthony Swiger, interview by author, videotape recording, 29 June 1995, Augusta Collection.

24. The actual time period in which Edden and this wife, Caroline Riddle, cohabitated was three weeks (Cuthbert 1982).

25. William S. and Ceil Baring-Gould, eds., *The Annotated Mother Goose* (1962; reprint, Cleveland: World Publishing, 1967), 86-87. A later, similar rhyme has an ending where the fiddler says: "If I should give (up) my fiddle, / They'll think I have gone mad; / For many a joyful day, / My fiddle and I have had."

26. Millie Hammons, interview, 1 September 1993.

27. Ibid. See also Anthony Swiger, interview, 29 June 1995, Augusta Collection.

28. Gus McGee, interview by author, Elkins, W.Va., 30 March 1994, Augusta Collection.

29. Currence and Minnie Hammonds field recorded songs with interview by author, Huttonsville, W.Va., 2 August 1983, Augusta Collection.

30. Cuthbert and Jabbour, eds., 1984.

31. Marion O'Brien, interview, 21 August 1989.

32. Cuthbert and Jabbour, eds., 1984. Booklet accompanying recording of music.

33. If from Ulster, the Hammonses are heirs to a particularly strong bardic tradition. One early king there had three thousand bards at his disposal, confiscated through wars in neighboring kingdoms. An ancient Northern Irish verse indicates the respect that area had for musicians:

Musician, herald, bard, thrice may'st thou be reknowned,
And with three several wreaths immortally be crowned.
Bonwick (1894), 41

Minstrelsy was sanctioned through government statues and guilds into the late eighteenth century in the region. Cohen and Greenwood, *The Buskers: A History of Street Entertainment* (London: David and Charles, 1981, 42-44.

34. Byrne 1940, 53.

35. Currence Hammonds, interview by Michael Kline, Davis and Elkins College oral history class, date unrecorded, Augusta Collection.

36. In central West Virginia, poor farm is the standard term for a home for paupers operated by the state or county.

37. Ernie Carpenter, interview by author, Sutton, W.Va., 23 September 1988, Augusta Collection.

38. Cuthbert 1982, 46-49. Edden Hammons plays fifty-two tunes during two sessions in the collection of Louis Watson Chappell.

39. *The Edden Hammonds Collection*, recording with descriptive booklet, West Virginia Univ., 1984.

40. Cuthbert 1982, 47-48.

41. Fleischhauer and Jabbour, eds., 1973.

42. *Shakin' Down the Acorns*, Rounder Records, 0018.

43. *Old-Time Banjo Anthology*, two volumes, Marimac, AHS-004 and AHS-005, cassette recordings.

44. *The Fiddling of Burl Hammons: The Diller Collection*, AHR-017, and *Old-Time Banjo: The Diller Collection*, AHR-019.

45. Correspondence from Gus Meade, 31 July 1989, and Marion O'Brien interview, 21 August 1989.

Chapter 5. Go Ye Forth and Preach the Gospel

1. Zimmerman Papers, West Virginia State Archive, 116

2. The original Scots signers of the National Covenant of 1638 and the Solemn League and Covenant of 1643 were resisting the Church of England. They, and people who were followers of the principles of the original signers, were termed "covenanters."

3. Jones 1960, 19-20.

4. Sutton 1919.

5. Price 1963, 494, 516.

6. John Powell, preface to George Pullen Jackson, *Spiritual Folk-Songs of Early America* (1937; reprint, Gainesville: Univ. of Florida Press, 1952), viii.

7. Ibid. The "Why should the devil" quote comes from William Chappell, in *Old English Popular Music*, ed. H. Ellis Wooldridge (London: Chappell, 1893), ix.

8. Jackson 1933, 54.

9. For a full discussion of the religious experience of this period in the American back country, see James G. Leyburn, *The Scotch-Irish: A Social History* (Chapel Hill: Univ. of North Carolina Press, 1962), 271-95.

10. Don Yoder, *Pennsylvania Spirituals* (Lancaster: Pennsylvania Folklife Society, 1961), 4-5.

11. Fischer 1989, 703-8, describes how the "field meeting" of the north British/Scottish border was prevalent among backcountry inhabitants. M.W. Zimmerman (Papers), who chronicled early religion in West Virginia, states: "The camp-meeting system, always so popular with the Methodists, was introduced it is claimed by the Presbyterians. Many trace common usage of folk music in a religious context to the period of the 'Great Awakenings' a time of mass religious conversion" (Blaustein 1975, 17).

12. Yoder 1961, 41, and Jackson 1933, 215.

13. Jackson 1937, 7.

14. Yoder 1961, 1-7.

15. Jeff Todd Titon, *Powerhouse For God* (Austin: Univ. of Texas Press, 1988), 219-24.

16. This piece has been found in northern West Virginia and western Pennsylvania by Bayard 1982, and is in Jackson 1952, 12, as "I Believe In Being Ready."

17. Currence Hammonds, field recording by author, Huttonsville, W.Va. 3 January 1977, Augusta Collection.

18. Millie Hammons, field recording by author, Adolph, W.Va., 31 August 1993, Augusta Collection.

19. The words menstruation and moon are the same in many languages (Harding 1971, 20-24).

20. European peasants believe that the moon menstruates during its period of waning, and know it as "moon blood." Ibid., 55.

21. Traditional verse to song, "When the Saints Go Marching In," recorded by the Lilly Brothers of Raliegh County. See the Lilly Brothers and Don Stover, County, 729.

22. As sung by Maggie Hammons Parker. Recording, *The Hammons Family, A Study of a West Virginia Family's Traditions*, 1973.

23. Jackson 1952, 276.

24. Surveyors confirm Elmer's thinking on this point. Elmer himself was a surveyor, as were several of his West Virginia ancestors. He had an old brass ship's compass that came down through his family, which he used for surveying.

25. Elmer Mollohan, interview by author, Hacker Valley, W.Va., 11 October 1989.

26. William Griffee Brown, *History Of Nicholas County, West Virginia* (1954; reprint, Richwood, W.Va.: Comstock, 1981), 281-391.

27. Ibid., 144-45.

28. Brown, in Bean, et. al, 1996, 36.

29. Hamill 1945.

30. Harold Wentworth, *American Dialect Dictionary* (New York: Thomas Y. Crowell Company, 1944), 123. See also Hans Nathan, 1996.

31. I collected this song from Everett White, who had it from his Braxton County grandfather, Nelson Wine. See AHR-007 for recorded version. Nelson Wine was collected by Cox, 1925.

32. Fischer 1986 makes numerous religious comparisons and distinctions among people of these two regions.

33. At the early Colonial date of 1691, in Princess Anne County, Virginia, during one term of court there were three indictments for fiddling and dancing on the Sabbath (Bruce 1907, 161). In the 1690s, a slave was paid to fiddle at a house while the master, a clergyman, was away. The dance lasted from Saturday night until 7 A.M. Sunday morning. Needless to say there was hell to pay when he returned home. From Accomac County Records, see Philip Alexander Bruce, *Social Life of Virginia in the Seventeenth Century* (Lynchburg: J.P. Bell Company, 1907), 186-89.

34. Butler 1990, 19.

35. Ibid.

36. Sutton 1919, 276.

37. Ernie Carpenter, interview by author, Sutton, W.Va., 9 February 1989, Augusta Collection. There are stories from Tennessee where people have found fiddles enclosed in the walls of old houses. Presumably this was done by fiddlers so as not to be tempted by their instruments (Wolfe 1972, 17).

38. Newman Ivey White, ed., *The Frank C. Brown Collection of North Carolina Folklore*, 7 vols., (Durham: Duke Univ. Press, 1952-64), 637-38. Brown identifies this in black tradition in this Civil War–era song, titled "I Picked My Banjo Too." The fourth of nine verses says:

> I was born in North Carolina
> And raised up as a slave,
> And no one ever told me
> I had a soul to save.
>
> *7th Verse*
> Until he called for mourners
> And tears stood in my eyes,
> I bowed beneath the altar,
> And I laid my banjo by.
>
> *8th Verse*
> I prayed for sovereign mercy,
> And Jesus filled my cup.
> I went home rejoicing,
> And I burned my banjo up.

39. Ernie Carpenter, interview, 17 January 1986.

40. Carl Davis, interview by author, Augusta Workshop Master Artist Visit, 8 April 1989, Augusta Collection. See also Milnes, *Fiddles, Snakes, and Dog Days*, 1997.

41. Sarah Singleton, interview by author, Salt Lick, Braxton County, W.Va., 26 October 1988. This motif has turned up often in the folktales of the Appala-

chian region, and "getting the call to preach" is considered a normal aspect of religious life among rural preachers of the region. See Fischer 1989, 719.

42. Dewees 1904, 10-11.

43. Pheoba Parsons, interview, 30 March 1989.

44. George Pullen Jackson, *Spiritual Folk-Songs of Early America* (1933; reprint, New York: Dover, 1964), gives a complete discussion of the history of shape-note music in the Upland South.

45. Clyde Case, interview by author, Duck, W.Va., 16 August 1988.

46. Jackson, 1964, *Spiritual Folk-Songs of Early America*, footnote to page 46.

47. The author assisted Michael Kline in recording this congregation's "lined out" singing for a radio production, *The Homeplace*, West Virginia Public Radio, 1981, Augusta Collection.

Chapter 6. Poor Little Omie Wise

1. Thelma Andrews, interview by author, Elkins, W.Va., 25 May 1993, Augusta Collection.

2. See Cuthbert, ed., 1982. Chappell's collection, made between 1937 and 1947, is the most important work because he made recordings. Several others, however, collected and published texts and music. John Harrington Cox, Ruth Ann Musick, Carey Woofter, Patrick Gainer, Marie Boette, and Jim Bush are ballad and folksong collectors in West Virginia who had success finding treasured old material (see bibliography).

3. White, ed. 1962, 690.

4. Before their deaths, D.K. Wilgus and Wayland Hand brought this document to light. Craven's text of "Poor Naomi" was first reprinted by *The Randleton News*, Randleton, N.C. See White, ed. 1962, 692-93. Craven's text is published in *The Viking Book of Folk Ballads of the English-Speaking World*, ed. Albert Friedman (New York: Viking Press, 1966), along with a tune transcribed from Victor 21625 (1927).

5. See Mattie Taylor, "Conversations with Aunt Harriet" in *Kentucky Folk-Lore and Poetry Magazine* (October 1928), 4.

6. See H.M. Belden, ed. *The University of Missouri Studies* 15, no. 1 (January 1, 1940), 322-24; also Vance Randolph, *Ozark Folksongs*, (1946; revised by Univ. of Missouri, 1980). For a thorough discussion of early regional variants, see Belden (above) and Malcomb Laws, *Native American Balladry* (Philadelphia: American Folklore Society, 1964).

7. Leroy Wingfield, interview by author, Beverly, W.Va., 28 May 1992.

8. This information was collected from oral tradition by the Chapmans, but there are also confession precedents in the North Carolina accounts. See White, ed., 1962, 693.

9. The Chapmans graciously turned over a folder of written notes to me that they had made about their conversations with area residents.

10. Randolph County, West Virginia, Courthouse Records.

11. Ibid.

12. In the local dialect, names ending in *a* are pronounced as though they

end in *ie.* Thus, Ruhama becomes Ruhami and Naoma becomes Naomi, or they may be shortened to Amie and Omie.

13. See Laws 1964, F-4.

14. See recording, "Little Omie," in *The Hammons Family: A Study of a West Virginia Family's Traditions*, 1973. The author collected a similar version in Fayette County, West Virginia, that places the incident in that region. See *Folksongs and Ballads*, vol. 3, AHR-009. The author collected another variant in McDowell County, West Virginia, that has Lewis being captured in "old Mt. Airy town." See Dock Scott field recording by author, War, W.Va., 29 April 1994, Augusta Collection.

15. The author collected a written copy or "ballad" of the song from Mrs. Howard Louk, of Huttonsville, which is similar to the Robison text, including the standard line, "In Randolph County now her body lies."

16. *West Virginia Folklore* 7, no. 4, (Summer 1957), 66-67. This collected version indicates widespread belief of the West Virginia claim to the song and incident.

17. From Amanda Ellen Eddy, Rivesville, West Virginia, published in *West Virginia Folklore* 7, no. 4 (Summer 1957). This same issue published "Little Loney," from a Mrs. Howard Glasscock of Fairmont, West Virginia, which is a version based of the older Craven text from North Carolina.

18. Marie Boette, *Singa Hipsy Doodle and Other Folk Songs of West Virginia* (Parsons, W.Va.: McClain Printing, 1971), 129.

19. See Jim Comstock, ed., *West Virginia Songbag* (Richwood, W.Va.: Comstock, 1974), 449-501, and *The West Virginia Encyclopedia*, vol. 23 (Richwood, W.Va.: Comstock, 1976), 5142. These and other West Virginia references (notes 16 and 17 above) perhaps tell us more about nativism affecting regional literature than about historic incidents commemorated through folk song.

20. See "Discovery Rekindles Murder Mystery, 'Ballad of Naomi Wise' Written to Chronicle the Murder," *Inter-Mountain* (Elkins, W.Va., 14 September 1992, and "Ballad of Naomi Wise Filled With Local Lore," *The Allegheny Journal* (W.Va.), 9 August 1973.

Chapter 7. Oral Traditions

1. Andrew Picken, *Traditionary Stories of Old Families, and Legendary Illustrations of Family History*, 2 vols. (London: Long and Green, 1833), I: v-vi. In Allen and Montell, *From Memory to History* (Nashville: American Association for State and Local History, 1981), vii.

2. Byrne 1940, 283.

3. Words from Melvin Wine. Sherman Hammons sang, "Yea, ho, the John B. Hosey" on the chorus and said the words were about a man named John B. Hosey, who ran a large flock of sheep on the head of Williams River in Pocahontas County.

4. Currence Hammonds, interview by Michael Kline, Davis and Elkins College oral history class. Augusta Collection. Christeson 1973 notes the tune bears considerable resemblance to "Rachel Rae," found in some of the older Scottish tune collections as well as in White's *Solo Banjoist* (Boston, 1896).

Some fiddlers play the first part of this tune differently and use a portion of "The Forked Deer," as published in *Virginia Reels* by George Willigin in Baltimore in the 1840s. It is a version that is very perplexing for the accompanist. Forked Deer is a floating title (Bayard, 1986). A minstrel-era version was titled the "Forkedair Jig," and the earliest Forked Deer title was published in Knauff's Virginia reels, Vol. 1, No. 4, 1839 (see, Cuthbert and Jabbour, 1984).

  5. Dan Ben-Amos, quoted in George Schoemaker, ed., 1990, 3.

  6. Thompson, B557.3, from Tom Peete Cross, *Motif-Index of Early Irish Literature* (Bloomington, Indiana, 1952). Currence Hammond's tale was produced on a West Virginia Public Radio show, *The Homeplace* by Michael Kline. Burl Hammons tells his similar story on the recording *Shakin' Down the Acorns*, Rounder-0018.

  7. Joseph Wright, *An Elementary Middle English Grammer* (London: Oxford University Press, second edition 1928) 34. "The io became ie in early ME. Then it became a rising diphthong medially written ie, ye." Examples are "dyep" for "deep," "dyere" for "dear" or "deer," and "lyese" for "lose."

  8. With the passing of Old English, some words with strong forms changed. Oke, as the past tense of ache, became ached, and trut became treated. These forms were common in Old English, and spent about 100 years changing into Middle English. Thus, clomb or clumb became climbed. Phoeba still uses clumb, fit for fought, and rid for rode. She also uses Middle English forms like hissen to show possession like mine, where the n sound shows the possessive form. Paul D. Brandes and Jeutonne Brewer, *Dialect Clash in America: Issues and Answers* (Metuchen, N.J.: Scarecrow, 1977), 291; quotes from Hans Kurath and Sherman Kuhn, eds., *Middle English Dictionary* (Ann Arbor: Univ. of Michigan Press, 1952).

  9. Buchan 1984, 250. See also Archie Green, "Hillbilly Music: Source and Symbol," *Journal of American Folklore* 78, no. 309 (1965): 204-5.

  10. Many old timers use the term tush, especially to describe the tusks or "tushes" on a wild hog, but not limited to that species. The word is archaic, was first found in the year 1050, and was used until the nineteenth century, but it is still used among older people in West Virginia.

  11. Henry W. Hill, Arthur F. Hill, and Alfred E. Hill, *Antonio Stradivari, His Life and Work* (1902; reprint, New York: Dover 1963), 59, 224.

  12. Bud Sandy, interview, 5 November 1987.

  13. I collected these verses from Everett White, Florena Duling, and Myrtle Hammons (Augusta Collection), and from Phyllis Boyens, who sang with her father, Nimrod Workman. Rounder-0076.

  14. See Wolfe, ed., 1991, 52.

  15. See W.K. McNeil, *Southern Mountain Folksongs* (Little Rock: August House, 1993), 72-73.

  16. *The Fiddling of Burl Hammons*, AHR-017.

  17. Fischer 1989, 685-86.

  18. Bennett documented this tradition in Newfoundland. See Margaret Bennett, *The Last Stronghold: Scottish Gaelic Traditions in Newfoundland* (Breakwater Press, 1989), 68.

  19. Fischer 1989, 665, makes the case that the clan system of the north

British border country, and the extent of nicknames needed to keep people straight within such a system, was a tradition carried to the American back country by the north British and Scots-Irish people who were the major immigrants to Appalachia.

20. Hardway 1994, 155.

21. Murrell Hamrick may be heard on AHR-020, *Old-Time Fiddling in Randolph County.*

22. Byrne 1940, 121.

23. Currence Hammonds, interview by author, Huttonsville, W. Va., 11 September 1979, Augusta Collection.

Chapter 8. Black George

1. The "Ought to Ought" rhyme is widely reported. See Jeff Todd Titon, *Early Downhome Blues* (Urbana, Chicago, London: Univ. of Illinois Press, 1977), 15. Another racial rhyme collected by the author in Braxton County:

> On a cold frosty morning, the nigger 'peared good
> With his axe on his shoulder, he went to the wood;
> He had nothing to eat but a little hog fat,
> And the white folks they kind of grumbled 'bout that.

This was collected by Talley (see Wolfe, ed., 1990).

2. The first documented instance of African Americans playing the fiddle occurs in the late seventeenth century. See Epstein, 1977, 21.

3. Blaustein 1975, 18.

4. Jabbour 1993, 29.

5. We get a good idea of how music spread on the river through Collins's journals (Roush 1985, 1986).

6. Frank George, interview by author, videotape recording, 23 August 1995, Augusta Collection.

7. Charles Wolfe, *The Devil's Box* (Nashville and London: The Country Music Foundation Press and Vanderbilt Univ. Press, 1997), 68-77.

8. Fleischhauer and Jabbour 1973. The following is reported by Sutton (1919, 311), presumably about a relative of Lacy's, and who could easily have been present. It documents house dance parties and violence among the Granny's Creek African Americans in 1916: "During the Christmas holidays of 1916, while at a dance at a house on Granny's creek, Hank Haymond, a colored man, shot Wm. Lacy, colored. The wounded man was taken to a hospital at Clarksburg, but lived only a few hours."

9. See *The Fiddling of Burl Hammons: The Diller Collection*, AHR-017.

10. Currence Hammonds told me he learned fiddle and banjo tunes directly from ex-slaves in the Huttonsville area. Several of Currence's tunes, like "Sandy Boys" and "Rock Old Liza Jane," had words about old "massa." Currence Hammonds, interview by author, 18 March 1977, Augusta Collection.

11. Cauthen 1989, 12, from Gilbert Chase, *America's Music: From the Pil-*

grims to the Present. (New York: McGraw Hill, 1955), 435. Cauthen documents early black influence on Alabama fiddling.

12. See Jabbour in Worley and Webb 1994.

13. "Breakdown" has been used since the early nineteenth century to signify a type of slave dance. Abrahams documents the word coming from the "breaking down" or harvesting of the corn, part of the corn shucking rituals and frolics that he documents widely throughout the South. See Roger Abrahams, *Singing the Master* (New York: Penguin Books, 1992), 102, 309.

14. Marshall Stearns and Jean Stearns, *Jazz Dance: The Story of American Vernacular Dance* (New York: Shirmer Books, 1979), 49-50. See also Susan Spalding 1995 for African American influences on Appalachian dance forms.

15. Blaustein 1975, 24.

16. The Jim Crow genealogy begins in African American tradition, from which the tune came. Alleged to have been based on a real person, Jim Crow became a blackface song and dance act in 1832. His persona, the rough plantation darky, is the antithesis of the northern black "dandy." He roved with troublemaking mummers in Philadelphia in 1834, he turns up on the British stage as early as 1836, and he ends up representing his race in discriminatory law. See Eric Lott, "Blackface and Blackness: The Minstrel Show in American Culture," in *Inside the Minstrel Mask: Readings in Nineteenth-Century Blackface Minstrelsy,* ed. Annemarie Bean, James V. Hatch, and Brooks McNamara (Hanover and London: Wesleyan Univ. Press, 1996).

17. Bayard 1969, xv.

18. Ibid. Bayard refers to Richard Henebry, *A Handbook of Irish Music* (London: Longmans, Green & Co., Ltd., 1928) 67.

19. Wolfe, ed., 1991.

20. Bud Sandy, interview, 5 November 1987.

21. Hobart Blake, interview by author, 26 May 1988, Augusta Collection.

22. George Melton (heard on AHR-013) says he learned his tunings from Tyson Moss, who claimed to have learned them from "Nigger Milt." George Melton, interview by author, tape recording, Rosedale, W.Va., 25 March 1988, Augusta Collection.

23. James C. Klotter, "The Black South and White Appalachia," in Turner and Cabbell 1985, 51.

24. Maynard Blake, interview by author, 23 June 1988, Augusta Collection.

25. Melvin Wine, interview by author, Copen, W.Va., 8 October 1987, Augusta Collection. A ditty to this tune is sung by Rita Emerson, of Gilmer County, as "Chippy Get Your Hair Cut."

26. Bud Sandy, interview, 5 November 1987.

27. Tallmadge 1983 quotes John Edmund Stealey III, "Slavery and the Western Virginia Salt Industry," *The Journal of Negro History* 59 (April 1974), 105-31.

28. Robert Winan's study reported in Karen Linn, *That Half Barbaric Twang: The Banjo in Popular Culture* (Urbana: Univ. of Illinois Press, 1991), 42.

29. John P. Hale, *Trans-Allegheny Pioneers,* 3d edition (1886; reprint, Radford, Va., 1971), 150.

30. Louis Chappell published thirty variants of "John Henry" and numerous fragments along with extensive oral history in his exhaustive study of the legend in *John Henry, A Folk-Lore Study* (Port Washington, N.Y.: Kennikat, 1932). Reprinted in Comstock (WVS), 1974.

31. Conway 1995, 138; and Lott, in Bean, Hatch and McNamara, 1996, 5.

32. Paul Gartner, "Wilson Douglas—A Determined Mind," in *The Old-Time Herald*. 5, no. 2 (Winter 1995-1996), 38.

33. Jim Knicely sings the line: "The worst man that lived was old Rockefeller," field recording by author, 21 February 1991, Augusta Collection.

34. Conway 1995, 102.

35. James T. Laing, "The Negro Miner in West Virginia," in Turner and Cabbell, 1985, 71.

36. Brooks Hardway, interview, 17 September 1988.

37. This instrument is now in the Augusta Collection.

38. Melvin Wine, interview, 8 October 1988.

39. Everett White, interview by author, 20 December 1988, Augusta Collection. Everett, a fine ballad singer, may be heard on AHR-007.

40. Julia Johnson, interview by author, Long Run, Braxton County, 11 April 1988, Augusta Collection.

41. Ernie Carpenter, interview by author, Sutton, W.Va., 2 November 1987, Augusta Collection.

42. Green 1965.

43. Titon 1977, 203-10.

44. Ibid., 200, and Green 1965, 207.

45. Tribe 1984 details Hutchinson's career. His music may be heard on a reissue, *Frank Hutchison*, Rounder, 1007, and *The West Virginia Hills*, Old Homestead, OHCS-141.

46. For strong documentation of this, see Abrahams 1992.

47. Titon 1977, 245-54.

Chapter 9. Dancin' and Fightin'

1. Milton W. Humphreys letter published in the *Journal of the Braxton Historical Society* 19, no. 4 (December 1991), 15.

2. William Christian ("Rattlesnake Bill") Dodrill, *Moccasin Tracks and Other Imprints* (1915; reprint, Parsons, W.Va.: McClain, 1974), 62.

3. The formalities (bow to your partner, etc.) at the beginning of this caller's dances show aspects of the quadrille figures that were popularized in the nineteenth century. In *West Virginia Square Dances* (Country Dance and Song Society of America, 1982), Bob Dalsemer notes that dances in West Virginia lack the formalities found in dances stemming from nineteenth-century quadrille figures. While whole quadrille figures are not evident in Braxton County, this vestige of the form exists. Burman-Hall 1974 reports the disappearance of the "courtesy movements" in Southern square dancing. Wolfe 1972, 18, quotes an interview with Sam McGee, who observed three figures to a set in his youth (1910) in rural Tennessee. In Braxton County years ago, two figures, or "changes," made up the set, but that is only in memory today.

4. Jack Mayse, interview by author, 4 May 1988, Augusta Collection.

5. Currence Hammonds, interview by Michael Kline, tape recording, Elkins, W.Va., 12 January 1982, Augusta Collection. In sixteenth- and seventeenth-century England, longways dances (reels) were common. Once established in this country, the reels or longways dances died out in the nineteenth century, with few exceptions, such as in New England. Surprisingly, longways dances called "contras," after a French form, lingered among the Puritans (Blaustein 1975, 11-14) and have now been revived nationally.

6. Ibid. A description of dances in one small Braxton County village, circa 1920, notes, "Everyone in Bower could dance." Annie Dulaney, "I Remember Bower," *Journal of the Braxton Historical Society* 3, no. 3 (25 September 1995), 29-37.

7. This seems to be a standard price for the time period. A "set," however, included two dances. See Donald Andrew Beisswenger 1997, 60.

8. Ibid.

9. Epstein 1977, 211-12.

10. Ivor Evans, ed., *Brewer's Dictionary of Phrase and Fable* (New York: Harper and Row, 1989), 247. "The place where barnyard fowls are fed is the walk, and if there is more than one cock, they will fight for the supremacy of this domain."

11. Abrahams 1992, 212, 313, documents this practice in Southern plantation life.

12. Winter 1996, 224.

13. Phil Jamison, "The Cakewalk," in *The Old-Time Herald* (November 1992-January 1993), 13-16. An extension and public demonstration of the form can be seen in the Mummers Parade held every year in Philadelphia where, until recently, men in black-face strutted about with hands held aloft in what is the classic cakewalk strut. Because of public indignation during the era of civil rights consciousness, objection to white mummers strutting in blackface brought about a discontinuation of the practice. Today, white strutters do it in whiteface, adding still more racial twists to the tradition.

14. Christeson 1973, 181.

15. Ralph Durrett, *Talbott Community* (self published, 1989). The author of this local history of a Barbour County community remarks on the frequency of cake and pie socials followed by cakewalks at schoolhouses just after the turn of the century. He also says it was customary at one time to include a contest for the prettiest girl. Voters had to pay a nickel to vote. This led to so many arguments and fights by the contestant's beaus that the contests were discontinued. All of the above activities were usually involved in fund raising efforts for community organizations.

16. Brooks Hardway, interview, 17 September 1988.

17. Howard Hamrick, interview by author, Valley Head, W.Va., 17 November 1992, Augusta Collection.

18. Russell's banjo music may be heard on *Old-Time Banjo Anthology*, vol. 1, Marimac, AHS-4.

19. Ott Scott, interview by author, Lewis County, 4 April 1988, Augusta Collection.

20. Ibid.

21. James M. Beall, in *Journal of the Braxton Historical Society* 24, no. 3 (September 1996), 16-17.

22. Maynard Blake, interview, 23 June 1988.

23. Phoeba Parsons, interview, 30 March 1989.

24. *Nicholas Chronicle*, 23 July 1914

25. The Mullins family, as with the Hammons family, had immigrated from Kentucky to Wyoming County and then to Webster County about the time of the Civil War (Hardway 1994, 16).

26. Marion O'Brien, interview, 21 August 1989.

27. *Nicholas Chronicle*, 29 July 1914.

28. Nicholas County Court Records, 30 October 1914.

29. In the eighteenth century, in areas where the law was either distant or nonexistent, it was the practice to fight it out to determine a victor. This Hammonds/Fletcher feud embraces vestiges of this line of thought as demonstrated by Maston Hammons's reluctance to cooperate with the law even though he faced certain conviction. William Price (1901, 564-65) reports an incident in a pre-Revolutionary Randolph County land dispute (roughly thirty miles from the above incident) where this appeared to be the only recourse in settling the controversy: "it was finally decided to settle the dispute by fair fight, fist and skull," and "The ground was chosen for the contest," In this dispute, an Andrew Crouch defeated a William White and assumed legal ownership of the land.

30. Christian's banjo playing is on *Old-Time Banjo Anthology*, vol. 1, Marimac, AHS-4.

31. Leyburn 1962, 45-46. Leyburn traces this cultural trait to Scots-Irish history and social custom. He notes that the chronic insecurity of life before (and well after) 1600 produced a deep-seated practice of settling one's own disputes through one's own efforts. This "might makes right" attitude stems from centuries of living under that rule in feudal Scotland.

32. Currence Hammonds, interview by Michael Kline and Bob Dalsemer, 2 July 1979, Augusta Collection.

Chapter 10. Hard Times and Jo-Heads

1. Blackie's guitar playing may be heard on *Blackie Cool: Back Memories*, AHR-002C.

2. Woody Simmons, interview by author, videotape recording, Mill Creek, W.Va., 13 August 1996, Augusta Collection.

3. Howard Hamrick, interview, 17 November 1992.

4. Kenton Sears, interview by author, Sutton, W.Va., 10 December 1991, Augusta Collection.

5. French Carpenter to Ken Davidson, 8 March 1965.

6. Dena Knicely, interview by author, tape recording, Friar's Hill, W.Va., 5 June 1990, Augusta Collection.

7. Clyde Case, interview by author, 7 November 1987, Augusta Collection.

8. Linn 1991, 32.

9. Ibid., 5-39.

10. Jenes Cottrell made numerous banjos with torque converters from old Buick transmissions for rims and sycamore and walnut necks. See Sylvia Cottrell O'Brien, videotaped interview by author, Clay County, W.Va., 21 March 1995.

11. Conway (1995, chap. 4) documents recent makers of this type of instrument. Glassie (1968, 22-24) points out that some makers in North Carolina continued to cling to the old style of both instrument and playing technique. He observes that "The interaction of popular and folk cultures has not resulted exclusively in modifications of folk culture." Glassie shows how in some aspects of folk culture, e.g. food, it works the other way around.

12. See notes to *Old-Time Banjo Anthology*, vols. 1-2, AHS-004 and 005, 1991.

13. Jim Bollman, Dick Kimmel, and Doug Unger, "A History of Vega/ Fairbanks Banjos," *Pickin' Magazine* (June 1978).

14. The overwhelming evidence attributes this style of playing to African origins. Epstein (1977, 30) notes an instance in 1694 where a black is described while playing a "banza": "the instrument was played by plucking and striking the strings." Tallmadge (1983, 172) reports a Georgia instance where, in 1838-39, a banjo is thumped. Scholars agree that the downstroke used by old-time banjo players is of African origin (see Conway 1995, chap. 5).

15. White, ed., 1962, 427.

16. See Epstein 1977, 359-62.

17. Conway 1995, 163, fig. 92. Interestingly enough, most words ending in "a" get changed to the "r" or "y" sound, thus, if you planted the word bania in West Virginia, it would soon be called a "banyer," which is getting close to banjer.

18. Jennings Morris, interview by author, Cowen, W.Va., 25 January 1990, Augusta Collection. Morris wanted to learn to play in picking styles after hearing classical players, such as Van Eps, Ossman, and Bacon, on 78 rpm recordings.

19. Wolfe, ed. 1991, *Thomas W. Talley's Negro Folk Rhymes*. This work shows that a great many old-time tunes have lyris and motifs found in black tradition.

20. Tunes by the "Old Christmas," "Old Christmas Morning," and "Christmas Morning" titles are known in the Wine, Humphreys, Hammons, and Carpenter families. Old Christmas (January 6) came about upon Britain's acceptance of the Gregorian calendar to replace the older Julian.

Chapter 11. Hog Harps, Waterswivels, and Fence Scorpions

1. William Walker, ed., *Christian Harmony* (Christian Harmony Publishing, revised 1958), 339.

2. This last anecdote was related by Loyal Jones of Berea, Kentucky.

3. Cathleen Hinkle, of Greenbrier County, more than ninety years old, convinced me that dulcimers and fiddles, played together, are hard to beat. Interview by author, Lewisburg, W.Va., 10 February 1994, Augusta Collection.

4. Lola Cutlip, interview by author, 26 April 1988, and Hobart Blake, interview, 26 May 1988, Augusta Collection.

5. The word dulcimer appears in the King James Version of the Bible in chapters three, five, ten, and fifteen of the Book of Daniel. Though believed to

refer to the hammered dulcimer, it is only a vague reference to a stringed instrument. There is no evidence to support the existence of the hammered instrument in biblical times. Also referred to are viols, etc., that are of much later invention.

6. The best collection of these instruments is at the Henry C. Mercer Museum at Doylestown, Pennsylvania.

7. L. Allen Smith, *A Catalog of Pre-Revival Appalachian Dulcimers* (Columbia and London: Univ. of Missouri Press, 1983).

8. The word "sheitholt" translates to fine-wood.

9. Patrick Gainer, *Folk Songs from the West Virginia Hills* (Grantsville, W.Va.: Seneca Books, 1975), 169. Gainer was attacked for shoddy scholarship, specifically by David Whisnant, who in the *Appalachian Journal* 5, no. 1 (Autumn 1977), makes the claim that Gainer's book "is too superficial to be of much use." Gainer responded in "Issues and Resources in Folk Music in West Virginia," in *West Virginia Folklore Journal* 20, no. 1. Although tape recorders were in wide use at the time of his collecting activities, Gainer preferred to transcribe the words and music he was collecting and then publish it. As early as the 1940s, John and Alan Lomax were redefining "authentic" folk music in a way that differed from Gainer's later work, and using recordings as a best means of presenting traditional folk music to the public. See Rosenberg, 1993, 13-14.

10. In *The Nicholas County News Leader* in 1968, accompanying a picture of old dulcimer maker Henry B. Bryant, Gainer says, ". . . what we think of as the dulcimer of today is not sailing under its true name. The Asiatics had a three-string viol called the rebab, and later the rebec, which is probably the true ancestor of what American pioneers called the dulcimer. . . . Where the names became corrupted is a problem for the scholars of antiquity, for Mr. Bryant and the many others who remember the three-stringed instrument of their youth will continue to call it a dulcimer, and the word 'Rebec' will remain lost with the ages."

11. In his introduction, John Jacob Niles (*The Ballad Book of John Jacob Niles* [Dover 1970]) describes his theory of the dulcimer's origins: "As one who has played the dulcimer much of his life and made all the dulcimers he uses, I am convinced that the traditional mountain dulcimer is a development of two instruments—one, the rebec, a medieval English instrument of three strings played with a bow, and the other, the crowd, a Celtic instrument, having from three to six strings, also played with a bow. In my collection, I have a dulcimer of 4 strings, intended to be played with a bow; the bow, with a few remaining horsehairs, came with the instrument." Also see Michael Murphy, *The Appalachian Dulcimer Book* (Folksay Press, 1976), 19. Murphy writes: "There are several reasons why the Appalachian dulcimer's ancestry is difficult to trace with precision. Currently, there are no old living dulcimer makers or players." In fact, in central West Virginia alone there were numerous old dulcimer makers, and scores of old traditional players in 1976 when this book was published. Despite this oversight, Murphy establishes strong ties between the Appalachian dulcimer and the German, French, Swedish, Norwegian, and Icelandic instruments of the fretted zither family from which the mountain dulcimer is related/descended.

12. Margaret Downie, *History of the Rebec* (Ph.D. diss., West Virginia Univ., 1982).

13. Ralph Lee Smith, *The Story of the Dulcimer* (Cosby, Tenn.: Crying Creek Publishers, 1986).

14. Eaton 1973, 202. Eaton notes: "Might it not be possible that the Kentucky dulcimer was influenced directly by the Pennsylvania German instrument, just as some of the spinning wheels found in the Highlands were undoubtedly copied from models originally made in Pennsylvania?" and "It might reasonably be that the first dulcimer of the (Appalachian) Highland type was an adaptation from the German zither." Don Yoder (1968, 192) lists Eaton, Glassie 1968, and Raines' *The Land of Saddlebags* as published sources of Pennsylvania German influence on Appalachian culture.

15. Charles Seeger, "The Appalachian Dulcimer," in *Journal of American Folklore* 71, no. 279 (January-March 1958), 40-51.

16. Smith R.L. 1986, 9, 37, and Smith, L.A. 1983, 20, 21, 29.

17. Smith, L.A. 1983, 116.

18. Dena Knicely, interview, 21 February 1991. See John Rice Irwin 1973, 70; L. Allen Smith 1983, 20, 21, and 29; and Ralph Lee Smith 1986, 8, 19, and 37, for fretted zithers and dulcimers with bows.

19. Brown 1981, 287, and Dodrill 1915, 76.

20. Dodrill 1915. Dodrill provides some early sketches of the county. Some of Barnett's descendants, the Davis family, did make and play dulcimers.

21. Ibid., 77-8. Dodrill describes Birch River in 1849, listing only two settlers on the river in Webster County besides the Baughman family.

22. Jim Costa, personal collection.

23. Noah Seymour Dasher, *Dasher Family History* (1924) unpublished.

24. Smith, L.A. 1983, 108-11.

25. A straight-sided, fretted zither-type instrument reportedly from Randolph County, may indicate some existence of an older tradition there (author's collection).

26. Patty Looman of Mannington has a collection of fretted dulcimers from the northern part of the state that were gathered by her mother, who traded farm supplies at the family's feed store for musical instruments throughout the early to mid twentieth century.

27. Lola Cutlip, interview by author, 26 April 1988, Exchange, W.Va., Augusta Collection.

28. Smith 1979. The music for the state song, "The West Virginia Hills," learned by all West Virginia school children, was written by one of these Germans, Reverend Engle, at Exchange, Braxton County, in 1885. The old organ on which Reverend Engle composed the song now resides at Davis and Elkins College in Elkins, having arrived as part of the "Comstock Collection."

29. Earl Gerwig, *Gerwig Genealogy*, 1974.

30. Smith 1983, 103-6.

31. Prichard was identified by L. Allen Smith. Jim Costa found an old instrument with a complete, intact label bearing Pritchard's name. Ralph Lee Smith found C.N. Prichard (1839-1904) in census records, listed as an "instrument maker."

32. Junior Lloyd, interview by author, Napier, W.Va., 20 December 1987, Augusta Collection.

33. Beatrice Metheny, interview by author and Stan Gilliam, videotape recording, Lower Mill Creek, Braxton County, Augusta Collection.

34. Reva Fincham, interview by author, 26 April 1988, Augusta Collection.

35. Reva Fincham may be heard playing on *West Virginia Hills: Traditional Dulcimer Music*, AHR-011.

36. Hobart Blake, interview, 26 May 1988.

37. John Davis, interview by author, Sugar Creek, Braxton County, 14 November 1987.

38. Carl Davis, interview by author, 7 March 1988, Augusta Collection.

39. See Milnes, *Fiddles, Snakes, and Dogdays* video, 1997, and *The West Virginia Hills: Traditional Dulcimer Music*, AHR-011.

40. Walter Miller, interview by author, 18 April 1988, Augusta Collection.

41. Paul McKinny, interview by author, 11 June 1991, Vermillion, Ohio, Augusta Collection. Walter Miller and Freeman McKinney are recorded on *West Virginia Hills: Traditional Dulcimer Music*, AHR-011.

42. Smith, L. Allen 1983; Smith, Ralph Lee 1986.

Chapter 12. The Magic String

1. A more reasonable view is presented by Gene Wilhelm Jr., "Appalachian Isolation: Fact or Fiction," in *Appalachia: Its People, Heritage, and Problems*, Frank S. Riddel, ed. (Dubuque, Iowa: Kendall/Hunt, 1974).

2. Jeff Todd Titon, *Early Downhome Blues* (Urbana, Chicago, London: Univ. of Illinois Press, 1977), 201.

3. Green 1965, 207. Green briefly describes the pre-hillbilly era of recorded music. The machine being held by Neal Hammonds in the family photograph is made by Columbia, Model A J, introduced just after the turn of the century. Sometimes carrying a Columbia brand, more often it was sold through Sears and other mail-order houses, under various brand names.

4. Linn 1991, 19.

5. *The Fiddling of Burl Hammons: The Diller Collection*, AHR-017.

6. Laws 1964, F-17.

7. See Roush, ed., 1985 and 1986.

8. Phoeba's modesty prevents her from saying it was the penis bone of a raccoon. This was an amulet of the Indians with whom the Cottrells were trading. It's common for old-timers in central West Virginia to keep one in their pocket for use as a toothpick.

9. See Rosenberg 1993, 14.

10. Cunningham 1990 and 1987. Also see Simpkins, O. Norman, "The Celtic Roots of Appalachian Culture," in *Appalachia: Its People, Heritage, and Problems*, Frank S. Riddel, ed. (Dubuque, Iowa: Kendall/Hunt, 1974).

11. Conway 1995, *xxii*. Conway bases her Celtic-American classification on work by Cunningham (1987). The term "British-American" was widely used by notable scholars, like Samuel Bayard and Cecil Sharp, to represent people of

mixed Irish and Anglo stock (Burman-Hall 1974). More recently, this has fallen into disfavor.

12. This statement was made in a report on West Virginia Public Radio on the 1990 census. Grady McWhiney in *Cracker Culture* (Tuscaloosa: Univerity of Alabama Press, 1988), 3, chides historians for not considering the Germanic heritage of Anglo-Saxons. He then proceeds throughout his book to refer to southern Americans as "Celts," without any regard for their Germanic and Anglo heritage.

13. Gary Gene Smith 1979, 11.

14. Fleischhauer and Jabbour, eds., 1973, 5.

15. Delores Cogar Bright, "The Cowger Family," in *Journal of the Braxton County Historical Society*, 14, no. 3 (September 1986). Gauger was a German who emigrated to Philadelphia in 1736.

16. Fleischhauer and Jabbour, eds. 1973, 5. Currence Hammonds spoke of banjo player Norman Cogar (interview, 2 July 1979). Two Webster County fiddlers with the Cogar surname were documented by Tom Brown (see Cuthbert 1982, 107-8). An unusual dulcimer with a carved top and back in the Looman private collection is attributed to the Cogar family of Webster County. Two Cogar fiddlers in Braxton County, John and Pat, were excellent fiddlers. Forty folk songs and ballads were collected from Lafe Cogar of Calhoun County by Chappell (see Cuthbert 1982, 18-19).

17. Currence Hammonds, interview, 3 January 1977. Bernard Baughman, Currence Baughman, and their sister, Elizabeth Baughman Hammonds, were ballad singers from Webster and Randolph Counties. Elizabeth and her father, David, played dulcimers, and he made them. Mose Coffman and Lee Hammons recognized gifted fiddlers who were Baughmans, including Dave Baughman.

18. Bayard 1982, 8.

19. See Gainer 1975, and John Jacob Niles, *The Ballad Book of John Jacob Niles* (Dover, 1970). As recent as September 1996, in a national music magazine, it was claimed that the Appalachian dulcimer is descended from instruments known in England and Scotland. See David A. Sturgill, "The Appalachian Dulcimer," in *Bluegrass Unlimited*, 31, no. 3 (September 1996), 47-49.

20. David Whisnant, *All That Is Native and Fine* (Chapel Hill and London: Univ. of North Carolina Press, 1983), demonstrates how ballad collectors, and others from points far afield, used the dulcimer as an idealized symbol of mountain life.

21. See Dietz and Olatunji, *Musical Instruments* of Africa (1965).

22. See John Minton, *West African Fiddles Deep in East Texas*, in Patrick B. Mullen and Alan B. Govenar, eds., *Juneteenth Texas: Essays in African-American Folklore*, Publications of the Texas Folklore Society 54 (Denton, Texas: Univ. of North Texas Press, 1996). See also John Rice Irwin 1979, 17, and Vaughn Webb, ed. 1993, 48, for examples of Appalachian gourd fiddles.

23. Malone 1968, 27.

24. Ibid., 5.

25. Conway 1995.

26. Allen Batteau, *The Invention of Appalachia*, (Tucson: Univ. of Arizona Press, 1990), 1.

27. See Jack E. Weller, *Yesterday's People* (Lexington: Univ. of Kentucky Press, 1965), and Harry M. Caudill, *Night Comes to the Cumberlands* (Boston and Toronto: Little, Brown and Co., 1962).

28. See, Norman Adams, interview by author, videotape recording, Gassaway, W.Va., 21 July 1995; Carl Davis, interview by author, videotape recording, 22 March 1995; Carl Degler, interview by author, videotape recording, Elkins, W.Va., 15 February 1995; Phyllis Marks, interview by author, videotape recording, Glenville, W.Va., 20 April 1995; Glen Smith, interview by author, videotape recording, Elizabeth, W.Va., 15 February 1995. Also see Halpert 1995.

29. Couples dancing, including the polka, waltz, schottische, varsouvienne, mazurka, redowa, galop, and two-step, vied with group dancing from 1840 on (Blaustein 1975, 25).

30. John Lilly, while working at the Augusta Heritage Center, initiated this effort through developing the national organization Old-Time Music on the Radio.

Bibliography

Abrahams, Roger D. *Singing the Master: The Emergence of African American Culture in the Plantation South.* New York: Penguin Books, 1992.

Allegheny Journal, The, (W.Va.), 9 August, 1973.

Allen, Barbara, and Lynwood Montell. *From Memory to History.* Nashville: American Association for State and Local History, 1981.

Artley, Malvin Newton. "The West Virginia Country Fiddler: An Aspect of the Folk Music Tradition in the United States." Ph.D. diss., Chicago Musical College, 1955.

Baring-Gould, William S., and Ceil Baring-Gould, eds. *The Annotated Mother Goose.* 1962. Reprint, Cleveland: World Publishing Company, 1967.

Batteau, Allen. *The Invention of Appalachia.* Tucson: Univ. of Arizona Press, 1990.

Bayard, Samuel Preston. *Hill Country Tunes, Instrumental Folk Music of Southwestern Pennsylvania.* 1944. Reprint, New York: American Folklore Society, 1969.

———. *Dance to the Fiddle, March to the Fife, Instrumental Folk Tunes in Pennsylvania.* University Park and London: The Pennsylvania State Univ. Press, 1982.

Beall, James M. "Jesse Knew Now to Avoid Trouble." *Journal of the Braxton Historical Society* 24, no. 3 (Sept. 1996): 16-17.

Bean, Annemarie, James V. Hatch, and Brooks McNamara, eds. *Inside the Minstrel Mask: Readings in Nineteenth-Century Blackface Minstrelsy.* Hanover and London: Weslyan Univ. Press, 1996.

Beisswenger, Donald Andrew. "Fiddling Way Out Yonder: Community and Style in the Music of Melvin Wine." Ph.D. diss., Univ. of Memphis, 1997.

Belden, H.M., ed. "Ballads and Songs Collected by the Missouri Folk-Lore Society." *The University of Missouri Studies.* 15, no. 1 (1 January 1940): 322-24.

Benet, Stephen Vincent. "The Mountain Whiporwill, Or, How Hillbilly Jim Won the Great Fiddler's Prize." From *Selected Works of Stephen Vincent Benet.* Garden City, N.Y.: Rinehart & Company, 1925.

Bennett, Margaret. *The Last Stronghold: Scottish Gaelic Traditions in Newfoundland*. St. Johns: Breakwater Press, 1989.

Blaustein, Richard Jason. "Rethinking Folk Revivalism: Grass-Roots Preservation and Folk Romanticism." In Neil V. Rosenberg, ed., *Transforming Tradition*. Urbana: Univ. of Illinois Press, 1993.

———. "Traditional Music and Social Change: The Old Time Fiddlers Association Movement in the United States." Ph.D. diss., Indiana Univ., 1975.

Blethen, Tyler, and Curtis Wood Jr. *From Ulster to Carolina: The Migration of the Scotch-Irish to Southwestern North Carolina*. Cullowhee, N.C.: Western Carolina Univ., 1983.

Boette, Marie, *Singa Hipsy Doodle and Other Folk Songs of West Virginia*. Parsons, W.Va.: McClain Printing, 1971.

Bollman, Jim, Dick Kimmel and Doug Unger. "A History of Vega/Fairbanks Banjos." *Pickin' Magazine* (June 1978): 26-48.

Bonwick, James. *Irish Druids and Old Irish Religions*. 1894. Reprint, New York: Dorset Press, 1986.

Brandes, Paul D., and Jeutonne Brewer. *Dialect Clash in America: Issues and Answers*. Metuchen, N.J.: The Scarecrow Press, Inc., 1977.

Bright, Delores Cogar. "The Cowger Family." *Journal of the Braxton County Historical Society* 14, no. 3 (September 1986): 1-5.

Brown, Frank C., *The Frank C. Brown Collection of North Carolina Folklore* (see White, Newman Ivey, ed.).

Brown, William Griffee, *History of Nicholas County West Virginia*. 1954. Reprint, Richwood, W.Va.: Dietz Press, 1981.

Bruce, Philip Alexander. *Social Life of Virginia in the Seventeenth Century*, Lynchburg: J.P. Bell Company, 1907.

Buchan, David. *Scottish Tradition: A Collection of Scottish Folk Literature*. London, Boston: Melbourne and Henley, 1984.

Burman-Hall, Linda C. "Southern American Folk Fiddling: Context and Style." Ph.D. diss., Princeton Univ., 1974.

Burt, Struthers. *Philadelphia: Holy Experiment*. New York: Doubleday, Doran & Company, 1945.

Bush, Michael E. "Jim," *Folk Songs of Central West Virginia*, 5 vols., 1977.

Butler, Jon. *Awash in a Sea of Faith: Christianizing the American People*. Cambridge and London: Harvard Univ. Press, 1990.

Byrne, W.E.R. *Tale of the Elk*. Richwood, W.Va.: Mountain State Press, 1940.

———. "The Story of the Christmas Tree." *Journal of the Braxton County Historical Society* 1, no. 1 (25 March 1973): 5-10. First published in Byrne 1940.

Carpenter, French, to Ken Davidson. March 1965. Gus Meade Papers, courtesy of Steve Green.

Carr, Virginia R. "Adam O'Brien." *Journal of the Braxton County Historical Society* 11, no. 3 (25 September 1983).

Caudill, Harry M. *Night Comes to the Cumberlands*. Boston and Toronto: Little, Brown and Co., 1962

———. *A Darkness at Dawn*. Lexington: Univ. Press of Kentucky, 1976.

Cauthen, Joyce H. *With Fiddle and Well Rosined Bow: Old Time Fiddling in Alabama.* Tuscaloosa: Univ. of Alabama Press, 1989.

Chappell, Louis W. *John Henry, A Folk-Lore Study,* Port Washington, N.Y.: Kennikat Press, Inc., 1932. Reprinted in Comstock, *West Virginia Songbag* (Richwood, W.Va.: Comstock, 1974).

Christeson, R.P. *The Old-Time Fiddler's Repertory.* Columbia: Univ. of Missouri Press, 1973.

Cohen, David, and Ben Greenwood. *The Buskers: A History of Street Entertainment.* London: David and Charles, 1981.

Comstock, Jim, ed. *West Virginia Heritage Encyclopedia,* Richwood, W.Va.: Comstock, 1976.

———. *West Virginia Women.* Richwood, W.Va.: Comstock, 1974.

———. *West Virginia Songbag.* Richwood, W.Va.: Comstock, 1974.

Conway, Cecelia. *African Banjo Echoes in Appalachia: A Study of Folk Traditions.* Knoxville: Univ. of Tennessee Press, 1995.

Courlander, Harold. 1963. Reprint, *Negro Folk Music, U.S.A.* New York: Columbia Univ. Press, 1991.

Cox, John Harrington. *Folk-Songs of the South.* Harvard Univ. Press, 1925.

Crayon, Porte. "The Mountains." *Harper's New Monthly Magazine* 45 (June to November, 1872).

Cunningham, Rodger. *Apples on the Flood, The Southern Mountain Experience.* Knoxville: Univ. of Tennessee Press, 1987.

Cuthbert, John A., ed. *West Virginia Folk Music.* Morgantown: West Virginia Univ. Press, 1982.

Cuthbert, John A., and Alan Jabbour, eds. *Edden Hammons, His Life and Music.* Booklet with recording. Morgantown: West Virginia Univ. Press, 1984.

Dalsemer, Robert G. *West Virginia Square Dances.* Country Dance and Song Society of America, 1982.

Dasher, Noah Seymour. Dasher Family History. 1924 (unpublished).

Davenport, Henry B., *Tales of the Elk and Other Stories.* 1943. Reprint, Gauley Bridge: Thomas Inprints, 1992.

Davis, Amy. "Old-Time Music at Augusta, An Innovative Approach to a Tradition," Master's thesis, Wesleyan Univ., 1983. Augusta Collection.

Deitz, Betty Warner, and Michael Babatunde Olatunji. *Muscial Instruments of Africa.* New York: John Day, 1965.

Deitz, Dennis. *The Greenbrier Ghost and Other Strange Stories.* Charleston, W.Va.: Mountain Memories Books, 1990.

Dewees, Col. D.S. *Recollections of a Lifetime.* Calhoun County, W.Va.: Eden, 1904.

Dodrill, William Christian (Rattlesnake Bill). 1915. Reprint, *Moccasin Tracks and Other Imprints.* Parsons: McClain, 1974.

Downie, Margaret. "History of the Rebec." Ph.D. diss., West Virginia Univ., 1982.

Dulaney, Annie. "I Remember Bower." *Journal of the Braxton Historical Society* 3, no. 3 (25 September 1995): 29-37.

Durrett, Ralph. *Talbott Community.* Self published, 1989.

Eaton, Allen H. *Handicrafts of the Southern Highlands*. 1937. Reprint, New York: Dover, 1973.

Ely, William. *The Big Sandy Valley*. 1887. Reprint, Catlettsburg, Ky.: Heritage Books, 1987.

Epstein, Dena J. *Sinful Tunes and Spirituals, Black Folk Music to the Civil War*. Urbana and Chicago: Univ. of Illinois Press, 1977.

Evans, Ivor H., ed., *Brewers Dictionary of Phrase and Fable*, 14th ed. New York: Harper and Row, 1989.

Fischer, David Hackett. *Albion's Seed*. New York, Oxford: Oxford Univ. Press, 1989.

Fleischhauer, Carl, and Alan Jabbour, eds. *The Hammons Family, A Study of a West Virginia Family's Traditions*. Washington: Library of Congress, 1973.

Foley, Daniel J. *The Christmas Tree*. Philadelphia and New York: Chilton Co., 1960.

Friedman, Albert B. *The Viking Book of Folk Ballads*. New York: Viking Press, 1956.

Gainer, Patrick. *Folk Songs from the West Virginia Hills*. Grantsville, W.Va.: Seneca Books, 1975.

————. "Issues and Resources in Folk Music in West Virginia." *West Virginia Folklore Journal* 20, no. 1 (1975): 2-6.

Gamble, Rev. J. Lee, and Charles H. Greene, *Seventh Day Baptists in Europe and America*. Plainfield, New Jersey: American Sabbath Tract Society, 1910.

Gartner, Paul. "Wilson Douglas—A Determined Mind." *The Old-Time Herald* 5, no.2 (Winter 1995-1996).

Gerwig, Earl W. "Gerwig Genealogy." West Virginia and Regional History Collection.

Glassie, Henry. *Pattern in the Material Folk Culture of the Eastern United States*. Philadelphia: Univ. of Pennsylvania Press, 1968.

Green, Archie. "Hillbilly Music: Source and Symbol." 1965, *Journal of American Folklore* 78, no. 309 (1965): 204-28.

Hale, John P. *Trans-Allegheny Pioneers*. 3rd ed. 1886. Reprint, Radford, Va.: Robert Ingle Steele, 1971.

Halpert, Herbert. "The Devil, the Fiddle, and Dancing." In *Fields of Folklore, Essays in Honor of Kenneth Goldstein*, edited by Roger D. Abrahams. Bloomington: Trickster Press, 1995.

Hamill, Kenny. *West Virginia Place Names*. Piedmont, W.Va.: West Virginia Place Name Press, 1945.

Hamrick, Wilton M., and Ronald V. Hardway. "The Baughman Family: Part II." *The Webster Independent* 2, no. 2 (Fall/Winter 1984-85).

Harding, M. Esther. *Woman's Mysteries, Ancient and Modern*. 1935. Reprints, New York: G.P. Putnam's Sons, 1971.

Hardway, Ronald V. "History of Webster County." In *Heritage of Webster County, West Virginia, 1994*. Upper Glade: Webster County Historical Society, 1994.

————. "The Last Pioneers" *The Webster Independent* (Webster County Historical Society) 9, no. 1 (Fall/Winter 1994-1995): 1-45.

————. "The Final Frontier: Pioneers of Webster County." *Journal of the Braxton County Historical Society* 9, no. 4 (25 December 1981); 10, no. 1 (25 March 1982): 6-23; 10, no. 2 (25 June 1982): 32-46; 10, no. 3 (25 September 1982): 62; 10, no. 4 (25 December 1982): 91-93.

————. "The Baughman Family: Part I and II." *The Webster Independent* 2, no. 2 (Fall/Winter 1984-85): 2-12, 13-19.

Haymond, Henry. *History of Harrison County West Virginia, from the Early Days of Northwest Virginia to the Present.* Morgantown: Acme Publishing Company, 1910.

Hill, W. Henry, Arthur F. Hill, Alfred E. Hill. *Antonio Stradivari, His Life and Work.* 1902. Reprint, New York: Dover 1963.

Hislop, Alexander. *The Two Babylons.* 1916. Reprint, New York: Loizeaux Brothers, 1956.

History of Calhoun County, West Virginia. Spencer, W.Va.: Don Mills, Inc., and Calhoun County Historical Society, 1989.

Humphreys, Milton W., letter to his brothers. 10 April 1866. *Journal of the Braxton Historical Society* 19, no. 4 (December 1991): 14-20.

Inter-Mountain, The. Elkins, W.Va. 14 September 1992.

Irwin, John Rice. *Musical Instruments of the Southern Appalachians.* Exton, Penn.: Schiffer Publishing, 1979.

Jabbour, Alan, ed. *American Fiddle Tunes* (booklet with recording). Washington: Library of Congress, AFS L62, 1973.

————. "The Fiddle in the Blue Ridge." In Worley, Beth, and Vaughn Webb. *Blue Ridge Folk Instruments and Their Makers.* A catalog from an exhibit of the same name. Ferrum, Va.: Ferrum College, 1993.

Jackson, George Pullen. *White Spirituals in the Southern Uplands.* 1933. Reprint, Hatboro, Pa.: Folklore Associates, 1964.

————. *Spiritual Folk-Songs of Early America.* 1937. Reprint, New York: Dover, 1964.

————. *Another Sheaf of White Spirituals.* Gainesville: Univ. of Florida Press, 1952.

Jamison, Phil. "The Cakewalk." *The Old-Time Herald.* November 1992-January 1993.

Jones, Maldwyn Allen. *American Immigration.* Chicago, London: Univ. of Chicago Press, 1960.

Karpeles, Maud (see Sharp 1952).

Kephart, Horace. *Our Southern Highlanders.* New York: Macmillan Co., 1929.

Laws, Malcomb. *Native American Balladry.* Philadelphia: American Folklore Society, 1964.

Leyburn, James G. *The Scotch-Irish: A Social History.* Chapel Hill: Univ. of North Carolina Press, 1962.

Linn, Karen. *That Half Barbaric Twang: The Banjo in American Popular Culture.* Urbana: Univ. of Illinois Press, 1991.

Lott, Eric. "Blackface and Blackness: The Minstrel Show in American Culture." In *Inside the Minstrel Mask: Readings in Nineteenth-Century Blackface Min-*

strelsy, edited by Annemarie Bean, James V. Hatch, and Brooks McNamara. Hanover and London: Wesleyan Univ. Press, 1996.

MacAlpine, Neil. *A Pronouncing Gaelic-English Dictionary*. 1832. Reprint, Glasgow: Alexander MaClaren and Sons, 1957.

Malone, Bill C. *Country Music U.S.A.: A Fifty Year History*. Austin and London: American Folklore Society, 1968.

McNeil, Douglas. *The Last Forest, Tales of the Allegheny Woods*. 1940. Reprint, Parsons, W.Va.: Pocahontas Communications Cooperative Corporation, 1990.

McNeil, W.K. *Southern Mountain Folksongs*. Little Rock: August House, 1993.

McWhiney, Grady. *Cracker Culture*. Tuscaloosa: Univ. of Alabama Press, 1988.

McWhorter, Lucullus Virgil. *The Border Settlers of Northwestern Virginia, from 1768 to 1795*. Hamilton, Ohio: Republican Publishing Company, 1915.

Miles, Emma Bell. *The Spirit of the Mountains*. 1905. Reprint, Knoxville: Univ. of Tennessee Press, 1975.

Miller, Sampson Newton. *Annals of Webster County, West Virginia: Before and Since Organization, 1863*. Buckhannon, W.Va.: West Virginia Wesleyan College, 1969.

Milnes, Gerald. "Old Christmas and Belsnickles." *Goldenseal* 21, no. 4 (1995): 26-31.

———. "Uncle Jack McElwain (1856-1938)." *The Old-Time Herald* 4, no. 1 (Fall 1993): 34-37.

———, producer. *Helvetia: The Swiss of West Virginia*. Augusta Heritage Center, AHV-93, 1993. Videotape.

———, producer. *Fiddles, Snakes and Dogdays*. Augusta Heritage Center, AHV-097, 1997. Videotape.

Milnes, Gerald, and Michael Kline. "Tales of the Elk River Country." *Goldenseal* 12, no. 2 (Summer 1986).

Minton, John. "West African Fiddles Deep in East Texas." In Mullen, Patrick B., and Alan B. Govenar, eds. *Juneteenth Texas: Essays in African American Folklore*. Denton, Texas: Texas Folklore Society, 1996.

Murphy, Michael. *The Appalachian Dulcimer Book*. Folksay Press, 1976.

Murphy, Michael J. *Tyrone Folk Quest*. Belfast: Blackstaff Press, 1973.

Musick, Ruth Ann. *Ballads, Folk Songs, and Folk Tales from West Virginia*. Morgantown, W.Va.: West Virginia Univ. Library, 1960.

Nathan, Hans. "The Performance of the Virginia Minstrels." In Bean, et al., 1996.

Nicholas Chronicle, The. Summersville, W.Va. 23 October 1914, 29 October 1914, 23 July 1914, and 29 July 1914.

Nicholas County News Leader. 1968 (date unrecorded).

Niles, John Jacob. *The Ballad Book of John Jacob Niles*. New York: Dover, 1970.

Oxford English Dictionary, The Compact Edition. Oxford: Oxford Univ. Press, 1989.

Price, William T. *Historical Sketches of Pocahontas County, West Virginia*. 1901. Reprint, Marlinton: Price Brothers, 1963.

Randolph, Vance. *Ozark Folksongs*. 1946. Revised, Univ. of Missouri, 1980.

Rice, Otis K. *The Allegheny Frontier, West Virginia Beginnings, 1730-1830*. Lexington: Univ. Press of Kentucky, 1970.

Riddel, Frank, S., ed. *Appalachia: Its People, Heritage, and Problems*. Dubuque, Iowa: Kendall/Hunt, 1974.

Rorrer, Kinney. *Rambling Blues: The Life and Times of Charlie Poole*. Danville, Va., 1982.

Rosenberg, Neil V., ed. *Transforming Tradition*. Urbana and Chicago: Univ. of Illinois Press, 1993.

Roush, Herbert L., Sr., ed. *The Adventures of T.C. Collins—Boatman: Twenty-four years on the Western Waters, 1849-1873*. Baltimore: Gateway Press, 1985.

———. *The Biography of T.C. Collins, Written by Himself*. Baltimore: Gateway Press, 1986.

Ruland, Josef. *Christmas in Germany*. Bonn: Hohwacht, 1978.

Seeger, Charles. "The Appalachian Dulcimer." *Journal of American Folklore* 71, no. 279 (January-March 1958): 40-51.

Seventh Day Baptists in Europe and America. Vol. 2. Plainfield, New Jersey: Seventh Day Baptist General Conference, 1910.

Sharp, Cecil J. *English Folksongs from the Southern Appalachians*. 1932. Reprint, London, New York, Toronto: Oxford Univ. Press, 1952.

Shoemaker, George H., ed. *The Emergence of Folklore in Everyday Life*. Bloomington: Trickster Press, 1990.

Smith, Gary Gene. *The Smiths of Brush Run*. Self published, 1979.

Smith, L. Allen. *A Catalog of Pre-Revival Appalachian Dulcimers*. Columbia and London: Univ. of Missouri Press, 1983.

Smith, Ralph Lee. *The Story of the Dulcimer*. Cosby, Tenn.: Crying Creek Publishers, 1986.

Spalding, Susan Eike. "You've Got to Get the Dancing in Your Feet: Old Time Dancing in African American and European American Communities in Southwest Virginia." *Journal of the Appalachian Studies Association* 7 (1995): 29-40.

Stearns, Marshall, and Jean Stearns. *Jazz Dance: The Story of American Vernacular Dance*. New York: Shirmer Books, 1979.

Stecher, Jody. "Cross Tuning Workshop." *Fiddler Magazine* 4, no. 2 (Fall 1996): 29-31.

Stewart, Bob (R.J.). *Where Is Saint George? Pagan Imagery in English Folksong*. London: Blandford Press, 1977 and 1988.

Stoutamire, Albert. *Music of the Old South: Colony to the Confederacy*. Rutherford, N.J.: Fairleigh Dickinson Univ. Press, 1972.

Sturgill, David A. "The Appalachian Dulcimer." *Bluegrass Unlimited* 31, no. 3 (September 1996): 47-49.

Sutton, John Davison. *History of Braxton County and Central West Virginia*. Sutton, W.Va.: 1919.

Tallmadge, William. "The Folk Banjo and Clawhammer Performance Practice in the Upper South: A Study of Origins." In *The Appalachian Experience*,

Proceedings of the 6th Annual Appalachian Studies Conference. Boone, N.C.: Appalachian Consortium Press, 1983.

Taylor, Mattie. "Conversations with Aunt Harriet." *The Kentucky Folk-Lore and Poetry Magazine* (October 1928): 1-5.

Thompson, Stith. *Motif-Index of Folk Literature.* 6 vols., Bloomington and Indianapolis: Indiana Univ. Press, 1955.

Thonger, Richard. *A Calendar of German Customs.* Great Britain: Oswald Wolff Ltd., 1966.

Titon, Jeff Todd. *Early Downhome Blues.* Urbana, Chicago, London: Univ. of Illinois Press, 1977.

———. *Powerhouse for God.* Austin: Univ. of Texas Press, 1988.

———. "Reconstructing the Blues: Reflections on the 1960s Blues Revival." In *Transforming Tradition*, edited by Neil V. Rosenberg. Urbana and Chicago: Univ. of Illinois Press, 1993.

Tribe, Ivan M. *Mountaineer Jamboree, Country Music in West Virginia.* Lexington: Univ. Press of Kentucky, 1984.

Turner, Ella May, ed. *Stories and Verse of West Virginia.* 1923. Reprint, Richwood, W.Va.: Comstock, 1974.

Turner, William H., and Edward J. Cabbell, eds. *Blacks in Appalachia.* Lexington: Univ. Press of Kentucky, 1985.

Wagner, Ann Louise. *Adversaries of Dance: From the Puritans to the Present.* Urbana and Chicago: Univ. of Illinois Press, 1997.

Walker, William, ed. *Christian Harmony.* n.p.: Christian Harmony Publishing, revised 1958.

Waller, Altina L. *Feud: Hatfields, McCoys, and Social Change in Appalachia, 1860-1900.* Chapel Hill: Univ. of North Carolina Press, 1988.

Webster Echo, 15 January 1904.

Weller, Jack E. *Yesterday's People.* Lexington: Univ. of Kentucky Press, 1965.

Wentworth, Harold. *American Dialect Dictionary.* New York: Thomas Y. Crowell, 1944.

West Virginia Folklore 7, no. 4 (Summer 1957).

Whisnant, David. *All That Is Native and Fine.* Chapel Hill and London: Univ. of North Carolina Press, 1983.

White, Newman Ivey, ed. *The Frank C. Brown Collection of North Carolina Folklore.* 7 vols. Durham: Duke Univ. Press, 1952-64.

Wiggins, Gene. *Fiddlin' Georgia Crazy, Fiddlin' John Carson, His Real World, and the World of His Songs.* Urbana and Chicago, Univ. of Illinois Press, 1987.

Wilgus, D.K., ed. "An Introduction to the Study of Hillbilly Music." *Journal of American Folklore* 78, no. 309 (July-September 1965): 195-203.

———. *Anglo-American Folksong Scholarship since 1898.* 1959. Reprint, Westport, Conn.: Greenwood Press, 1982.

Wilhelm, Gene, Jr. "Appalachian Isolation: Fact or Fiction." In Riddel, ed., 1974.

Winter, Marian Hannah. "Juba and American Minstrelsy," In *Inside the Minstrel Mask: Readings in Nineteenth-Century Blackface Minstrelsy*, edited by

Annemarie Bean, James V. Hatch, and Brooks McNamara. Hanover and London: Wesleyan Univ. Press, 1996.

Winans, Robert B. "The Black Banjo Playing Tradition in Virginia and West Virginia." *Journal of the Virginia Folklore Society* 1 (1979): 7-30.

Withers, Alexander Scott. *Chronicles of Border Warfare*. Cincinnati: Robert Clark, 1895.

Wolfe, Charles. *Tennessee Strings, the Story of Country Music in Tennessee*. Knoxville: Univ. of Tennessee Press, 1977.

————. *The Devil's Box*. Nashville and London: The Country Music Foundation Press and Vanderbilt Univ. Press, 1997.

————, ed. *Thomas W. Talley's Negro Folk Rhymes*, rev. ed. Knoxville: Univ. of Tennessee Press, 1991.

Worley, Beth, and Vaughn Webb. *Blue Ridge Folk Instruments and Their Makers*. A catalog from an exhibit of the same name. Ferrum, Va.: Ferrum College, 1994.

Wright, Joseph. *An Elementary Middle English Grammar*, 2nd edition. London: Oxford Univ. Press, 1928.

Yoder, Don. *Pennsylvania Spirituals*. Lancaster: Pennsylvania Folklife Society, 1961.

————. *Discovering American Folklife*. Ann Arbor: UMI Research Press, 1990.

Zimmerman, M.W., Papers. West Virginia State Archive.

Field Recordings: Interviews and Music

Audio tape recordings by author, Augusta Collection, unless otherwise noted.

Adams, Norman. 21 July 1995. Videotaped interview. Gassaway, W.Va. G. Milnes. Augusta Collection.

Andrews, Thelma, and Eloise Mann. 25 May 1993. Elkins, W.Va.

Blake, Hobart. 26 May 1988. Burnsville, W.Va.

Blake, Maynard. 23 June 1988. Exchange, Braxton County, W.Va.

Bright, George. 30 March 1980. Sutton, W.Va.

Carpenter, Ernie. 12 February 1981. Sutton, W.Va. M. Kline and G. Milnes. Augusta Collection.

Carpenter, Ernie. 8 January 1983. Interview. Sutton, Amy Noel Davis. Augusta Collection.

Carpenter, Ernie. 17 January 1986. Sutton, W.Va.

Carpenter, Ernie. 2 November 1987. Sutton, W.Va.

Carpenter, Ernie. 23 September 1988. Sutton, W.Va.

Carpenter, Ernie. 9 February 1989. Sutton, W.Va.

Carpenter, Ernie. 5 June 1991. Sutton, W.Va.

Case, Clyde. 7 November 1987. Duck, Braxton County, W.Va.

Case, Clyde. 16 August 1988. Duck, Braxton County, W.Va.

Case, Clyde. 17 November 1989. Duck, Braxton County, W.Va.

Coffman, Mose. 23 February 1991. Sweet Springs, W.Va.

Cottrell, Senate. Date unrecorded. Braxton County, W.Va. Field recording. Fern Rollyson. Augusta Collection.

Cutlip, Lola, and Reva Fincham. 26 April 1988. Exchange, Braxton County, W.Va.

Davis, Carl. 7 March 1988. Raccoon Creek, Braxton County, W.Va.

Davis, Carl. 22 March 1995. Videotaped interview. Raccoon Creek, Braxton County, W.Va. G. Milnes. Augusta Collection.

Davis, John. 14 November 1987. Sugar Creek, Braxton County, W.Va.

Degler, Carl. 15 February 1995. Videotaped interview. Crystal Springs, Randolph County, W.Va. G. Milnes. Augusta Collection.

Dillon, Thomas. 26 July 1956. Recording LWO 2471. Library of Congress.

Douglas, Wilson. 8 December 1988. Clendenin, W.Va.

Duling, Florena. 1989 (exact date unknown). Field recording. Grant County, W.Va. F. Duling. Augusta Collection.

George, Frank. 23 August 1995. Videotaped interview. Walton, Roane County, W.Va. G. Milnes. Augusta Collection.

Hammonds, Currence. 3 January 1977. Huttonsville, W.Va.

Hammonds, Currence. 18 March 1977. Huttonsville, W. Va.

Hammonds, Currence. 2 July 1979. Taped interview. Huttonsville, Randolph County, W.Va. Michael Kline and Bob Dalsemer. Augusta Collection.

Hammonds, Currence. 10 July 1979. Taped interview. Huttonsville, W.Va. John McCutcheon and G. Milnes. Augusta Collection.

Hammonds, Currence. 12 January 1982. Taped interview. Appalachian Studies class. Davis and Elkins College. Michael Kline. Augusta Collection.

Hammonds, Currence. Date unrecorded. Taped interview. Appalachian Studies class. Davis and Elkins College. Michael Kline. Augusta Collection.

Hammonds, Currence and Minnie. 2 August 1983. Field recording, singing, and interview. Huttonsville, Jack Bernhardt and G. Milnes. Augusta Collection.

Hammons, Millie. 31 August 1993. Adolph, Randolph County, W.Va.

Hammons, Millie. 1 September 1993. Adolph, Randolph County, W.Va.

Hamrick, Howard. 17 November 1992. Valley Head, Randolph County, W.Va.

Hardway, Brooks. 17 September 1988. Elizabeth, Wirt County, W.Va.

Hinkle, Cathleen. 10 February 1994. Lewisburg, W.Va.

Jarvis, Ward. 2 April 1980. Stewart, Ohio.

Johnson, Julia. 11 April 1988. Long Run, Braxton County, W.Va.

Knicely, Dena and Jim. 5 June 1990. Taped interview. Friar's Hill, Greenbrier County, W.Va. Jim Costa and G. Milnes. Augusta Collection.

Knicely, Dena and Jim. 21 February 1991. Friar's Hill, Greenbrier County, W.Va.

Lloyd, Junior. 20 December 1987. Napier, Braxton County, W.Va.

Marks, Phyllis. 20 April 1995. Videotaped interview. Glenville, W.Va. G. Milnes. Augusta Collection.

Mayse, Jack, and Waneta Mayse Brown. 4 May 1988. Sutton, W.Va.

McGee, Gus. 30 March 1994. Elkins, W.Va.

McKinny, Paul. 11 June 1991. Vermillion, Ohio.

McMillon, Ray. 28 April 1988. Riffle, Braxton County, W.Va.

Metheny, Beatrice. 28 January 1994. Videotaped interview. Lower Mill Creek, Braxton County, W.Va. G. Milnes and Stan Gilliam. Augusta Collection.

Miller, Walter. 18 April 1988. Craigsville, W.Va.

Melton, George. 25 March 1988. Braxton County, W.Va.

Mollohan, Elmer. 11 October 1989. Webster County, W.Va.

Morris, Jennings. 25 January 1990. Cowen, W.Va.

O'Brien, Marion. 21 August 1989. Bolair, Webster County, W.Va.

O'Brien, Sylvia. 21 March 1995. Videotaped interview. Clay County, W.Va. G. Milnes. Augusta Collection.

Parsons, Phoeba. 30 March 1989. Bear Fork, Calhoun County, W.Va.

Propst, Rob. 4 November 1974. Pendleton County, W.Va. Fiddle music and interview. Nick Royal. Augusta Collection.

Ross, Avis and Jim. 26 June 1988. Flatwoods, Braxton County, W.Va.

Sandy, Bud. 5 November 1987. Burnsville, W.Va.

Sandy, Bud. 4 April 1988. Burnsville, W.Va.

Sandy, Bud. 31 July 1988. Burnsville, W.Va.

Santy, Mamie. 29 April 1987. Chloe, Clay County, W.Va.

Scott, Dock. 29 April 1994. Video recording. War, McDowell County, W.Va. G. Milnes. Augusta Collection.

Scott, Ott. 4 April 1988. Lewis County, W.Va.

Sears, Kenton. 10 December 1991. Sutton, W.Va.

Simmons, Robert. 17 March 1992. Moyers, Pendleton County, W.Va.

Simmons, Woody. 30 August 1995. Videotaped interview. Mill Creek, Randolph County, W.Va. G. Milnes. Augusta Collection.

Simmons, Woody. 13 August 1996. Videotaped interview. Mill Creek, Randolph County, W.Va. G. Milnes. Augusta Collection.

Singleton, Sarah. 26 October 1988. Salt Lick, Braxton County, W.Va.

Slaughter, Omar. 20 April 1995. Videotaped interview. Braxton County, W.Va. G. Milnes. Augusta Collection.

Smith, Glen. 15 February 1995. Videotaped interview. Elizabeth, Wirt County, W.Va. G. Milnes. Augusta Collection.

Stover, Hazel. 2 October 1995. Videotaped interview and singing performance. Clay, W.Va. G. Milnes. Augusta Collection.

Swiger, Anthony. 29 June 1995. Videotaped interview. Randolph County, W.Va. G. Milnes. Augusta Collection.

White, Everett. 20 December 1988. Enterprise, Harrison County, W.Va.

White, Everett. 22 February 1994. Enterprise, Harrison County, W.Va.

Wine, Melvin. 8 October 1987. Copen, Braxton County, W.Va.

Wine, Melvin. 23 June 1988. Copen, Braxton County, W.Va.

Wine, Melvin. 19 November 1988. Copen, Braxton County, W.Va.

Wingfield, Leroy. 28 May 1992. Beverly, Randolph County, W.Va.

Woods, Arthur. 2 October 1996. Field notes. Webster County, W.Va. G. Milnes. Augusta Collection.

Discography

The following 33 rpm lp-recordings, cassettes, and compact disc recordings represent music considered in this volume. They were published on various commercial and educational labels, and are/were publicly available. Numerous recent self-produced and privately produced recordings also exist, representing the musicians of the region.

Blackie Cool: Back Memories. Augusta AHR-002C.
Ernie Carpenter: Elk River Blues. Augusta AHR-003C.
Jenes Cottrell and French Carpenter: Old-Time Songs and Tunes from Clay County, West Virginia. Charleston, W.Va., Folk Promotions.
Wilson Douglas: Boatin' Up Sandy. Marimac AHS-1.
Foggy Valley: Traditional Fiddling of Randolph County (anthology). Augusta AHR-020.
Folk Music and Lore of the Civil War (anthology). Augusta AHR-014.
Folksongs and Ballads, Volume 3 (anthology). Augusta AHR-009.
Folksongs and Ballads, Volume 4 (anthology). Augusta AHR-010.
The Fuzzy Mountain String Band. Rounder 0010.
Frank George. Kanawha 307.
W. Franklin George: Swope's Knobs. APRC 001.
Ed Haley: Parkersburg Landing. Rounder 1010.
Ed Haley: Forked Deer, Volume 1. Rounder 1131, 1132.
Ed Haley: Grey Eagle, Volume 2. Rounder 1133, 1134.
The Fiddling of Burl Hammons: The Diller Collection. Augusta AHR-017.
Edden Hammons Collection. WVU, Sound Archive 001.
The Hammons Family. Library of Congress L-65, 66.
The Hollow Rock String Band. Kanawha 311.
Delbert Hughes: The Home Recordings. Augusta AHR-015.
Frank Hutchison: The Train That Carried My Girl from Town. Rounder 1007.
Frank Hutchison, Vol. 1, 1926-29. Document Records 8003.
Frank Hutchison, Williamson Brothers and Curry, Dick Justice, Vol. 2, 1927-29. Document Records 8004.

John Johnson: Fiddlin' John. Augusta AHR-001C.

The Kessinger Brothers. County 536.

Kessinger Brothers: Complete Recorded Works, Vols. 1, 2, and 3. Document Records 8010, 8011, 8012.

The Legend of Clark Kessinger. County 733.

Clark Kessinger: Sweet Bunch of Daisies. County 747.

The Lilly Brothers and Don Stover: Early Recordings. County 729.

The McCumbers Brothers: Hillbilly Hobo. Old Homestead 90065.

Phyllis Marks: Folksongs and Ballads, Volume 2. 1991. Augusta AHR-008.

The Music Never Dies: A Vandalia Sampler (anthology). Elderberry Records 1988.

Old-Time Banjo Anthology, Volume 1. Marimac AHS-4.

Old-Time Banjo Anthology, Volume 2. Marimac AHS-5.

Old-Time Banjo: The Diller Collection (anthology) Augusta AHR-019.

Old-Time Fiddling of Braxton County, Volume 1 (anthology). Augusta AHR-012.

Old-Time Fiddling of Braxton County, Volume 2 (anthology). Augusta AHR-013.

Blind Alfred Reed: How Can a Poor Man Stand Such Times and Live? Rounder 1001.

Harvey Sampson and the Big Possum Stringband: Flat Foot in the Ashes. Augusta AHR-004C.

Shakin' Down the Acorns (anthology). Rounder 0018.

Woody Simmons. Elderberry ER 007.

Glen Smith: Say Old Man. Marimac AHS-3.

Israel Welch: Tearin' Down the Laurel. Augusta AHR-018.

The West Virginia Hills: Early Recordings from West Virginia. Old Homestead CS 141.

The West Virginia Hills: Traditional Dulcimer Music (anthology), Augusta AHR-011.

Everett White: Folksongs and Ballads, Volume 1. Augusta AHR-007.

Melvin Wine: Hannah at the Springhouse. Marimac AHS-2.

Melvin Wine: Vintage Wine. Marimac AHS-6.

Melvin Wine: Cold Frosty Morning. Poplar LP1.

Nimrod Workman. Rounder 0076.

Oscar and Eugene Wright. Rounder 0089.

Index

Page numbers in italics refer to photographs.